LANDSCRIPT 3

Topology

LAN RIP

L A N D S C R I P T IS A PUBLICATION ON LANDSCAPE ÆSTHETICS INVITING AUTHORS FROM DIFFERENT DISCIPLINES TO INVEST THOUGHT ON ESTABLISHED MODES OF PERCEIVING, REPRESENTING, AND CONCEIVING NATURE. STEERED BY AN EDITORIAL BOARD COMPRISED OF INTERNATIONAL EXPERTS FROM VARIOUS FIELDS, WHICH WILL ENCOURAGE A CRITICAL AND CONTROVERSIAL DIALOGUE, ITS GOAL IS TO ACT AS A REVELATOR OF CONVENTIONAL PERCEPTIONS OF LANDSCAPE AND TO CULTIVATE THE DEBATE ON ÆSTHETICS AT A SCHOLARLY LEVEL. THIS DISCUSSION PLATFORM AIMS AT REKINDLING A THEORETICAL DEBATE, IN THE HOPE OF FOSTERING A BETTER UNDERSTANDING OF THE IMMANENCE OF LANDSCAPE ARCHITECTURE IN OUR CULTURE, FOCUSING CRITICALLY ON THE WAY WE THINK, LOOK, AND ACT UPON SITES.

Professor Christophe Girot, Albert Kirchengast (Chief Editors)
Institute of Landscape Architecture ILA, D–Arch, ETH Zürich

EDITORIAL BOARD

SUBMISSION GUIDELINES

Manuscript proposals are welcome in fields appropriate for *Landscript*. Scholarly submissions should be formatted in accordance with *The Chicago Manual of Style* and the spelling should follow American convention. The full manuscript must be submitted as a Microsoft Word document, on a CD or disk, accompanied by a hard copy of the text. Accompanying images should be sent as TIFF files with a resolution of at least 300 dpi at 8 × 9-inch print size. Figures should be numbered clearly in the text. Image captions and credits must be included with submissions. It is the responsibility of the author to secure permissions for image use and pay any reproduction fees. A brief letter of inquiry and author biography must also accompany the text.

Acceptance or rejection of submissions is at the discretion of the editors. Please do not send original materials, as submissions will not be returned.

Please direct submissions to this address:

Landscript
Chair of Professor Christophe Girot
Institute of Landscape Architecture ILA, ETH Zürich
Wolfgang-Pauli-Strasse 15, HIL H 54.2
8093 Zurich, Switzerland

Questions about submissions can be emailed to:
kirchengast@arch.ethz.ch

Visit our website for further information:
www.girot.arch.ethz.ch

D S C
T 3

CHRISTOPHE GIROT
ANETTE FREYTAG
ALBERT KIRCHENGAST
DUNJA RICHTER (EDS.)

TOPOLOGY

TOPICAL THOUGHTS ON THE CONTEMPO-RARY LANDSCAPE

In this publication, masculine forms are used in the interest of readability. The feminine participles are implicitly included.

Foreword

Wilhelm Krull

"We have walked through the great outdoors countless times and, with varying degrees of attention, observed trees and bodies of water, meadows and grain fields, hills and houses, and thousands of variations of light and clouds—but looking at one thing, or at these or those things together, does not mean we consciously see a 'landscape.' Such fragmented content of our visual field is not what should be capturing our attention. We need to be aware of a new whole, an entity that goes beyond individual elements, that is not bound to their specific meanings, and does not mechanically assemble them into a design—that is when landscape happens."—1

Choosing a holistic perspective rather than viewing individual elements, as emphasized by Georg Simmel in his "Philosophie der Landschaft," is also an aspect of the theoretical position asserted by Christophe Girot and his colleagues at the Institute for Landscape Architecture at the ETH Zürich. Many current landscape architecture projects, according to their diagnosis, are defined by economic considerations or ecological fashions. But as the contributions in this book emphasize, landscape architects should neither be satisfied with their role as decorators who spruce up the leftover, open spaces around infrastructure facilities, nor with their role as nature conservationists who try to heal landscape or defend it from interventions. Instead, there should be a design-based approach from

1 Georg Simmel: "Philosophie der Landschaft," in: *Die Güldenkammer*, 11/1913, pp. 635–644 (my translation).

the beginning, which understands landscape in all its complexity. The topology concept, the term given to the theory of site and topos, precisely characterizes this approach. Working topologically means examining in detail the planned site of intervention, understanding it in relation to other aspects—such as landscape, infrastructure, or built structures—organizing the space landscape architecturally, and considering people. "Space" in this sense is not understood as a mere physical and geographical dimension, but as a multidimensional network generated by culture and in many respects historically variable.—[2] Reintroducing aesthetics is essential to this approach, and equal status must be given to economic and ecological factors. Landscape is more than a functional space; the poetic and symbolic significance it possesses is vital to understanding it holistically.

2 See Hille von Seggern, Julia Werner: "Entwerfen als integrierender Erkenntnisprozess," in: Hille von Seggern, Julia Werner, Lucia Grosse-Bächle (eds.): *Creating Knowledge*, Berlin 2008.

This approach greatly boosts the status of landscape architecture. It no longer responds to the planning decisions of others, but has a fundamental, integrative—topological—function, by connecting a specific landscape's different dimensions. It is understood, of course, that this integrative capacity can only result from including all participating disciplines as a "partner-based orchestration of institutions and professions that directly or indirectly design the space giving priority to aesthetics."—[3]

3 See the funding application to the Volkswagen Foundation and the publication: Christophe Girot, Anette Freytag, Albert Kirchengast, Suzanne Krizenecky, Dunja Richter: *Topologie/Topology*, issue 15 of the publication series "Pamphlet," Zurich 2012.

Through funding initiatives, the Volkswagen Foundation wants to encourage research focused on emerging, high-risk areas, and to transcend boundaries—whether between science and practice, between specific professional cultures, or between different countries. We are happy to support Professor Christophe Girot's plan to develop a theoretical position in landscape architecture that uses the topology concept to cross the borders between disciplines and methodologies. This is even more the case, because the declared objective of the project is not only to benefit the discipline through theoretical and critical debates and question its self-image, but also to influence design practice and establish a new and fundamental, "landscape-oriented" attitude in urban planning, which will hopefully have a sustainable effect on the quality of our urban life. The mission statement should be a design concept that is holistic and rooted in our daily life, and which also connects scientific and cultural aspects.

One of the cornerstones for this project was the workshop entitled "Topologie—Zur Gestaltung der gegenwärtigen Landschaft" (Topology—On Designing Landscape Today) held from October 11–13, 2012 in the Semper Aula of the ETH Zürich. The main lectures of the conference, which defined the project, were revised and are now available as collected essays in this book. Numerous experts from various disciplines and professional perspectives—ranging from philosophy to history, garden design, sociology, and architecture—were invited to discuss the integrative effect of landscape architecture. They also proposed ways in which a holistic spatial design that integrates the usefulness and the beauty of landscape on equal terms might be achieved. It became clear that contemporary landscape architecture lacks a theoretical foundation, partly due to the fact that academic training has been deficient since the nineteen-seventies. Theoretical professorships have not been not replaced, while fundamental questions and an analysis of new theoretical approaches and artistic design processes have remained superficial or are lacking completely. The consequences are design concepts that are often scarcely reflected theoretically or scrutinized critically. For this reason, Christophe Girot and his team, first and foremost Anette Freytag, but also her colleagues Albert Kirchengast, Suzanne Krizenecky, and Dunja Richter have taken on the ambitious goal of not only shifting aesthetic issues and design to the core of the theoretical debate, but also of anchoring them in academic curricula and improving university education in professional landscape architecture. For this, it is necessary to promote a theory of landscape architecture, architecture, engineering, and urban design, which considers the relationship between various disciplines and merges economical, ecological, and aesthetic factors.

This publication, *Topology*, forms the basis for an international conference—also supported by the Volkswagen Foundation—held in June 2013 at Herrenhausen Palace in Hanover, among the unique landscape ensemble of the Herrenhausen gardens. Under the title, "Thinking the Contemporary Landscape. Positions and Oppositions," scientists and practitioners in landscape architecture and related disciplines participated in an inter-, and transdisciplinary dialogue as well as an exchange of fundamental ideas that go far beyond the design of landscape.

My thanks are due to the speakers at the Zurich event who were willing to revise their essays for this publication, as well as the editors of the book, including Albert Kirchengast who was responsible for editing the contributions. "Nothing thrives without care; and the most admirable things lose their value through inappropriate treatment," wrote the Prussian landscape architect Peter Joseph Lenné. This statement also undoubtedly applies to landscape architecture in general, and I am sure that the authors of *Topology* are giving it the very best of care.

Hanover, September 2013

How (Not) to Read This Book

Albert Kirchengast

The effort of reconstructing all the attempts that have sought to challenge the ideal of a linear flow of reading from the preface to the acknowledgements, undoubtedly deserves attention. This has taken either the form of narration (recently for instance in Jon Fosse's frugal dialogues and Jonathan Franzen's complex narrative strategy in his brilliant novel, *Freedom*), or of a graphic intervention (probably passé among graphic designers), or some "theoretical construct" (which still needs to be seen in print). But the concept of a book in Western culture still maintains that its content, and likewise its physical form should stubbornly unfold accordingly with headings, paragraphs, and other ingredients aimed at keeping the reader on track and entertained.

However, the way in which we understand text is not that linear, nor even direct; we can comprehend things in leaps, do somersaults, and a few loopdidoops too while reading. Some even believe in such a thing as the "decisive moment." Moreover: what was once practiced half seriously by highbrow hopefuls, as a way of "digesting", and taking a certain distance from knowledge, may, on the other hand become exposed methodologically, resulting in a break with underlying assumptions. This form of "comprehending" occurs as a paradigm shift, subsequently assuming an absolute distance from what is known, and even has the propensity to reinvent its starting point (see Kuhn).

The potential of such concepts at the onset of what has since become a form of tradition, meaning the constant dismantling and reconstruction of the Old-Modern, Western concept of science, is expressed in roughly the following manner: "Basic scientific and artistic decisions must by nature be made democratically" (Feyerabend, p. 10). Yet, following Paul Feyerabend in his stand, a democratic approach to the ideal of a creative scientist is only one side of the coin. The other side, of course, is the uncertainty brought about when the contours between science, politics, and economics tend to blur (see, for instance: Nowotny, Giddens, Crouch). Which is why Karl Popper decided to follow his own path. He too holds nothing sacred. Yet his Critical Rationalism indeed recognizes a necessity for correct knowledge: "Knowledge is the search for truth—the search for objectively true, enlightening theories" (Popper, p. 12). In order to entertain a suspicion against such "truth," science was obliged to search again and again for the falsification of theories that were valid in the first place. Skepticism in research is a virtue but, then again a concession is made by Popper to these "piecemeal engineers," who are allowed to feel reassured with an element of certainty "as if": as if they were holding on to something tangible. Could this mean that a fundamental longing for certainty, originating in our own *Lebenswelt*, undermines the research establishment? This would happily be supported by the newer sociology of scientific knowledge at any time. Yet, there is a true challenge in the idea of generating a creative scientific discussion, which would oscillates between relativism dampening the confidence in "useable results," and a simultaneous openness towards "negotiations" about an own starting point. The question we now face is how can such an approach to theory be pursued in a more or less theory-unfriendly academic world such as that of landscape architecture?

Some believe that the end to systematic thought has been long coming, when anything theoretical must appear episodic and be delivered with belligerent force in order to be noticed at all? In this case, "form" plays a significant role, as much as our reader at this very moment might believe to actually be holding just another (typical) book (see: Girot et al.). Form and comprehension cannot be separated from each other. Ultimately, postmodern forms of communication have become more than mere representatives of content. Rhetoric has now grown immensely in importance—despite being suspected of unfair intentions by some ever since it appeared with the ancient Sophists. The notion of performativity provided a postmodern tactic, still based on a rhetorical repertoire of forms, which survived the collapse of the Grand Narrative (Lyotard) and simply became a new one. This "rhetorical condition" should not be denied. But then, how can theory be pursued today in a market-sensitive design discipline, if one does not want to wholly engage in a non-teleological-political appeal that permeates all performativity? Are we here just to swindle out a better position for ourselves, or better yet, as an alternative, to buy one? After all, recognizing the status quo for the time being could help "to see all areas of culture not as authorities but as tools: as aids in a new description and new design of our egos and our environment" (Rorty, p. 11). Yet, what kind of tool could an anthology be, as one might at first glance consider this book, based on its appearance? What does such a collection of texts mean today; this loose succession of voices that might take on a life of their own in the reader's head?

First, an anthology is quite literally a "florilegium." And, as much as the first example of this type of assemblage might have involved the work of an, in this case, irrelevant Greek astronomer, *Topology* is of course far removed from the cosmic. Moreover, the etymology of florilegium is interesting; it quite figuratively implies that one has just visited a field of flowers. Flowers in a vase still refer to that today, which in turn suggests the beauty of the bouquet—as metaphor of the meadow, a moment enjoyed on a beautiful spring day. Hence, a place is evoked from a mere fragment of nature, full of memory and emotions, yet very real. This correlation of the part and the whole would actually not be the wrong metaphor for this endeavor. But how to arrange the content of this attempt, which contributes to the construction of a contemporary theory in landscape architecture? This is meant without arrogance and with pleasure by the fact, once again, that the first of its kind was also a collection of fragments. It would be more fitting to call this book a Chrestomathy rather than an anthology: *chrestos* means useful in ancient Greek. This book follows a didactic purpose. The manner in which it has developed its "maieutic dimension" is similar to a Socratic dialogue—in this instance about landscape—according to the often agonizing question of the not-yet, the not-knowing, and the non-assets; which in itself points to a utopian moment, in such a purposeful and result-oriented time as today. But then Socrates was not very appealing beyond his circle of students. Not only because of his looks, but because he touched upon what we call common sense. By simply observing his fellow peers—which they thought was much too banal a method, and thus did not understand nor appreciate—but he apparently hit a nerve. The result for Socrates was lethal. We will not go that far, even if we do take our endeavor very seriously.

Similarly to the way in which Socrates' considerations found its origins in the common world, *Topology* did not originate in landscape architecture, but in landscape itself. The "unity" of the modern landscape experience used to be general and aesthetic—until this was lost (Simmel, Ritter). Yet, today we are actually faced with the question of what it needs to integrate. Whether the "old" concept of landscape has to be discarded or not is the question? Not only has our natural landscape disappeared (a paradoxical term in itself), but traditional cultural landscapes as well. Does one have to reluctantly accept products, processes, and projects that do not go well together, but still cater to a historical ideal of life and work, relating to long-gone (agrarian) activities? Can this need be expressed in a different way, other than in the countless prefixes and suffixes currently imposed on the term “landscape”? *Topology* does not base its question on the finished “image” of a landscape's possible power of synthesis; it analyzes the process behind the power of reflection itself. In other words: “The unit is thus the product of an active participation in reflections that oscillate between the detail and the whole, in order to capture the relationship between the two” (Bubner, p. 63). In this self-reflexive back-step, which of course is also part of the aesthetic, the question focuses on the possible “details” that might form the basis of a new synthesis. In other words: what first needs to be considered, in order to understand this genesis of theory as a discussion, is to implement it with the purpose of design according to a “landscape model.” We reach once again the (admitted) preconditions of any theoretical construct: where we must first assume certain “topoi” in our speech that become indisputable. These are the building blocks, rediscovered in the form of participants invited to join a discourse organized in the form of a book. Who lead the discussion on design from their respective fields of expertise—do not in effect lead, but rather state their opinion about what they believe to be essential. Selecting those to be admitted to the discussion we encounter quasi-dogmatic positions, that have a strong channeling factor. But let us get back to the beginning, a (democratic) divergence of understanding and reading will be of assistance here: with every book supplied, there will be a new, self-responding synthesis by each reader.

Does this necessarily mean that anything goes? Due to *Topology's* core interest in landscape asthetics everything does not go. Following Immanuel Kant, aesthetics involves an access to a “whole” inasmuch as it escapes today's common reifying and positivistic gaze, concerned only with “functional parts” (see Kant §29, p. 193). “Our reaction to a landscape consists of older layers, which are beyond the human creative impulse. [...] This dialog leads to the question of whether and how things fit together. It is based on the hope of a harmonious whole by solving a purely physical problem" (Scruton, pp. 103, 113). In order to avoid misunderstandings, the topological viewpoint that understands aestheticized nature as its core ingredient is powered by *homo faber*. He, self evidently, does not set nature and culture in conflict (Blumenberg, p. 12). Quite the contrary, the major challenge for sophisticated design still lies in the fact that "within" landscape, those human needs (and products), which have always shaped our environment, can "disappear." Aesthetics—and more specifically, nature aesthetics—remains the core aspect: maybe this modern category has always formed somewhat of a counterforce in times of contingency. It draws on the peculiar glow that it produced itself to exist in a sober world; an aesthetic appearance, which constantly deals with the mystery of a difference between the factual and the possible. In the convoluted language of Theodor W. Adorno: "The beauty of nature is the trace of the non-identical in things under the spell of a universal identity" (Adorno, p. 114). The moments we experience in beautiful nature, and which are so essential to our daily lives, prove that not everything can be solved by mere facts. These moments are the energy, the fuel behind this project, and yet do not occur implicitely, but rather through the assertion that, as "whole people," we are ultimately dependent on our aesthetic experiences with nature (see Schiller, Heidegger). Proof of this could be the daily experience of beauty in nature where the beholder feels reassured. We recommend that our readers recall such moments before reading this book—those specific experiences make the texts start to "speak," and become the selected elements of the topological debate, which still does not exist but is announced in a markedly pragmatic Round Table, where different disciplinary approaches orbit with more or less distance around the single matter of this book. As little as these essays link the act of reading and reflecting to the notion of an "ideal" landscape—after all, they are merely text—so little should the discussion be silenced after reading through this book. And yet, as soon as the protagonists appear, raise their hands to speak, and design is considered, they should vanish behind their answers. Let the landscape architect vanish with them as well. This is not a competition of words.

The act of aesthetic reflection is grasped in a manner strikingly similar to the concept of *Topology*, within the omnipresent debate on landscape in cultural studies at the moment. Namely, not as a debate "landscape space," but rather its sense of "spaciousness" as a description of "spatial relations in terms of cultural and media issues" (Günzel, p. 13). Even in this instance it is about defining preconditions. Our discussion under the same key term, starting from the academic and theoretical discourse on landscape architecture, not only contributes to bringing the value of a discourse up to date in this discipline, but is a decisive step meant to redeem the debate on the constitution of landscape space from the point of view of design. The fact that it is preceded by a process of reflection on modern conditions of built space is obvious from the start (see Giddens). This only confirms the concept of landscape as a result of aesthetic reflection, which is based on nothing other than the act of distancing oneself from the object. By redefining this question, landscape architecture topology seeks to find nothing less than the core societal interest in the designed order of our dwelling space.

Consequently, naming this book *Topology*, rather than the more succinct title Landscape is not just a coquette strategy—a certain aspect of guardedness should be evident in this choice; a bit like circling the target again and again. At the same time, the word "topology" has something in common with its mathematical origins—the constant relation of surfaces to one another—again a wonderful metaphor. Of course, there is the risk of many other conceptual pitfalls. For instance *Topology* is not concerned with seeking out some genius loci, but is anchored in the informed discussion about a given site. As a contribution to this book shows how the "reading of a site" is now, however, the recourse to tools needed for an on-site, detailed topographic understanding of landscape, the site lays at the very basis of the related debate such as it is suggested paradigmatically in this book. As a theoretical construct in the proper sense it is not a manual. Nonetheless *Topology*, as a discussion about the understanding and designing of the world we inhabit, validates at the same time landscape architecture as a guiding force, because the discipline no longer stops at merely integrating the architectural. *Topology* has literally expanded the scale and dimensions of its current tasks—which lends startling virulence to a profession that, up until about one hundred years ago, was still nestled in the garden.

It was Aristotle, and not Socrates, who established the foundations of a discussion concerning "topoi." He provided the basics for a mutual understanding, which at least allowed for an exchange of content to take place. "First, then, we must see of what parts our inquiry consists. Now if we were to grasp with reference to how many, and what kind of, things arguments take place, and with what materials they start, and how we are to become well supplied with these, we should have sufficiently won our goal" (Aristotle, p. 3). However, one must not forget that Aristotle's *Topics* is only one element of his philosophical corpus, which clarifies the conditions for further reflection. At the same time this is fundamental to all: topoi provide agreements that allow for further agreements in a dispute yet to be held. This invitation to discuss such blurred topics today, is made for a discipline whose design knowledge can be traced back to the very roots of culture: to present the notion of topoi to others, without whom landscape architects could not operate today. At the end of the day, what if we could propose tangible results in design that could perhaps reach beyond the fashionable, beyond the personality cult of the designer, beyond plain formalism, in order to attain the wholeness once claimed by such a thing as landscape? Design therefore is understood as the taming of complexity, in other words: enabling the (successful) day-to-day life to unfold before our eyes. Incidentally, there is no need to introduce authors and content in the usual, protracted way here, since the process of appropriating the present texts, inflicted on the reader—texts that should each be read in full—belongs to a tactic that includes the reader. The "topological turn," as one of the last movements in the carousel of ideas in cultural studies, already attempts to optimistically demonstrate that landscape space is not an absolute—it only develops within a dialogue.

LITERATURE

Adorno, Theodor W.: *Ästhetische Theorie*, Frankfurt am Main 1973.
Aristotle: *Topics*, Montana 2004 (translated by W. A. Pickard–Cambridge).
Blumenberg, Hans: *Wirklichkeiten in denen wir leben. Aufsätze und eine Rede*, Stuttgart 1981.
Bubner, Rüdiger: *Ästhetische Erfahrung*, Frankfurt am Main 1989.
Crouch, Colin: *Post-Democracy*, Oxford 2004.
Feyerabend, Paul: *Wissenschaft als Kunst*, Frankfurt am Main 1984.
Giddens, Anthony: *The Consequences of Modernity*, Oxford 1990.
Girot, Christophe, Anette Freytag, Albert Kirchengast, Suzanne Krizenecky, Dunja Richter: *Topologie/Topology*, Zurich 2012.
Günzel, Stephan: *Topologie. Zur Raumbeschreibung in den Kultur- und Medienwissenschaften*, Bielefeld 2007.
Heidegger, Martin: "The Question Concerning Technology," in: id.: *Basic Writings*, edited by David Farrell Krell, London 1993.
Kant, Immanuel: *Kritik der Urteilskraft*, Frankfurt am Main 1974 (1790).
Kuhn, Thomas S.: *The Structure of Scientific Revolutions*, Chicago 1962.
Lyotard, Jean-Francois: *The Postmodern Condition*; Original: *La condition postmoderne*, Paris 1979.
Nowotny, Helga: *Es ist so—es könnte auch anders sein. Über das veränderte Verhältnis von Wissenschaft und Gesellschaft*, Frankfurt am Main 1999.
Popper, Karl R.: *Auf der Suche nach einer besseren Welt. Vorträge und Aufsätze aus dreissig Jahren*, Munich 1994.
Ritter, Joachim: *Subjektivität. Sechs Aufsätze*, Frankfurt am Main 1974.
Rorty, Richard: *Eine Kultur ohne Zentrum. Vier philosophische Essays*, Stuttgart 1993.
Schiller, Friedrich: *Über die ästhetische Erziehung des Menschen in einer Reihe von Briefen*, Stuttgart 2006 (1795).
Scruton, Roger: *Beauty*, Oxford 2009.
Simmel, Georg: "Philosophie der Landschaft," in: *Die Güldenkammer*, 11/1913, pp. 635–644.

The texts of this book are arranged alphabetically by the authors' last names.

Landscape Theories in Transition Shifting Realities and Multiperspective Perception

Annemarie Bucher

Landscape is considered to be the common place par excellence; an open space for thought and action that is, however, subjected to certain laws. The fact that this concept accumulates numerous phenomena, ideas, values, demands, and problems is not usually a problem in day-to-day life. But on the scientific and professional level, different disciplinary-specific concepts have developed around the understanding of landscape, which—because they are based on different systems of reference—have very different scopes, and come into conflict when they seek validity beyond their disciplinary limitations. In practice, this proves more and more a hindrance, because it is essential for planning, design, and development to have a broadly anchored and hence widely accepted understanding of landscape. Understanding landscape is not only fundamental to all those involved, actors and users alike; it is the result of a process of negotiation between the various positions. In the process, landscape theories—[1] play a role that is not to be underestimated. They not only offer insights, justifications, descriptions, and explanations for the "landscape phenomenon," they also create an environment for negotiations by localizing them within a larger intellectual and practical context.

Landscape was long caught in an "either-or" situation of the natural sciences and humanities. Either its natural phenomena were explained or its culturally construed

1 Under "landscape theories," I subsume all of the reflections and theory formulations that are meant to define or deal with landscape. Current landscape theories attempt to illustrate, make tangible, parts of landscape reality by means of statements.

idea interpreted. After the "topological turn,"—[2] however, landscape shifted towards the interest of cultural studies, where in particular transdisciplinarity, grounded theory, and methodological triangulation interlinked different explanatory and comprehension attempts. The current space of landscape is therefore no longer merely physical and geographical, but also cultural and social. Its conceptualization connects self-evident concepts and interests beyond disciplinary and methodological borders, and prioritizes relationships and entanglements over facts. Much has been discussed since the late twentieth century regarding the planning and designing of landscape. The discussion relates to wilderness parks as much as urban squares and, in the second instance, to the question of a common denominator. Various natural, suburban and urban, traditional, and post-industrial landscapes compete for quality and sustainability. Against this backdrop, a committed definition of landscape faded. It is uncontested however, that rapid change in use and design—instigated mainly by ecological pressures—greatly undermined any previously accepted concepts, terminologies, and visual images.

In face of this pressure to change, we are attempting to discover the causes and drivers of this change on the one hand, and on the other anticipating future needs and development tendencies through new visions and models. Yet the fundamental question remains: which understanding of landscape—which basis of theory—will form the basis? And what kind of landscape will be produced as a result?

The idea of landscape itself establishing how it should be perceived—and thus designed—is a modern development, which was greatly influenced by painting and painting's pictorial qualities: the framed picture represents observed landscape and turns it into an object to be viewed from an "aesthetic distance." The picture consequently becomes the way landscape is perceived ("pictorial vision"), and the gauge against which the reality of landscape is measured. Yet the "beauty" that is frozen in the picture is examined

2 The "topological turn" not only makes space the central category of analysis, but also promotes the spatiality of thought. See, inter alia Doris Bachmann-Medick: "Spatial Turn," in: id.: *Cultural Turns. Neuorientierungen in den Kulturwissenschaften* (2006), Reinbek 2009, pp. 284–328, and Karl Schlögel: *Im Raume lesen wir die Zeit. Über Zivilisationsgeschichte und Geopolitik*, Munich/Vienna 2003.

critically, due to the inescapable transformation of physical space and the shift of perspective in the age of post-industrialized, globalized society. It is more relevant at the moment for landscape not be chained to a predetermined aesthetic, but rather experienced casually in movement. It is laced with and structured by a dense network of pathways, streets, and tracks. This network creates a type of visual rhythm, forms points of intersections and a variety of complex relationships. Basing contemporary landscape purely on a traditional, pictorial mode of perception will inevitably fail. Because first of all, the traditional, pictorial perception is qualified when non-visual, sensual experiences are taken into account, and secondly, the processes of change and a multiplicity of perspectives makes the static image more dynamic. Landscape today is a multidimensional phenomenon that needs to integrate the non-visual as well as change, and that also demands different levels of reflection.

Differentiation and Contextualization Rather than Definition

It is now accepted, in the various sciences involved with landscape, that there is no single landscape concept that unifies all disciplines, nor do any representations or ways of presentation exist that are valid across the board. Instead, different ideas and views on landscape have materialized with different ranges and expiry dates.

This almost unimaginable diversity of landscape concepts and definitions reveals far more inconsistencies and contradictions than consensus and contingency. Against the backdrop of a universalizing understanding of landscape, which still shapes the landscape architectural practice, this complicates communication regarding landscape and hinders future negotiations. The ideal notion of landscape fades, becoming a pictorial label and a superficial sales pitch.

A typological understanding of landscape, on the other hand, is based on the specific site and its relationship, and tolerates contradictory definitions and perspectives. Instead of exclusionary general plans, there is an increasing amount of context-specific, temporary, process-based, participatory, design- and planning-related interventions—each with a landscape concept that responds to the specific site. And for this reason, such approaches can neither be right nor wrong (measured against an ideal), but rather plausible and sensible in relation to the actual situation. This reorientation of defining and assessing landscape was announced at the theoretical level: firstly, in a general differentiation of the landscape concept and in the question regarding its visibility; and, secondly, in concrete landscape theory in relation to practice.

Landscape not implying an image, an idea, or a physical-geographic space has long been a topic of cultural studies (green cultural studies). And the fact that this differentiation has far-reaching consequences on the practice level is an overdue subject of current discussion. The landscape concept has diverse interpretations and contexts of use. Work on the landscape concept—[3] has made the following dimensions visible and distinguishable:

I Landscape as physical, object-based space that exists beyond humans and is understood as object-based (natural perspective).

II Landscape as a space of action, space of residence, and social fabric (social perspective).

III Landscape as an abstract idea and cultural construct that shape perceptual conditions (ideal perspective).

IV Landscape as medium (image, film, text, code, and so on) that communicates the physical reality and or idea (media perspective).

3 See Annemarie Bucher: "Landschaft zwischen Bild und Begriff," in *Stadt und Land, Stadt oder Land, Land unter, Transscape*, vol. 11, November 2003, pp. 12–19; id.: "Landschaft als Sehfigur. Das wahrnehmende Auge, die Mittel der Darstellung und die Idee der Landschaft," in: Chris Wittwer (ed.): *Europäische Kulturlandschaften. Ein künstlerisches Forschungsprojekt*, Zurich 2003, pp. 59–72; id.: "Stadtlandschaften in Bewegung. Zur Wahrnehmung und Darstellung von Landschaft als Prozess," in: Stefanie Krebs, Manfred Seifert (eds.): *Landschaft quer denken. Theorien—Bilder—Formationen*, Leipzig 2012, pp. 167–184.

These four dimensions of landscape—their plausibility based on current scientific theoretical distinctions and philosophies—are not only distinguishable due to their theoretical orientation and conception, they are also interconnected by the complexity of the landscape phenomenon. Image, space, and ideas are inseparable, as the work by René Magritte has shown.

As obviously and frequently as these perspectives shape the intersections of the actual dealings with landscape, the relationships between them are comparatively not sufficiently reflected or discussed. The inflationary employment of beautiful landscape pictures to communicate a variety of implications is clear evidence of this. Traditional landscape pictorial conventions may well address a broad public, yet they also have less and less to do with the actual spatial reality they supposedly use as a point of reference in the first place. Blind spots in relation to these different realities—blind spots in theory—are preprogrammed here. They hinder not only an adequate sifting of the phenomenon, but also of the corresponding theoretical formulations.

As early as the nineteen-nineties, philosopher Wolfgang Welsch described the problem of turning a blind eye—the restriction of aesthetic perception.—[4] One of his core theories asserts that every aesthetic contains a conflicting anaesthetic—"a blind spot." "We do not see, because we are not blind, but rather we see, because we are blind to most."—[5] To see means to make visible—tangible to the senses—and thus it is exclusive. Making something visible is contingent upon making something invisible; it is shifting these things to a different dimension of perception that is not embedded in the consciousness. Because sensual perception is based on traditional patterns of perception, it excludes those things that are not cataloged therein. It declares them as nonexistent within the context of the given sensory concept. However, they are conceivable within the framework of Welsch's anaesthetic concept, and significant. In relation to landscape, these are the

4 Wolfgang Welsch: *Ästhetisches Denken*, Stuttgart 1998; id.: *Grenzgänge der Ästhetik*, Stuttgart 1996.

5 Welsch 1998, p. 31ff.

realms not contained within those of traditional perception, but are nonetheless significant within the framework of the overall phenomenon.—6 Hence, landscape should not only be perceived as aesthetic, but should also be considered and questioned critically on other levels.

6 In order to substantiate patterns of perception for suburban space, Thomas Sieverts has developed a concept that is similar to Welsch's concept of anaesthetics. In particular, Sieverts refers the anaesthetic to the "in-between city," because that is where traditional aesthetic sensitivity does not function.

This multiperspectivity was recognized as early as the second half of the twentieth century and responded to with corresponding conceptual approaches. A number of theories made attempts to capture and identify landscape in its complexity independent of disciplinary borders. They refer to the rapid change in design that was typical of contemporary times, as well as to the dynamization of perception and the problematizing of the models of the pictorial ideal. A sketchy review of exemplary perspectives and concepts on landscape in the second half of the twentieth century would easily demonstrate this fact.

J. B. Jackson: Change of Perspective to the Everyday Landscape

An initial impetus to reconsider landscape realities and the rigid conditions of perception came from the United States. In 1951, John Brinckerhoff Jackson (1909–1996)—7 founded the magazine entitled *Landscape*, which quickly became an important impetus for a critical and unbiased research of day-to-day cultural landscapes. Consequently, Jackson not only triggered an interdisciplinary debate on landscape, but also laid the foundation stone for cultural landscape studies.

7 Brigitte Franzen, Stefanie Krebs (eds.): *Landschaftstheorie. Texte der Cultural Landscape Studies*, Kunstwissenschaftliche Bibliothek, vol. 26, Cologne 2005.

Jackson protested as early as the mid-twentieth century that contemporary American landscape reality was not perceived "correctly." This led to him to the subject of landscape itself and also to its perception. In the USA, an everyday, vernacular landscape had developed that clearly differed from European cultural landscapes pictorially and structurally, and that also demanded a corresponding modi of perception. Therefore, he critically questioned the cultural history of landscape as a history of an idealized view of landscape, and called for examining landscape reality from an everyday perspective and recording it systematically. He developed a set of tools that would describe and locally anchor the sensorial and symbolic perception of landscape—the perception and meaning-production of landscape—by placing it in the context of American day-to-day reality.—[8] This shift is not a singular phenomenon, but in combination with Pop Art, it is a precursor to postmodern architecture and Robert Venturi, Denise Scott Brown, and Steven Izenour's *Learning from Las Vegas*.—[9]

Jackson joins this cognitive process as a perceiving subject. He identifies other possible perceptual perspectives by reflecting and qualifying his own standpoint. The result of this fundamental critique of perception is, first, the ennoblement of the vernacular landscape, which, as a counterpole to the "Arcadian ideal," shifts everyday landscape into the center of focus; and, second, the qualification of the perceptual perspective, which is always to be interpreted in context and cannot claim universal validity. Hence, the question of landscape is directed at its cultural construction within a restricted scope.

According to Jackson, the landscape architectural practice was especially burdened by the fact that vernacular landscape is neither a part of the traditional ideal nor is it among the available parameters of perception. The eye is directed at the past, and thus only sees destroyed, formerly "beautiful landscapes" instead of the alive and hence positively charged, day-to-day contemporary landscape. This compels those involved to practice a defensive and conservative politics and design, to struggle against the new, and to preserve or reconstruct the old.

Jackson developed a new typology in order to establish a landscape that would be accountable to the present, which would make available landscape as a product of its history. He defined three types of landscape in a chronological sequence starting with the European and ending with the

8 See also John Brinckerhoff Jackson: "Der Pfad des Fremden" (1957), German in: Franzen, Krebs 2005.

9 See Martino Stierli, Hillar Stadler, (eds.): *Las Vegas Studio. Images from the Archives of Robert Venturi and Denise Scott Brown*, Zurich 2008.

American landscapes: Landscape One. Two and Three are not landscape facts as such, but rather structural perception aids and criteria for classification.

Landscape One is a mosaic of smaller functional landscapes that convey use, ownership, power relations, and technological circumstances, and hence are constant and rarely change. The epitome of such a territory is the medieval village where inhabitants all speak the same dialect, practice the same type of agriculture, maintain the same customs and traditions, and possess the same traditionally established rights and privileges.

But after the Renaissance, Landscape One was displaced by Landscape Two, which builds on the perspective of power, is directed at a single purpose, and—due to corresponding design aspects such as borders or enclosed spaces—is clearly defined and visible. This new visibility first led to a content-related differentiation, such as city versus countryside, field versus forest, or public versus private; and then to specifying external perspectives and the understanding of landscape as a natural scene to be either put on view or displayed.

According to Jackson, Landscape Three is a specifically American landscape that essentially demonstrates a return to the dynamic Landscape One, but with the static inscriptions of Landscape Two. This day-to-day landscape is not the result of planning, but more a pragmatic real space that was created by uses imported from overseas and the continuous adaptation of these traditions and practices to the conditions specific to the site. With this, Jackson attempted to overcome the problem of patchwork-like particularization and dynamization of spatial realities, and thus integrate different perceptual perspectives.

Broadening the perspectives to include the everyday landscape enabled Jackson to not only raise awareness of the dimensions of both the landscape concept and geographic space as laid out in theory and history, but also make it possible to recognize and use the networks contained therein. As a pioneer of a wider notion of landscape, Jackson subsequently provided a number of starting points for the further development of theory and also the establishment of a contemporary planning and design practice.—[10]

10 See Martin Prominski: *Landscape Design. On the Theory of Current Landscape Architecture*, Berlin 2004, and the programmatic anthology on *Microlandschaften*, published in 2006 by Stefanie Krebs and Brigitte Franzen. Stefan Körner undertook a differentiated interpretation, see Stefan Körner: "A New Landscape Theory? A Critique of the Concept, Landscape Three," in: *City and Green*, 55.10, pp. 18–25.

Gerhard Hard: Landscape as Cultural Vestige

In German-speaking countries, theories developed by the geographer Gerhard Hard (*1934)—[11] were an important impetus for a new understanding of landscape. He began in the nineteen-sixties to critically question the history, methods, and objects in geography and in particular landscape geography, by connecting them with the humanistic approaches and proposing an interdisciplinary understanding of landscape. Hard's critique of the classic geographical landscape concept and of the design- and planning-related landscape disciplines is based on a profound knowledge of linguistics and the philosophy of science ("scientific evidence"). As early as the nineteen-seventies and by means of linguistic studies and semantic analysis, he showed that the concept of "landscape" is rooted not in the scientifically objective spatial description, but in painting and the aesthetic perception of a chosen section of an area, and that it perpetuates precisely this aesthetic connotation. The understanding of landscape as a day-to-day phenomenon, in other words, on a general language level, is much more powerful than its scientific objective criteria and elements. Hard assumed that language a priori guides and pre-interprets human thought and action. Humans do not directly act on primary reality, thus it is always conveyed through symbols and media. This means that certain forms of our spontaneous knowledge of the world are articulated linguistically and then stored in the collective use of language, so that, consequently, words and their semantic fields reside in realities that, in turn, influence thought and action. Even in relation to landscape, Hard prioritizes the process of

11 Hard taught geography from 1969 to 1999 at the Bonn and Osnabrück Universities.

feedback of language to the subject and its reflection. He does not primarily question the nature or origin of landscape reality, but rather how the word "landscape" is used on a day-to-day basis.—[12] Thus, he believes that landscape is defined by the feedback effect of linguistic structures on the object—in this case, a spatial area—which represents a significant broadening of the viewing parameter, in which the spatial, media-related, and abstract dimensions of landscape all play a role.

12 See Gerhard Hard: *Die "Landschaft" der Sprache und die "Landschaft" der Geographen. Semantische und forschungslogische Studien*, Bonn 1970.

In response to the question of how one might proceed methodically here, Hard replied with the concept of "tracking."—[13] Instead of scientifically describing landscape with definitions and limitations, he made a case for landscape studies to be a type of "folk science," an everyday science that he developed further in line with the Kassel School—[14] and based on Carlo Ginzburg's evidential paradigm—[15] for landscape-related evidential science. Traces are evidence made "tangible" through understanding previous actions and processes. Cultural landscapes are full of the evidence of human intervention. Hard considered vegetation in particular to be important evidence, which is why he did not classify decorating a space with vegetation as a natural phenomenon, but rather interpreted and correspondingly decoded it as a trace of human intervention.

13 Gerhard Hard: *Spuren und Spurenleser*, Osnabrücker Studien zur Geographie, vol. 16, 1995. See also Annemarie Bucher, Jacqueline Parish: "Spurensuche, Zur Lesbarkeit der zeitgenössischen Landschaftsarchitektur und ihrer Paradigmatischen Funktion für die Landschaftsarchitektur," in: *Suchbewegungen, Zone 7*, edition 07, Berlin 2003, pp. 12–17.

14 The scientific-evidence-based landscape analysis in Kassel was particularly promoted by Karl Heinrich Hülbusch, see, id.: "Eine pflanzensoziologische 'Spurensicherung' zur Geschichte eines Stücks Landschaft," in: *Landschaft und Stadt*, 2/1986, pp. 60–72.

15 Carlo Ginzburg: *Spurensicherung. Die Wissenschaft auf der Suche nach sich selbst*, Berlin 1995.

This trace-guarding perception of landscape challenged scientific thought. It is based firstly on the assumption that culture comprises everything we do, "all the live long day," without thinking about it: everything can be evidence as long as one can see and interpret it. Secondly, the trace theory implies a multiple presence in space—a presence that also connects interpreting traces with leaving behind pre-traces and traces. Someone who simultaneously tracks and leaves tracks behind. The cycle of tracking and tracing closes. This way of viewing the world calls for particular attention to details and peripheries. When this concept is transferred to landscape, it means that landscape does not have to immediately impress the viewer as a spectacular "picture"; it already exists on the roadside or on ordinary park lawns—it is defined adequately by exactly such details. The trace theory, which includes a strong interactive component, has generally established itself in the space sciences.—16

16 See, for instance: Ulrich Veit, Christoph Kümmel, Sascha Schmidt (eds.): *Spuren und Botschaften: Interpretationen materieller Kultur*, Tübingen 2003.

Lucius Burckhardt: Landscape as An Object of Education

The Swiss sociologist and urban planner, Lucius Burckhardt (1925–2003), also responded to the visual impression of landscape with basic skepticism.—17 Landscape was a core concern in context with his fundamental critique of planning and design. He considered it a product of society rather than nature in need of design.—18

17 Lucius Burckhardt: *Die Kinder fressen ihre Revolution*, Cologne 1985; id.: *Wer plant, die Planung? Architektur, Mensch und Politik*, Berlin 2005; id.: *Warum ist Landschaft schön?*, Berlin 2006.

18 Burckhardt 2006.

Although landscape is man-made, most users take it for granted and thus think it cannot be altered. Burckhardt tried to change this, by not tying the landscape concept to physical space. According to Burckhardt, landscape does not exist per se; it is a concept projected onto the environment. He explicitly represented the theory that landscape is generated by the viewer: the generation of landscape by means of being viewed is a creative act; it is based on models and ideas by which spatial reality is accessed. The assumption that landscape is primarily a "generated object" has far-reaching practical and theoretical consequences. Since spatial landscape—as in the case of an English garden—is first produced through the eyes of a viewer, it is not only pictorial but also significantly structured by time. Burckhardt suggested taking walks as an instrument in order to adequately involve this dimension of time.—19 Strolling denotes a time-based organization of a space from a subjective perspective and enables the formation of spatial relationships. In the style of the great expeditions into the New World at the beginning of the Modern Age, he organized legendary landscape explorations into agglomeration landscapes where he allowed preformed expectations, longings, and realities to enter into a dialog with one another.

19 Ibid.

By developing the science of strolling (strollology), Burckhardt not only suggested a new perception of landscape in which direct physical experience was confronted with traditional visual expectations and patterns of perception, he also attempted to draw attention to the defects and errors in planning. He did not consider planning and design to be active processes of creation and organization that resulted in "good form" and "clear systems." The core impetus comes more from invisible networks within the system and leads back to it. Hence, planning and design is primarily the recognition and direction of the invisible impetus within systems. Burckhardt assumed that design was "invisible,"—[20] because the design is no longer determined by the objects and their technical, practical functions, but rather by marginal and basic conditions. Transferred to nature and landscape design this means that function does not determine the park, but rather the context of the social relationship to nature and the associated, invisible fabric of meaning. This makes the park a symbol of a nature culture beyond that of pure use.

20 See Lucius Burckhardt: "Design ist unsichtbar," in: id.: *Die Kinder fressen ihre Revolution*, Cologne 1985, pp. 42–48.

With these provocative theories and methods, Burckhardt attempted to activate users to participate in the design of the environment. His experimental spatial explorations and stollology were in particular integrated as methodological approaches by various other disciplines and developed further by others.—[21]

21 See also the strollology experiments by Martin Schmitz and Bertram Weisshaar.

André Corboz: The Palimpsest Metaphor

The approach by Swiss urbanism and architecture historian André Corboz (1928–2012) is based more on revising the terminology and recording instruments, rather than developing a new concept of landscape perception. His interest in a contemporary understanding of landscape is particularly motivated by observing changes in settlement areas. On the one hand, the traditional concepts of landscape and of city and countryside broke down in reality, but continued to influence social thought and action. On the other hand, Corboz no longer considered perception a reliable criterion. "The landscape that I look at disappears as soon as I close my eyes. The landscape that you look at from the same standpoint is different to the one I am seeing."—[22]

In order to be able to describe landscape, which had changed massively since industrialization, Corboz suggested a theory of territory that would describe a socially appropriated space and its inscriptions and qualities, and would also refer to the archeological concept of layer formations.—[23] This results in the metaphor of "territory as palimpsest." He distances himself explicitly from landscape because he does not believe that the gap between an economically and/or ecologically determined reality and the aesthetic idea can actually be closed. In contrast, the term territory is less loaded with definition. It is not determined by singular, aesthetic acts of perception from afar, but rather by the traces left behind by social action, which affect the spatial area and express its effectiveness and significance. These cultural inscriptions are, then, the determining powers that form and develop the cultural landscape.

These inscriptions have accumulated in layers throughout the course of history. Corboz uses the geographical and archeological principle of stratification in order to illustrate this, and adopted the metaphor of the palimpsest in 1983, in order to describe the long-term effects of these layers of meaning.—[24] Before paper was invented, writing surfaces were a scarce commodity—parchment was largely recycled by scratching off the old text and writing a new one on top of it. Hence, "palimpsest" is the term used to denote a writing surface that has been recycled many times and displays the traces of old texts that continue to effect how new texts are read. This principle can be compared to the surface of the earth, regarding the traces of use left behind by society and construction. While meaningful and valuable

22 André Corboz: *Die Kunst, Stadt und Land zum Sprechen zu bringen*, Basel 2001, p. 160.

23 Corboz 2001; id.: "Entlang des Wegs. Das Territorium, seine Schichten und seine Mehrdeutigkeit," in: Raymond Schaffert, Alain Léveillé, Georges Descombes (eds.): *Weg der Schweiz. Die Genfer Strecke. Von Morschach bis Brunnen*, Fribourg 1991, pp. 121–158.

24 This metaphor has not only been used for landscape purposes—it was also used quite exaggeratedly for multilayered phenomenon. The geographers Pierce Lewis and Denis Cosgrove raised concerns regarding this metaphor. They feared a compulsion to interpret the concept traditionally, and this in an age, where the hyper-textual structures in the digital realm were revolutionizing the classic notion of text.

inscriptions into the cultural landscape are protected and maintained, others are ignored or reconstructed. With his revision of the terminology apparatus, Corboz introduced a de-aestheticization and a critical re-politicizing of landscape that became a focus of broad interest.

Relational Landscape

Landscape "flows" with the times and changes constantly. And a critical reading of it remains essential. What can Jackson, Hard, Burckhardt, and Corboz contribute to the current debate? The original formulations of the four landscape theories outlined here may, in part, be outmoded, yet they still give clear insight into which philosophical trends and conceptual relationships should be taken into account regarding the new emerging complexity of the landscape concept. They have all critically questioned, in various ways, the core notion of the landscape ideal and suggested new points of view. Their critique of existing theory and of landscape was an attempt at searching for a way out. It was only logical that they sought to rethink the traditional concepts of perception, reorganize the respective landscape reality, and revise the fundamental terminology.

These approaches all demonstrate that landscape theory has not been based primarily on an "objective" definition of the landscape subject, but more on the critique of prevailing canons. On the one hand, this "critical" aspect refers to Immanuel Kant's "evaluative analysis," and on the other is based on Karl Marx's critique of a crisis-ridden social reality with the goal of improving it. Ultimately, they all point to how current landscape concepts escape all attempts at canonization, but can be better "situated"—meaning better identified—within their respective systems of reference.

Faith in a Community

Gion A. Caminada

A Personal Introduction

As a child, I was told how my grandfather used to go over the pass to Milan to school, later how, as a merchant, he drove animals south, and how during the Second World War, my father had to hold out up there to protect our homeland. I also remember the people walking up the steep path toward Greina with heavy packs on their backs, while we were scything our meadows. "They come from the city," my parents told me. People from Vrin rarely walked to Greina unless they absolutely had to. My father once took me as a little boy on a mountain tour. Back then, I thought the plateau with its meandering river was more curious than beautiful. What else should I have thought? In the spring and fall, I had to tend the cows up on the mountain. The environment was direct and close; neither romantic nor hostile. I also remember the corpses wrapped in plastic bags, which were flown down from the mountain by helicopter in winter. The village men told how tourists had gotten lost in a blizzard and froze to death. The circling helicopters were an exciting spectacle for us kids—more than the stiff, dead bodies.

Many years later, I stood as town council for the prevention of a reservoir in the Greina. My village colleagues did not understand how one could voluntarily turn down so much money: of course, the lure of money was powerful. Later, compensation funds were granted for the protected status of the Greina, the landscape was rescued, and in Vrin, nature started to be evaluated differently. Nature conservation was discovered and taken to heart, and suddenly—even for the people of Vrin—the Greina was considered beautiful, and I was no longer a traitor to my own people. Gradually, I became occupied with other perspectives of landscape. I read Burke on the sublime, and Rousseau's philosophy of glorified landscape. I dealt with natural historians, poets, and landscape painters. It was only by distancing myself in this way that I was able to understand the people of Vrin and *their* views on nature. I also began to realize that a romanticized portrayal of a relationship to nature, not based in purpose, was not fathomable to them (or to me). A farmer does not know this "elite status" of nature. He does not waste energy climbing a mountain for no reason; that's for city people. The mountain is only important for farmers as a source of existential necessities. Your energy has to be economized, planned, and this has been perfected over centuries of practice. Idealized descriptions of the life led by people who actually come from and live in the Alps are strange and incomprehensible to them. Especially when overstated as in Albrecht von Haller, for instance. In his book *Das Kalb vor der Gotthardpost* (The Calf in front of the Gotthard Post), Peter von Matt rightly questions why this eighteenth-century scientist violated the rules of scientific veracity. Haller had certainly witnessed the many diseases, the gnawing poverty, the high rate of child and maternal mortality, as well as this mountain population's truly very limited luck. Yet, there was nevertheless something very attractive about the simple country life for Haller, as well as for his predecessors, the Greek and Roman poets of the bucolic. In the ways of life of those living in remote areas, these mostly urban writers saw a strikingly immediate relationship to basic resources. I also experienced this immediacy as a child and teenager. Should I lament this time of my youth? This period of my life, which I can only now, through the distance of time, see as a type of magical of the elemental? What would have become of me had I not been sucked into precisely that "civilization," which underwent a fundamental division between nature and culture, and formed our present thoughts and actions?

Vrin, the life here, had a decisive influence on me—as well as on my architectural approach. A constitutive factor for the things experienced here is the recognition of their uniqueness, but the emotions and events that are associated with the place are also crucial. As elements of culture, they are my starting points for architectural design. If an architect recognizes the relevance in such complex phenomena, the significance of "contemporary" building priorities is significantly relativized—such as "object-based" aesthetics, with their exaggerated claim on effect and attention, or the tendency to specialize architecture, which prioritizes only selected interests. At the same time, the chance is opened for such priorities to lead to new options as broader-based processes, and, in turn, it is possible within the conflict between contemporary moments and the respective cultural base for architecture to be closer (once again) to the "elemental."

The guiding principle of architecture such as this is "difference." This difference arises from the distinctive relevance of the site. An "elemental" building works towards this and strives to create an added value to the local life. The core idea is to create spaces that are directly related to the people that inhabit them. I am of the belief that people need things to be manageable in order to develop effective incentive, and ultimately take responsibility for their own place and for the environment. And I am aware that this chance of comprehensibility does not apply to all aspects of human existence in this world. This not only involves a small, remote village, but also principles that I have developed from my own experience.

A reservoir was planned for the Greina plateau.

A place only arises through its difference to another. And only this can generate what people have always sought: identity and the sense of belonging. Otherness was never the actual goal, but rather the consequence of natural constraints and the opportunities to be gained from it. The constants of a place—such as climate, topography, or material resources—were the decisive factors. These context-forming conditions have been largely lost and the contours that frame a particular space have become frail. The amount of "somehow different" says nothing about the actual differentiation and diversity. Too much difference can undermine the difference.

Cultural effort is required if we want to regain the specific context. In our present way of life, difference promises to have a positive impact on the economy and thus on livelihood itself. Difference is not a concept that can be determined qualitatively; it depends on references constructed within a context. The method of consistently improving the existing context is more than just a challenge to rapidly spreading uniformity and the formation of stereotypes: it creates homes for humans.

As a rule, the still popular "building in context" is no longer governed by facts such as availability of materials and technical possibilities. Building is now governed by the two poles of modern architectural understanding: being "contemporary" or "timeless modern." But there are more comprehensive and credible ways of approaching this basic human need: for instance, a strong reference to a place and a community, to a social reality. People themselves would come more into focus, not as a design subject, but in conjunction with the interests of others.

In this process, I follow three main steps: perception—discourse—idea. Perception considers cultural, economic, or social realities as the most important potential. We can gain an overall view by a preferably precise and disciplined survey of the sensual (what do we see as somewhat sensitive?), structural (what do we see when we analyze something intellectually?), and the perceptual level (what is actually possible beyond the given?). The way in which this discourse is conducted allows participants to form a network, in which the individual feels a collective responsibility. The idea that can be gained from this perception and discourse is not the subjectively arbitrary; but rather the pursuit of a goal-oriented, independent conclusion. The architecture that evolves from this process could actually promise something like timelessness.

Vrin: The Idea of "Wholeness"

The small village of Vrin is economically fragile and affected by exodus. It can only continue to function as village in the long term, if the infrastructure necessary for the village community can be guaranteed. For the existence of the individual, it is vital to consider each and every economic possibility. The greatest potential lies in the reality of the place. Recognizing this and integrating it into a democratic structure is and always has been the greatest challenge for Vrin. This would promote autonomy and turn its "otherness" into livelihoods—both economically and in the sense of identity. This otherness is an absolute must for a peripheral existence; and, it is most likely the one quality that has given and, in another form, still gives the major city center its respective, specific appeal.

The village of Vrin.

The “barn costruction zone” is on the edge of the village.

A construction system was developed to build new barns.

The barn was replaced by a new building.

The slaughterhouse gives farmers the chance to direct market their goods.

Different cultural events take place in the town hall.

The telephone booth was built from wood.

The *Strickbau*

Strickbau is the local name for the wooden log construction method typical in the Alps region. The structure consists of stacked wooden beams that are stabilized by "interlocking" the logs at the corners, which creates a characteristic overhang. A Strickbau's floor plan usually consists of very corporeal, individual room modules or chambers, in which spatial tension is created by the interplay of bulk and enclosure. The essential research behind each construction type consists of exploring the limits of the construction while also adhering to its basic rules.

In a Strickbau construction, the process of developing and assimilating ranges from the physical structure to the atmospheric, especially with the interplay of plasticity and mass. Research on the Strickbau seems to follow a predetermined rhythm, but the findings are transferable to any other construction system. And working on a design idea within a local or regional context also creates a kind of sociocultural space: making a product generates both knowledge and meaning.

A "type" such as this takes a peculiar central position between form and idea. Although it can be described formally and thus also comprehended on a sensual level, type does not mean anything concrete; it rather forms the basis of something concrete. Hence, it is not only helpful to organize the confusing plethora of individual shapes, but also as an instrument of the design. The type is "the promise of architecture," in the words of Giorgio Grassi. Working with types allows one to create associations and, thus, to benefit from the experience of history without quoting it.

A type has to do with identity, with "being identical." The identity of a type consists in what it retains despite changes made to it. Identity is always understood and appreciated regardless of developments imposed on the object by functional, structural, or social constraints of a certain era. Yet, a type can be used in different situations, in contrast to a model, which is rigid, and where identity and variation are analogous. It is precisely this contrast between constants and variables that provides the space for research. The concept of repetition plays an important role. In contrast to classical science, where research findings cannot vary, the fine nuances in repetition, especially in architecture, are absolutely essential. While working on a type, there is the sense that each new design contains all past experiences, knowledge, and work, leaving one free to explore new horizons.

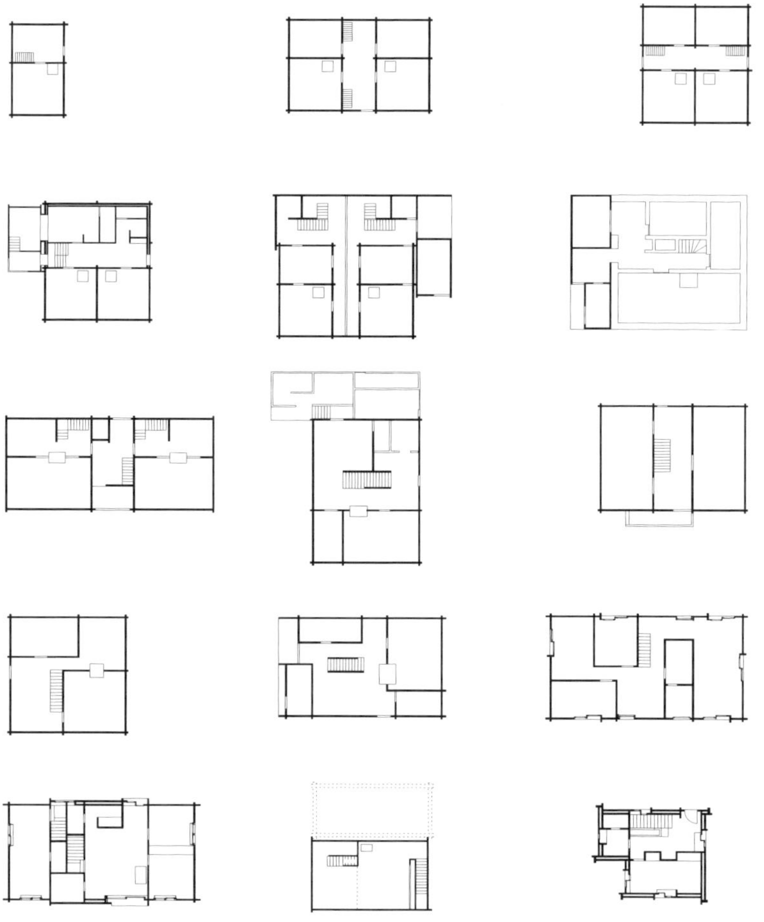

Floor plans.

My development of the Strickbau construction.

Strickbau construction with projecting corners.

Stiva da Morts

The people of Vrin wanted to change the way they dealt with their dead: they wanted a public mortuary. More and more people leave the village of Vrin at an old age and spend the last years of their lives in retirement or nursing homes. There is a problem now, however, when they die: the private funeral parlor where they used to be laid out for a period of mourning no longer exists due to social transformation in the village. While it would be a mistake to build a chapel of rest solely for this reason, it is justified by an acute reality: the displacement of death. And that was precisely the architectural challenge.

The *Stiva da Morts* is situated just outside the cemetery, where many believe the boundary between life and death lies. There are two entrances: through the cemetery and through the village streets. Visitors are free to decide which way to take. This aspect of "both" was the basis for all decisions during the construction process. The stiva da morts drew its meaning and purpose from the surrounding houses. It stands as such in the secular sphere but seeks references to the church, particularly through the way in which the material is processed. The timber used in stiva da morts is subjected to a similar refinement process, as was carried out on the stone of the church. This serves as a unifying element between the two structures. The change in dealing with the dead produced a new building type for the village, added a new element to the hierarchy of the buildings.

Topographical situation of the site.

Interior view of double Strickbau.

The Stiva da Morts is located between the village and church.

Disentis Abbey: Another Model Case

The abbey was always an excellent place to search for the best possible, but in recent decades it has become quiet around these communities. Now Disentis Abbey is a source of new impetus for the greater good. The core elements of this reactivation are an open monastic community, a boarding house for young people, and a monastery barn and production plant as a center for agricultural concerns.

Disentis Abbey, the monastery, monastery school, farmyard, and dairy will provide the space for education and experience. The most important and consistent themes that have always occupied the population will be revised at this special place. An educational facility is to develop here that will differ from the purely information society. Perhaps in terms of the Hellenistic programmatic *Prosoché* (alertness) concept of art, which is aimed at the perception of the moment, but also the widening of perspective. Building bridges between the past and the future is crucial. However, it is equally vital to focus on the here and now.

For this kind of education—one that attempts to comprehend as much of the world as possible and, hence, connect with it—the history-rich site is highly effective. The abbey is the context from which the effect of agriculture and the cloisters unfolds. For the abbey's students, both sites in unison depict everyday life in all its complexity.

The Boarding School

The new dormitory building is a social solitaire. It is the home for the girls of the monastery school. Our goal was to design rooms, which accommodate the young people and provide the space for living and exploring, and also let them live. The girls will have the chance to take possession of the constructed house. Thirty-one rooms are divided among the top four floors, and are grouped on each floor around a communal room. Each girl has her own retreat, without of course feeling isolated. The communal room is the girls' living room. They meet here, tell stories, make tea, or warm themselves at the brass-lined, oven-niche in the center of the room. The four meeting rooms each face a different direction. A staircase leads from each floor directly to the outside. This allows for very complex paths of motion. You can wander through the interior of the house or escape to the outside. The girls can choose to walk through the spaces alone, but unexpected encounters are also possible. The interplay of light and shadow enhances this setting. The house wants to be discovered. The school building was planned as a home for learning and the creation of community.

The boarding school and the benedictine monastery.

The stairs, cooking facilities, and the oven are located in the concrete core.

A typical room in the boarding school.

Salaplauna, the farmyard and alpine dairy, will be an agora for discussing agricultural issues in the region. This should help to recognize and appreciate one's own concerns, as well as those particular to the region.

Agriculture has a complex structure, and some of its aspects will be experienced in the new monastery barn. In addition to the production of food and the visualization of development processes, it will also be a platform for comprehensive discussions about agriculture-related political issues. This implied comprehensiveness of the agricultural form of existence can only be conceived of or obtained through an awareness of contexts that are of ecological, economic, and social complexity. To approach this goal, pedagogical reform principles will also be followed. In Salaplauna, even those who do not live in such communities should learn the importance of agriculture to fundamental existence.

The abbey farmyard consists of three main elements: the open-space barn for animals, the area for hay and straw, and a range of additional benefits based on new agricultural methods. This is where future prospects for agriculture are developed. The building is constructed entirely of wood. An elevated ramp runs through the entire building, so that the behavior of the animals can be studied without them being disturbed. It is possible to observe the animals moving around the barn, leaving the barn to go outside, or resting in their stalls. The abbey farmyard points us in a direction that will lead to a different relationship between humans and nature by sharpening our awareness.

Barn with the benedictine monastery.

An elevated wooden ramp runs through the barn.

The Alpine Dairy

In contrast to the barn, the dairy is made of stone: the building seems as though it wants to escape the ground. Rediscovering natural methods of production led to this archaic-looking form. The cheese cellars are located under the earth and form the core of the facility. They were designed to have an optimized spatial form and the specific climatic conditions necessary for the cheese maturation process. The building itself becomes part of the overall topography. Viewed from outside, the building should look familiar despite its unique shape. Various formal aspects seem to serve a different function from a distance, such as the tract projecting from the main building between dairy and cheese cellar or the freestanding fireplace. The forward-jutting roof, which protects the milk tank from the weather, creates associations with images of Alpine dairies and a familiarity with the local farming culture. The interior of the dairy is divided into three different sections: a public area, the industrial facilities, and the cheese cellar. The limited public accessibility to these facilities is in contrast with the traditional notion of cheese dairies, where products are typically on display. This transparency has been deliberately omitted. Only the core elements can be viewed, such as certain parts of the cheese storage areas or the copper material of the boiler.

It should be possible in Salaplauna to directly experience the positive aspects of agriculture in its entirety. The production of goods creates a production of knowledge, which in turn yields a third process, the production of meaning. A tripartite structure such as this is essential for the sustainable development of all habitats. The absence of a single aspect creates space for discord.

Cheese cellars form the core of the dairy.

The dairy is built of concrete.

The village, as a supporter of community, is an extremely complex structure. At best, the economic, social, aesthetic, and cultural aspects are in balance. If one of these elements disappears, not only are relations interrupted internally, but also those with the outside. Without a powerful inner core, an effective and credible partnership with the outside is not possible. This pair has always been in a mutually reciprocal flow. If the circuit is cut, the community will weaken and be threatened in the long term with extinction.

We can observe two different trends in building and architecture that lead to a loss of a sense of community. The first is aesthetic. The aesthetic objective is to achieve the greatest possible attention by creating a unique appearance. It is mainly directed outwards, and neglects internal hierarchies and their specific orientation, which are of great importance to the community and its function. Emphasizing the building's autonomy of design means that any connection to the specificity of site is ignored. The overall cultural significance of the building is stunted.

The second is the tendency towards specialization of architecture. It has a number of phenomena as preconditions: secularization and pluralization of notions of reality, individualization of lifestyles, the increase of media-based communication, internationalization of cultural forms, and in some respects also the democratization of political systems. Both tendencies—the one that claims rights to an art form, and the one regarding specialization—lead to the emancipation of architecture from social and cultural realities.

We cannot recover what has disappeared. We can, however, strive to regain past advantages, in part with old, in part with new forms and orientations. An architectural approach that follows a direction such as this is not to be found in property or construction projects, but in people themselves, in their present as well as in their emerging new values and ideas about life. This search reveals a strong-willed, self-confident, self-critical person, shaped by keen interest, who first searches for his or her self-realization in a manageable "ownness," which is his or her domain, and at the same time proves that this does not have to come at the expense of solidarity and community. Fundamental relationships need points of intersection, places where they converge. Public inns used to be the central space for many kinds of encounters, even for the secular part of most celebrations that fall between birth and death. Celebrations are a source of strength for the community, not least in the fact that they took place in the semi-public atmosphere of the inn.

Photo of the model for the project in Valendas.

The Engihuus consists of components built in different eras, with a recently constructed addition. It wants to expand the space for festive and profane gatherings, for small and large events, and for planned or accidental meeting. The inn is unfamiliar with the inhibiting thresholds of seminar rooms. Its rooms are soaked in a different atmosphere; they are more open and want to attract people without needing a programmed event. A carefully installed guesthouse in the center can attract people even from the last hamlet and provide openness for encounter. As a hub of relationships, it promises to strengthen the community, but also something unknown, new, the ingredient of hope and confidence. The challenge in Valendas is to develop a place that can help to recover some of the lost sense of community. This is not an utopist architectural claim; it takes steps to provide a "better" world within a given context. It aims to strike a balance between everyday and non-everyday events. In it and with it, the closeness and the distance to the things of this world are remeasured. An exclusive focus on the global world—which, due to a lack of outlook, ultimately remains a fictional relationship—is as irrelevant for the reconquest of community as is the transition to an insular, individualistic existence.

The Elegance of Topology

Christophe Girot

I would therein describe men, if need be, as monsters occupying a place in Time infinitely more important than the restricted one reserved for them in space, a place, on the contrary, prolonged immeasurably since, simultaneously touching widely separated years and the distant periods they have lived through—between which so many days have ranged themselves—they stand like giants immersed in Time.

Marcel Proust, last words of *Time Regained*

The Other Model

In the early summer of 2011, three researchers from the theory laboratory at my Chair met with me at the Monte Verità near Locarno in Switzerland.—1 We spent three intense days questioning the current state of affairs in landscape architectural theory. The question asked was whether a simple term existed, which was capable of expressing both a poetic and constructive understanding of landscape? In architecture, for instance, the term "tectonics" has helped to establish a general theory of design and construction. A similar term for landscape could help define a structured sense of place and time, and return to a more original intelligence of terrain. Such an all-embracing term capable of expressing the fundamental essence of a landscape with discernment is still lacking.

1 Anette Freytag, Albert Kirchengast, and Dunja Richter joined me on a rainy weekend to examine, challenge, and debate about the state of affairs in landscape theory. Together, we tried to lay down the foundations of a new theoretical position and practical method of designing the contemporary landscape. Was it possible to develop a holistic approach, whether directly or indirectly, through a return to the primacy of aesthetics? Could a better understanding of a place through different benchmarks help to build relationships specific to a given landscape that could escape the banality of normative design? The goal was to establish a deeper understanding of natural and cultural structures within established design traditions.

We tend to refer to landscape in subjective terms, as if it were an amalgamation of things good and bad, beautiful and ugly, without a determined direction. And we agreed that the situation masks an overall absence of choice, method, and purpose regarding the making of a landscape. Agencies today tend to regulate and shape the landscape in such a normative way, that it is often difficult to note any sort of difference from one place to the next.

We come from a long-standing intelligence of terrain, and believe that this tradition could be reinstated with ingenious simplicity. Are we able to rekindle a renewed understanding of site in its physicality, and elegance that could translate back into a sense of design? Modeling tools of unprecedented precision are now able to replicate the physical properties of a site. They show specific aspects of a landscape that cannot be depicted in a plan. Does this mean that these aspects are insignificant, or that the plan in fact seriously limits the range of possible interpretation of a place? The modeling tools rely on large three-dimensional data sets that are unwieldy to decipher and difficult to convert into meaningful workable formats, despite the fact that they are aesthetically pleasing to look at. But does this mean that we should ignore them, and that a valid and workable understanding of landscape can only be based on the use of a plan? Despite the difficulty and challenge that these data sets represent, it is clear that a renewed approach to landscape through such modeling can provide a stronger, well-informed basis for design. In this age of big data, there is a need for a new insightful method that can retrieve the spirit of terrain with elegance. What are the physical aspects that truly matter in design and that so far have eluded the plan? How does one sift through such data sets, in order to touch on the spirit of a landscape? Abstraction has always been the problem with a plan, and the landscape overlay method, which has now become the rule and standard procedure in landscape architecture, cannot design properly because it always confuses deductive analysis with the poetics of place.

Point-cloud models are unwieldy and the information they deliver—although highly precise topographically—remains partial, virtual, and superficial. These models should in no way be confused with the tangible physical reality of a site, but understood rather like its spirit. They depict many of the physical, material, and temporal qualities of a place that are of vital interest to us. How does one mine these qualities out of a model, and how can it better contribute to design? A point-cloud model resulting from laser scans is fascinating, but of very little use when it is not combined and scaled with other techniques of observation and design. It appears on the computer screen as a pixelated membrane, producing a luminescent ensemble of textures, including details of reliefs, vegetation, and infrastructure. From a topographical point of view, the model is stunningly precise and beautiful in its wafer-thin representation. Landscapes captured in this mode reproduce a pointillistic veil of scintillating electronic point-clouds that look like dew drops minutely covering the entire surface of the land. The models reveal a highly complex assemblage of topography and infrastructure, blending cultural and technical artifacts with natural outcroppings, torrents, and gorges. Beyond the visual fascination the image confers, the features of interest depend on our particular agenda. We can derive a new approach from the models at our disposal, which challenges a certain planimetric status quo in terms of landscape planning and design.

The Other Mind

We all agreed on the choice of one term referring to the physical and poetic reality of a landscape, suggesting a sense of wholeness, namely "topology." Its etymological roots lie in the ancient Greek for place (*topos*), and language (*logos*). Although topology is generally understood as a mathematical construct relating to the continuity and connectivity of surfaces, it can also incorporate a more general understanding about the genealogy of a constructed landscape. Highly precise electronic models inform us better about the physical interrelation of complex surfaces with forces and changes in the environment. It is not the quantity of data produced by a model that is relevant to topology, but rather the quality and precision of information that can be mined and retrieved from it. The word "elegance" stems from the Latin *elegans,* which finds its roots in *legere* (to pick out or to choose). The elegance of topology could be best defined as the refined art of picking out the essential features of a site. How does one teach such elegance, with or without a model? Topology is about the intelligence of a site perceived, and shaped by society topically. It defines a discerning approach to the physical and natural conditions of a landscape, guided by the technical, ethical, and aesthetic choices. Topology sets the physical, cultural, and temporal reality of a given place through a series of reflected deontic and cognitive choices.

The mapping overlay techniques, developed originally by Ian McHarg and used at present by most agencies around the world, have tended to transform landscape irrevocably into a set of rather abstract and categorical items and zones on a plan. Topology challenges this approach in that it must be local, precise, and culturally specific. The normative overlay system, derived from McHarg's method has tended to considerably reduce and flatten the reality of landscapes as we understand them today. Can the physical model, which can of course supplement many other models and layers, become the canvas of a new approach to design, one that would be much more specific in its understanding and interpretation of place? The elegance of topology could reflect a landscape tradition that is eminently physical, aesthetic, and artistic, and that seems to have been forgotten. It can open a wide range of possibilities across disciplinary fields such as engineering, planning, architecture, and art, by preserving the cultural thread of a place, while discerning key aspects of a given terrain knowledgeably and elegantly.

True-color point-cloud, St Moritz, Szwitzerland.

Section through true-color point-cloud, Göschenen, Switzerland.

Section through true-color point-cloud, Brissago, Switzerland.

SSGRID
697379.58
07274.97
346.61
SWISSGRID
lon 697383.81
lat 107274.97
elev 343.25
SWISSGRID
lon 697388.71
lat 107274.97
elev 341.35
SWISSGRID
lon 697393.44
lat 107274.97
elev 338.91

Plan view of true-color point-cloud, Brissago, Switzerland.

Topology must be understood as a holistic approach to a landscape that has always been in the making; a landscape that seems so fragmented and zoned today that we seem to lack an awareness of its past qualities. Topology enables a more general understanding of landscape as a symbolic cultural entity, woven into physical and spatial relationships at the dimension of a territory. Understanding territorial continuity physically helps better identify qualitative priorities in a landscape. Young landscape architects must return to the field, to learn once more how to operate knowledgeably in a landscape. The tendency in recent decades has been to push landscape education towards a higher degree of abstraction and reduction, with an emphasis on communication skills and pattern recognition, rather than physical design skills. This probably has its merits in terms of advocacy and didactics, but has led to a more subjective rather than constructive approach to landscape design, whereby personal impressions, images, and narrations come to play an increasingly important role in describing the existential reality of a site. Consequently, it seems particularly important to return to the concrete physical reality of a site, learning how to identify the character, potential, and inherent qualities of a landscape. Students must strive to gain a better understanding of terrain and foster stronger disciplinary skills before launching into a design. Acquiring skills and proficiency in topology has always been central to the art of landscape architecture. What kind of proficiency is actually needed today? Can we still sketch an idea on a piece of paper, or must our entire design universe be confined to the pixels and vectors of a computer screen? Which generation, if any, works a plan on velum as a palimpsest in the masterful manner of the architect Carlo Scarpa, where every step of the design process transpires through a single sheet of paper? Topology should encapsulate these steps, which assess the physical and temporal reality of a site by consciously weighing a series of decisive choices to avoid applying normative changes blindly.

Topology works as a method of design while maintaining elegance and precision at different scales. Some projects show how it works effectively with regards to large-scale territories. It is effective when applying new techniques intelligently and precisely, particularly in the vicinity of flooding river basins and coastal regions, where the quality and mastery of virtual modeling is of the utmost relevance. We now have the necessary technical know-how to react creatively to such large-scale challenges, and need to improve our constructive approach to landscape in these domains. Topology, understood as a philosophy, but also as a specific intelligence of terrain, will play a major role in the design of landscapes to come. With precise tools and a new attitude towards analysis and design, many of our idiosyncratic habits will be questioned, such as granting the preeminence of program over terrain. To illustrate this point, I can recall the Grands Atelier Project I worked on a decade ago, where the French government decided to embark on a project requiring a flat four-hectare site for an experimental architectural laboratory. They chose a steep hillside for the project, requiring a geologically complicated flattening of the site, which was considerably in excess of the budget. It would have been advisable not to go ahead with such a project on that site, had better knowledge about the terrain and its physical properties been integrated in the program. This lack of understanding about terrain is quite typical of our modern age and has been detrimental to landscape in general, where it is always assumed that a site can be made flat to assume a program.

The Other Foot

Ironically, in light of remarkable developments in landscape modeling, few schools seem to have placed emphasis on topology and a better understanding of what constitutes the physical and cultural basis of landscape design. We are apparently content with a status quo that has prevailed in landscape architecture over the last forty years? How often must we look again at the "brilliant" plans of Tschumi and Koolhaas for the Parc de la Villette competition of the early nineteen-eighties, to reiterate our belief in the preeminence of program over terrain? Both projects at Parc de la Villette approached this very flat site programmatically as if it were a blank sheet of paper. It is indeed convenient to ignore the challenges presented by a given terrain and to pursue a conceptual approach to landscape design, as long as the bulldozer follows and flattens accordingly. But such principles go hand in hand with an absence of discernible aesthetic theory about site topography and locality; in the case of the Parc de la Villette the aesthetic is only in the program. Can anyone talk, let alone teach about the beauty or ugliness of a given place, or are we just seduced by our own concepts independently of a site? We have become disconnected from the sites we supposedly care for, and are unable to formulate a clear opinion about them, because we lack the proper tools and training to do so. These fundamental questions shed a light on the plight of landscape architecture today, which is apparently attempting to save the natural world programmatically without adequate tools or the necessary landscape theory. Many reasons explain such shortcomings, which are bound up with a weakened understanding of the symbolic power of landscapes globally. The waning respect for symbolic value, in favor of programmatic functionalism has greatly affected the credibility and scale of landscape operations worldwide with repercussions that are essentially educational, economic, and social. Large engineering offices have taken over the vast environmental planning and management projects that we should be doing, developing ecosystems services to the detriment of design. Moreover, quantitative methodologies and programs inherent to these services have nothing to do with design and the feeling for place. Topology is first and foremost about understanding the aesthetic substrate of a site, and acting where it matters most in nurturing design. It serves as the basis of a more immanent understanding of landscape in society. It is about combining the technical and the aesthetic elegantly in a physical conception of place, embracing higher social and cultural values that go with it. A point-cloud model is just the starting point of a set of informed physical choices regarding a site, which enable precise "surgical" interventions into a terrain that are based on a long-standing tradition, where art and technique blend into a single elegant topology. The loss of a sense of the whole in a landscape is not due to the world we inhabit, but rather to the methods we employ. This calls for a renewed attention to terrain, and is only possible if a fundamental change of attitude in society happens, and the blind faith in our current methods of design is challenged.

The schism between an originally shared aesthetic appreciation of landscape and a more subjective and interpretive form of observation can be traced back to the Romantics. The "lakists" saw landscapes as the narcissistic embodiment of individual mystical values. Topology could breed a new generation of "cloudists," capable of founding deeper meaning through an informed understanding of landscape past, present, and future. They should remain wary of whimsical and emotive interpretations of nature, and take distance from assertive scientific analysis aimed at describing and prescribing an entire spectrum of landscape environments. A better understanding of the inherent physical appeal of a given site will be gained through proper methods and tools. Topology is based on the meaning of a terrain, not only technically, but also culturally and symbolically, because it relates to the genealogy of place. This leads to a better understanding of landscape, where subjective interpretation and scientific empiricism are subordinated to the reality of given situation. Models used for topology have the advantage of being eminently physical. They are informative and can be filtered for various design purposes, presenting an undistorted 3D representation of the world, which is geo-tagged. The models themselves have little meaning unless they are combined with other fields of knowledge about a place. They are used by engineers for advanced surveying, and are appreciated for their incredible precision. For engineers, they merely depict an existing situation in high resolution and three dimensions, but for the landscape architect, these models have an inherent aesthetic appeal in addition to the actual terrain information they provide.

Work completed over the past decade on an artificial mound in Sigirino, Switzerland for the AlpTransit Company shows how efficiency and precision in topology help define better solutions and answers to questions of environmental aesthetics and integration. Many of us seek sustainability in our designs; in the case of the Sigirino mound, the 3D point-cloud model enabled a piece of environmental "haute couture," where the project became precisely interwoven and confined to the existing mountainous terrain. Extensive data sets made it possible for the landscape architect to determine the exact contact point between the artificially fabricated mound delineated by a gabion drainage line and the steep rocky slopes of the Monte Ferrino with its rivulets, rubble, and cascades. This understanding of the precise physical reality of a terrain enabled a particular approach, which could be termed "topological elegance," where the entire team of landscape architects, environmentalists, and engineers reached a compromise, and agreed on a common solution.

Tools of topology as such do not provide an interpretation of site, but they help assess a given situation very precisely. By focusing on the problem at hand, the situation can be assessed accurately, it is then up to the design team to discuss and determine the appropriate course of action. In the case of the Sigirino mound, verification led to the avoidance of dynamiting mountain rock faces, while linking the project to an existing network of paths and slopes. The form of a landscape project is constantly influenced by the strong physical conditions of a site, and has to adapt to external conditions. Topology creates a unique design approach that is quite different from the programmatic and analytical methods acclaimed before. Landscape architects can benefit tremendously from surveying and modeling techniques that are usually the privilege of engineers; these can add value to a better design and aesthetic approach to terrain. One can literally visit each rock, each tree, each house on such a point-cloud model, placing viewer, the client, the designer at the heart of the landscape and the intended design. We can look at a singular design project as it evolves under a variety of scales and aspects, with a surgical precision that will come to revolutionize the notion of landscape design simulation and participation.

The Other Eye

For centuries, landscapes were considered the product of ideal representations of the world captured within a picture frame. The epitome of such paintings, were the seventeenth-century idealized perspective works by Nicolas Poussin and Claude Lorrain. Earlier perspective studies in the Renaissance focused on building the illusion of pictorial depth through precise proportional triangulation. For this formidable task, the construction of a landscape image always preceded the choice of place. The custom actually goes back to the logic of the *ars topiaria* initiated by the Romans, who drew frescoes illustrating Virgil's *Bucolics* on the walls of their Pompeian atria years before these landscape ideals were ever applied to a garden. To master perspectival illusion in the Renaissance, the rest of the landscape was occluded, while attention was focused on a single point on the horizon. The grand illusion of perspective happened to the detriment of broader aspects in the environment, including the landscape itself, which became seriously distorted around the edges of the picture frame. In Leonardo da Vinci's *Annunciation* or even more so the *Mona Lisa*, the distant landscape warps towards the edge of the frame. (da vinci) We have all grown accustomed to looking at landscapes in a perspectival manner, and it feels almost natural today. However, beautiful landscape vignettes produced by Claude's glass are nothing more than ambient scenery reflected on a dark parabolic mirror. Beyond the immediate charm of this reflection for the beholder, it also stands as the living proof of a tangible perspectival reality. This brings to mind the earlier "Tavoleta" experiment staged by Brunelleschi at the beginning of the fifteenth century, who also used a mirror, which was considered a high-tech product at the time, to reflect a constructed drawing of the Florence Baptistery in perspective. In order to achieve this perspectival epiphany effectively, the beholder needed to literally lie down on his belly at the entrance of the cathedral nave and peek at the Baptistery through a small hole bored in the door on the aforementioned painting. The reflected image confirmed the validity of perspective as an effective mental construct that could be projected onto the world, and the symbolic significance of the observer's prostration in the cathedral nave to attain this revelation was by no means fortuitous. In effect, perspective can detach the subject from the reality of a place for the sake of a projected ideal. Consequently, ideals have had a beautifying but distorting influence upon our gaze over the past five hundred years.

This phenomenon of the idealized gaze could now be counteracted by topology, with an elaborate landscape model preceding any image. This presents a considerable challenge to our conventional way of thinking and designing. The plan, section, and perspective are here to stay, but they can no longer precede the renewed understanding of terrain. If we agree that a model of the existing terrain will supersede the idealized image, it shows the inherent relativity and complexity of landscape transformation. A virtual point-cloud terrain model can be applied to landscapes at different scales, viewed relative to several points of view and sets of interest within an overall genealogy of design. The

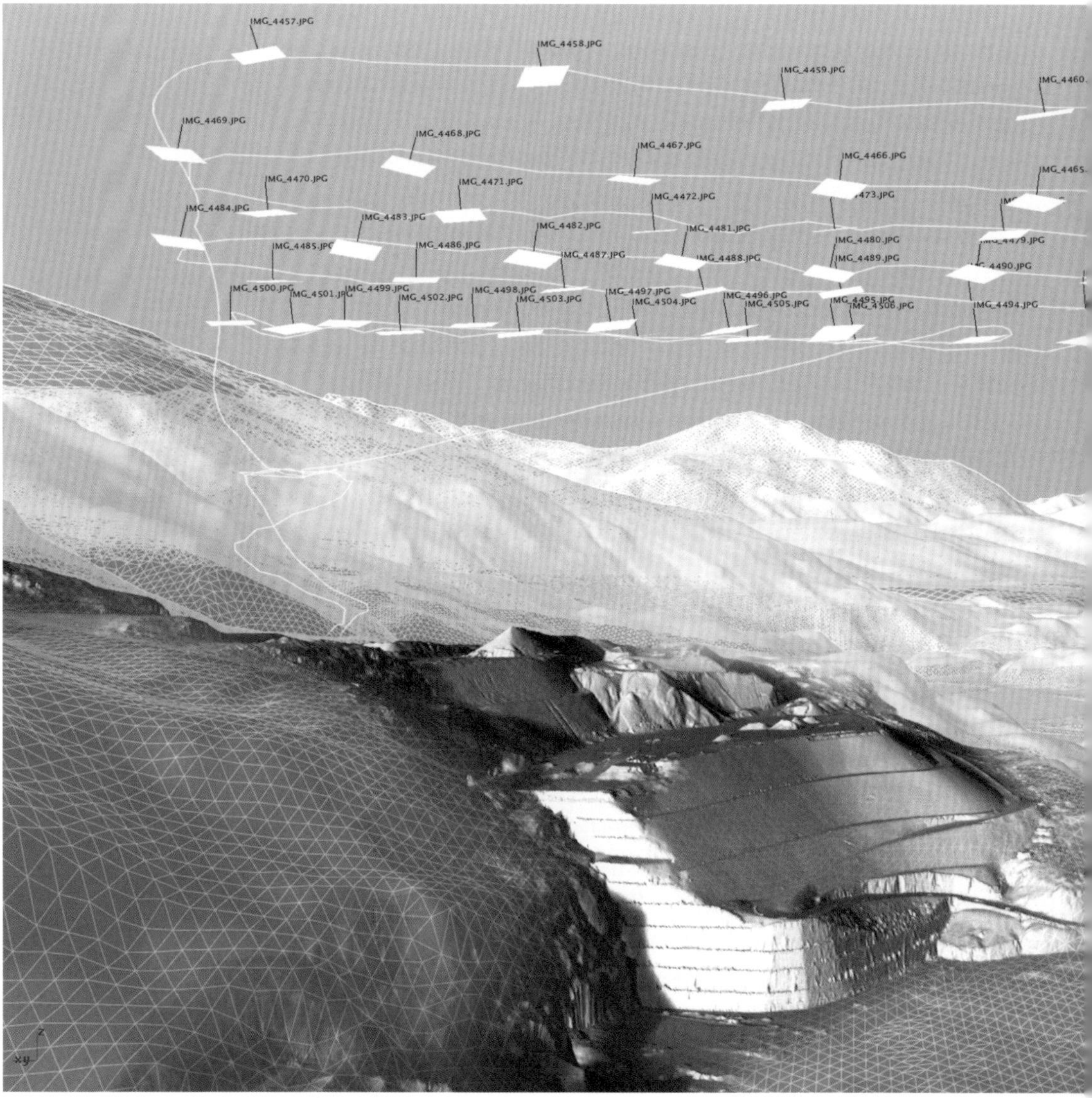

Drone survey over the Sigirino Depot construction site.

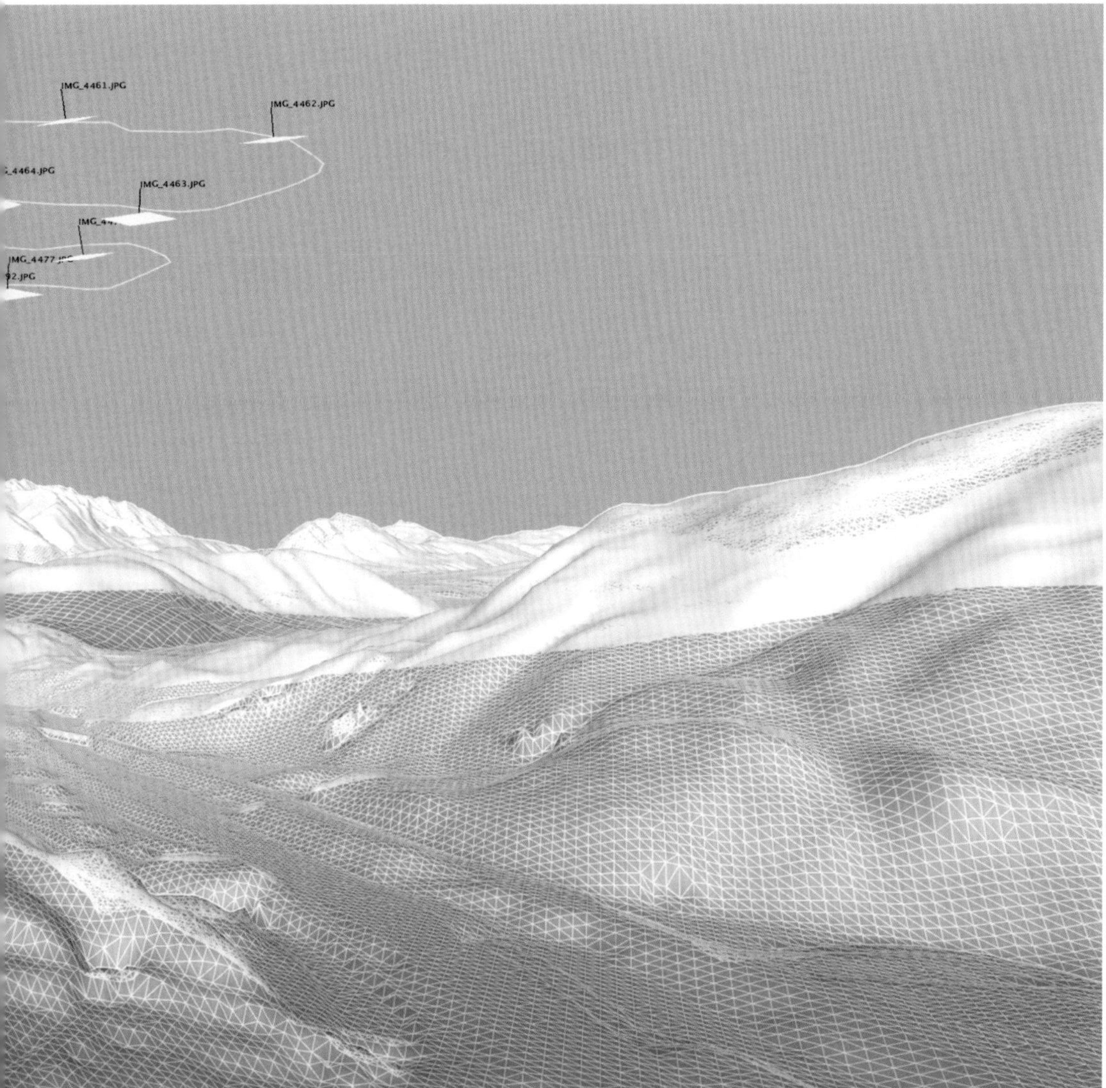
IMG_4461.JPG
IMG_4462.JPG
IMG_4463.JPG

Sigirino Depot project embedded in the digital terrain model.

Visualization of the Sigirino Depot project.

elegance of topology encompasses various landscape forms and artifacts within its present scope, while asserting the potential for possible transformations.

Research in "Landscape Chronology" developed at the Chair shows how past landscape sceneries obtained from photographs and paintings can be effectively embedded into 3D point-cloud models. The site of St. Moritz which is consistently documented photographically was chosen as a laboratory for model studies over successive periods of time. Beyond landscape design innovation, these models can also be used to simulate urban growth, and test acoustic phenomena, water, air and snow flow, as well as vegetation over time. Topology is about the primacy of the actual terrain over an idealized vision; and letting a terrain speak in this manner brings something quite new to the discipline. There remains the challenge of how to recover meaning in a landscape with which we have seemingly lost touch. It is precisely the apparent level of abstraction and displacement through the point-cloud model that leads to the elegant selection of what matters in a location. In topology, it is the surface of the model in its intricate folds and structure, and not the ideal image that becomes the generative force of design.

French perspective painters were trained by Italian masters, and subsequently influenced the English landscape tradition a century thereafter. The elaborate triangulation behind each picture preceded the setup of the scene and its narrative. Once painted, the scene preceded by several decades the parks and gardens it inspired in England. Think also of Baldassare Lanci's instrument in the Renaissance used for surveying and perspective by Vignola at Villa Lante. The elaborate device was used, quite literally, to project perspective upon an existing hillside. Applied in this instrumental manner, perspective worked perfectly well and gave a majestic illusion of depth in a single direction through the deformation of volumes as they receded from the picture frame into the real space of the garden. The gardens of Vaux le Vicomte, Versailles, and Herrenhausen are perfect examples of further applications of these geometric principles at the scale of a park. The question remains, however, as to how such a perspectival approach employed over the last five hundred years has related back to the rest of the landscape outside of the picture frame, and how this affected the devolution of countless other places. The answer is probably to be found in the grid-like landscape of North America laid out by Thomas Jefferson, or the polder landscapes of North Holland like the Beemster.

The Other Landscape

Picturesque depictions convey meaning to people, both poetically and symbolically, through sets of perspectival conventions, blending optics and mathematics with aesthetics. These meaningful, almost sacred constructs, took centuries of mastery and theory to establish the landscape aesthetic we now revere—such as the great landscapes of Castle Howard, Rousham, and Stowe, and later Central Park and Buttes Chaumont, to name but a few. They show the extraordinary power of idealized landscape perspectives once the mastery of the tools and the theory have been established. The question is not to arraign, nor to replace perspective *per se*, but to understand how it was conceived over time and to reveal the paradox we are part of today. From the point of view of landscape, the perspective system that we have inherited formally prioritizes the image and construct, over the reality of the terrain and model. This is more evident in pseudo-perspectival assemblages, such as photomontages and collages, which emphasize the atmospheric aspects of a landscape of a landscape where an seductive oneiric sense creates scenes that are scarcely believable. Perspective is like a construct that is counterintuitive to normal landscape perception, because it challenges the immediacy of terrain as our gaze pans the land.

The drawing and plan, and even more so the camera image and its multiple derivatives, elude landscape as a whole when it comes to perspective; they provide information about a small scope of terrain that becomes idealized, while the rest remains marginal and ignored. A landscape cannot reduce itself to such a perspectival metonym, or fragment, nor can it cobsist of a set of in-betweens; landscape must encompass a much fuller topological description of the environs. The discrepancy between a perspective image and a site as a whole tends to cripple our apprehension of the world. By entrusting the landscape model with its point-clouds, topology yields a renewed sense of the world that subsequently leads towards a renewed sense of aesthetics. When speaking of a model, the cloudist does not brandish the entire spectrum of existing facts about the world, but rather shows an elegant and knowledgeable selection of agents to be considered, shaped, and modified through masterful design. The anticipation of modeling over perspective will bring about a fundamental epistemic shift, whereby the observer will learn to master and appropriate a site in all its *physis*, gaining a deeper sense and conviction about its inherent wholeness, which is both local and specific.

Cultural questions raised by topology are of key importance because they include other forms of knowledge and help cloudists master and differentiate design decisions. They challenge the status quo, but also question the very places that are devoid of such ideals. In this instance, it is the earth itself that "speaks" to us in a meaningful way about all its complexity, history, and structure. The model is not a fac totum, but a measurable constant that refers to distinct points in the world; the cloudist knows that the model and the world will always remain distinct from one another, but through it he will gain a greater mastery and understanding of terrain.

It is precisely this distance between world and subject, that topology questions openly and diachronically. Landscape is the canvas of multiple successive changes, and present-day modeling relates to this culture of change through sets of conventions and signs that eventually enable better choices on the terrain. The point-cloud model shows an abundance of contextual evidence that is at times quite overwhelming, not to say uncomfortable, for most of us who do not master the technique of grading properly. But when it comes to the actual reading and mastering of territorial conditions, topology draws a clear distinction between the tangible reality of a physical terrain model and the evanescent approximation of a photomontage and its eidetic dream. The challenge is to change what has been part of landscape practice over the past decades, presenting a combination of highly abstract programmatic plans, coupled with dreamlike images that simply shortcut any account of the terrain. The established representations of the picturesque relied heavily on an aesthetic theory born from earlier pictorial conventions mastered over previous centuries as an epistemic modality to access the world. The topological model enables the mastery of an entirely different kind of physis, typically non directional and open to a landscape, in its entirety, adding a level of knowledge to a project that will help bridge the gap between terrain and older conventions. In the case of projects like the Sigirino Mound for the AlpTransit Company, the Zimmerman Garden in Brissago, or the River Park at Dordrecht, the images and sections result directly from the mastery of a point-cloud model. Topology learns to master a landscape that is eminently physical and bound to the terrain; it understands first and foremost the rules that apply to a real situation. In that sense, one could oppose the eidetic to the topological, the lakist to the cloudist. The knowledge that topology claims results from local evidence gleaned on-site and considered in all its physical complexity. The new method presents an epistemic challenge, because its mastery necessarily questions the primacy of image over model, and moreover our very own conditioned perspectival sensitivity towards a place. The role reversal between model and image proposed by topology is highly destabilizing, yet very liberating and promising for design; it requires

City and agriculture, Design Studio Dordrecht, The Netherlands.

Urban park, Design Studio Dordrecht, The Netherlands.

Agriculture polder, Design Studio Dordrecht, The Netherlands.

that we question the modalities of aesthetic preconceptions that we have learned to trust for a long time by mastering a physical approach of another kind. Topology can work for landscape architecture in the same way as tectonics did for architecture, mastering the fundamental design aspects of a place through informed modeling and structure. It can can promote new forms of spatial relationships, leading at term to an aesthetic that is not necessarily linked to the ideals of the picturesque, but rather rooted in the gritty reality of today. Topology must first infiltrate the technical and master the elegant enhancement of a landscape *in situ* and *de visu*, before postulating some theory. This mastery is all about returning to the constructive genesis of a place, with a focus on changing physical, temporal, and cultural aspects. Landscape elements can be manipulated physically in such models, or mastered just as they are in all their immanence and purpose. Through topology, design questions and works the model first before reverting to any image. The fact that image follows the model and no longer precedes it harks back to our sedentary origins when the first landscapes were simply drawn with a stick, rope, and chalk directly onto the ambient terrain.

There is a dichotomy between our understanding of landscape in the scientific sense, as a functional normative network of ecological systems, and the existence of a place, as it appears cognitively, poetically, and emotionally for people. Topology operates with elegance at the interface of science and philosophy, combining the reading of layers of history with a mastery of present uses. A point-cloud model offers more holistic truth than a layered plan, although both remain incomplete representations of a world that work in many ways. The difference between topology and palimpsest is essentially epistemic and physical. The palimpsest involves a synthesis of layers, traces, and erasures compressed on the surface of a plan, which are meant to be understood as a two-dimensional representation of different times on the surface of the earth, whereas topology, through a 3D physical model, directly represents the embodiment of landscape in a much fuller synchronic dimension. Some of our predecessors were already able to operate topologically at a different scale, albeit without reverting to a model, but always keeping the reality of a terrain in check. Lenné worked on a vast but incomplete green ring, embedded in the gritty periphery of Berlin, Olmsted skillfully fought sand dunes behind the Presidio in San Francisco to secure Golden Gate park and the Panhandle, Alphand modeled an idealized landscape with precise contours out of the slums surrounding abandoned gypsum quarries in Paris, and Burle Marx created a previously non-existent beach in Copacabana. Topology is about the mastery of terrain and the creation of timeless landscapes inextricably linked to their respective site, culture, and environment.

The Dordrecht studio, which ran at the ETH in 2011–2012, based its approach on the mastery of highly accurate, virtual terrain models, showing the impact of shifting intertidal waters in the Dutch Delta of South Holland over time. The intertidal zone of Dordrecht, once mastered and modeled, became a virtual laboratory for testing a range of scenarios for high risk flooding. Precise modelling combined with the mastery of terrain grading at ten-centimeter hight intervals made it possible to create simulations of a wide range of landscape futures. The designs were fed directly into the virtual 3D model, which in turn generated new landscapes that merged waterways, urban areas, and agricultural terrain into an entirely new understanding of the Dutch territory. The method, based on the simulation of exact variations in water levels across a very vast territory, helped show possible adaptations to very real flooding threats for South Holland. The use of photomontage was banned in the studio, and students were asked to work on-site directly with sand models in order to remain focused on the physical reality of this sensitive topography—illustrations of the project were generated from the model later only once the landscape had been entirely thought through topologically, mastered and modeled. Without such precision on the terrain, it would not have been possible to simulate credible flooding scenarios for Dordrecht. Topology is about design in an age of geographic information, where one must master the available tools in order to meet the challenges ahead. This heralds a return to topology, and a better understanding of landscape formation, because although the appearance of a place appears to change, its essential make-up prevails over time. The studio method for Dordrecht showed how precise topological readings could help master the inherent forces at work in a landscape. The elegance of topology relies on the use of powerful indicators that bring a landscape's atavistic qualities to the forefront. In the case of Dordrecht, students mastered the founding blocks of a new Dutch landscape identity that were synonymous with notions of collective effort and trust in the ambient terrain.

The Dordrecht studio was focused on the topological mastery of an extraordinary mosaic of landscape potentials, set within a few meters of sea level. In some cases, the earth was forced to yield to the brute force of water, in others the modulation of terrain would alter its course. River flow and tidal flow shaped sedimentation at specific boundaries that were sometimes designed, sometimes not, which in turn shifted settlement patterns over time. Through the mastery and control of landscape, topology can play a fundamental role in the cultural understanding of this place marked by the memory of past cataclysms such as the St. Elizabeth's Flood of 1421. The patterns of cultivation that were established in polders during the centuries thereafter display the slightest variations in natural sedimentation. This ebb and flow between culture and nature stabilized gradually giving value and purpose to a place that was otherwise in a permanent state of natural flux. Here, the frailty of matter against the power of water is either tangent to the daunting force of flow or nothing. Holland is home to a thousand kinds of flatness, and landscape is its common cultural expression. Landscape, a term that originated in Holland as *Landskip*, is the product of a culture that frames a broader and more meaningful framework of natural signifiers. This topological truth beholds an extraordinary potential and points towards a knowledgeable recovery of terrain in which the sacred meaning of a place is amalgamated with the common banality of ambient circumstances. It shows how people remain in full possession of their land in the face of extreme adversity, turning dejected ordinary moorlands into something collectively remarkable.

The various projects developed in the Dordrecht studio show an elegant set of choices between prosperous agricultural islands, merging from an intertidal wildlife area and a new waterfront city facing the treacherous waters of the Maas. Between the mountain slopes of Switzerland and the moorlands of Holland, we have developed and mastered a range of topologies, adapting the shape of the land to the purpose of radical environmental change, transforming and recreating prosperous communities through a better and more precise feeling for landscape in the fullest sense of the word.

Landscape and Modernity

Stefan Körner

The concept of landscape is controversial in landscape architecture. The question is whether it is still a good basis for modern landscape design in spaces that are becoming increasingly urban. Its Arcadian aspect is considered problematic particularly when contemporary technologies and infrastructures are involved. It is hence seen as hopelessly outdated. Additionally, landscape has played a politically precarious role in the past.

"Transport Landscape".

Abandoning the landscape concept is, however, nothing new. In the nineteen-seventies, the need for planning was introduced and the term "open space" was adopted as an alternative to the word "landscape." It was especially criticized that landscape not only connoted something folksy, but that it was also bound to an elitist and "irrational," artistic-subjective design practice. It was countered with empirical surveys of needs in context with the objectifying and democratizing of planning (see Körner 2001).

The *Ästhetik des Angenehmen* (Aesthetic of Pleasantness) by Wulf Tessin (Tessin 2008) is a product of this tradition. This theory is specifically directed at the cool, minimalist landscape architecture that was fashionable in the nineteen-nineties, and was, in turn, landscape architecture's reaction to the ecological and nature conservation oriented landscape planning and nature conservation of the nineteen-seventies and eighties. It asserted the cultural dimension of human activities, in contrast to the popular naturalist trend in planning at that time. One did not symbolically or practically refer to nature, but to the city as a place of urban culture. This meant abandoning the idyllic countryside scenes that had previously served as design models, because, according to traditional perspectives, the city is the opposite of rural nature (see Körner 2001).

But following the debates of recent years and decades reveals that it would not have been possible, in either case, to dispose of the concept of landscape. In relation to the open spaces user, Tessin confirms the sustained importance of landscape-oriented patterns of perception. Moreover, and despite massive criticism of the traditional landscape concept, one is still building on its levels of significance in professional discourses. It is merely decorated with semantic appendages that result in constructions such as "total landscape" (Rolf Peter Sieferle) or "Landscape Three" (John Brinckerhoff Jackson). Some other terms are "urban landscapes," "periurban landscapes," "patchwork landscapes," and so on. Only urban planner Thomas Sieverts (2003), with his expression *Zwischenstadt* (*Cities Without Cities*), used a term that was clearly divorced from that of landscape: yet his ideas about how to design regions that were becoming increasingly urban continued to follow a still largely traditional concept of landscape (Körner 2005). Thus, it seems as if the concept of landscape is, in fact, more pluralistic. But here again, appearances are deceptive, because ultimately, attempts at redefining the landscape concept still revolve around an established, traditional core definition.

Before we begin to describe this core definition, on hand theories laid out by J. B. Jackson, one of the protagonists of the attempt to redefine landscape, we must first point out that the essential characteristic of landscape is not the definition of physical space, but the presentation of an idea that lies "behind" the notion of space and that shapes our perception. This is often confused or mixed up—also by Jackson. Landscape is primarily associated with a "metaphysically" charged form of perception, which *subsequently* leads to a specific, often ideologically derived interpretation of spatial realities—in precisely that sequence, and not vice versa. The space does not shape the perception, which would be a rather clumsy geographical determinism (that even Jackson would reject) and regarding normative design objectives, a classic naturalistic fallacy. It emerged in modern times as a new form of perception, and was ultimately loaded with traditional ideas of paradise and the remains of ancient European ideas of the cosmos. Ulrich Eisel in particular was able to present how the landscape concept is greatly informed by the Christian notion of individuality, which, in turn, relates to the concept of natural order (Eisel 1992, 2009; see also Trepl 2012).

In general, the symbolic meaning of landscape is initially associated with the Enlightenment. The modern subject, freed increasingly from immediate natural constraints, developed the capacity to build an aesthetic relationship to nature that had no specific purpose (Ritter 1989). Yet, in contrast wit this, English philosopher Thomas Hobbes (1588–1679) started a debate about how humans are capable of providing a reasonable social order due to a rational acknowledgement of their natural drive for self-preservation, by aggregating individual interests into a sensible whole. The fundamental aspects of this order, based on natural rights, is the surrender of some sovereignty to the state by means of a "social contract," and the increasingly democratically organized control of its associated exercise of power.

The new relationship with nature as landscape and the associated notion of a natural, freedom-related order first found its artistic resonance in landscape painting, and then in landscape gardening, which translated the painted ideal landscape into a physical reality.—1 The emergence of modern subjectivity led to the discovery of the productive inwardness of the individual. Landscape, therefore, was also used to refer to the romantic cultivation of human individuality. At the same time, Romanticism was a melancholic reaction to ancient Christian order being lost to the Enlightenment. From this perspective, a new disenchanted age emerged, in which the subject was left to fend for him or herself. In this context, nature became the last remaining relic of the sublime. This concept of melancholia and individual affirmation by perceiving sublime nature, finds its visual manifestation in the paintings by Caspar David Friedrich.

1 But the tradition of landscape gardening is not quite as enlightened liberal as it has always been portrayed. This was the case in England early on, where the landscape gardening nobility wanted to distance themselves from Absolutism, but stood for "good" feudalism, and also in Christian Cay Lorenz Hirschfeld, a German landscape garden theorist, elements can be found that could be classified in the tradition of conservative thought (Vesting 1998, Nagel 1997).

Caspar David Friedrich, Landscape with Rainbow.

In the perception of the sublime, the subject is forced into a state of self-reflection with respect to an omnipotent nature, and is able to assert him or herself in this emotional, existential situation by transforming it into an experience of desire. Art becomes a place of subjective productivity and landscape the symbol of a new art religion. The viewer takes pleasure in landscape, but in fact, the viewer is taking pleasure in him or herself. Landscape is an image of creation, and functions under the auspices of the ancient European notion of cosmos (Hard 2002) as the last bastion of a superior, integral order. If God is dead, all the individual parts are still integrated in a comprehensive nature (Trepl 2012, 126 f.). Hence, landscape is the projection surface for a new type of mythology, and the promise of a new paradise on earth (Piepmeier 1980, p. 19). Later, these notions of order were interpreted ecologically.

On the pictorial level, Arcadia is an expression of such a concept of paradise. It became, at least in Western culture, the universal ideal image of a picturesque, meaningful landscape with ample "green"—meadows, groves, single trees—peaceful grazing, few buildings, now and then a monument or gravestone, a temple or ruins. Landscape gardens were constructed according to these images, and their "degree of integrity" of cultural landscapes was assessed.

This reference to Arcadian iconography, and the estimation of landscape scenery from which it develops, is understood in landscape architecture today as a "romantic" and "backward" longing for idyllic, beautiful, and hopelessly outdated images and as representatives of an outmoded social order. Caspar David Friedrich's often nightmarish paintings are testimony of the "romantic" being far more complex than mere beauty and pleasant imagery. They also sowed the seeds for the critique of the new age, which was formulated in the course of conservative critique of civilization.—2

2 For this reason, open space protagonist Werner Nohl, made considerable effort to reinterpret the Arcadian as emancipatory, in his dissertation about forming a basis of an emancipated open space planning. He made it a symbol of a paradisiacal Golden Age in a democratic society and, at the same time, the pictorial elements of Arcadia were reinterpreted as very useable, in other words, "rationally justifiable" open space elements that result in a politically and pragmatically sensible park design (see Körner 2001, p. 331ff.).

Conservative Social Criticism and Heritage Protection

The idea of a natural order was thus transformed into the idea of an overarching, organic whole in which humans were to arrange themselves according to order. Order on a social level is something that grows and is not the product of the artificial-rational construct of a contract. This notion is supported by elements of Christian individualism, which state that the individual finds his or her place in the world by integrating into the whole. Thus, people do not necessarily find freedom in autonomy, but rather in the connection with specific wholes such as God, community, family, and nature. Landscape functions as a superordinate entity that expresses the respect for these wholes in aesthetic, comprehensive spatial impressions, which reflect society as a whole. These above-mentioned wholes are not merely abstract, but always individual in concrete situations and spaces. "Bound freedom" thus means finding one's own individual path, by filling general "meaning-horizons" with life in the respective contexts, and not fulfilling them with abstract "guidelines." In this way, not only personalities are created, but also landscapes as spatial individuals: One develops spaces on the earth's surface according to their present, specific potential (Eisel 2003).

The specific contexts have "grown" in a developing history and are reflected in local traditions and institutions, which is why conservative social criticism is primarily aimed at the further breakdown of traditions in modernity. Heritage protection saw its duties as preserving the pictorial landscape as an expression of the whole, and as not merely limited to the care and maintenance of customs and monuments. Moreover, to protect here meant not to conserve, but to develop the landscape in a sensible manner to prevent it from being overbuilt by industrial modernizations, in other words; homogenized, but with *Liebe zum Ort* (Love of the place) (Paul Schultze-Naumburg, architect, 1869–1949), in order to allow it to continue developing its local uniqueness and diversity. This is because landscape was understood as more than a mere symbolic construction, but also rationally as a cultural landscape and, thus, as a place and illustration of the day-to-day life of a specific area. Yet, categorizing uses in the symbolic structure landscape did not mean the uses needed to be subordinate, in other words, concealed; they could in fact redefine the actual landscape itself. It was essential, however, that this possessed enough character to allow for a new individuality to emerge. The site was important, but the creative power of the settlers and their culture was more important.

This is admittedly a very favorable description of heritage protection. But it also represented a variety of conservation and reactionary tendencies. Moreover, the ethnic interpretation of this design brief contributed to particularly northern Europeans feeling capable of progress and of having a close relationship to landscape. Nevertheless, it can be said of landscape design, that the protagonists who popularized it in their publications did in fact represent a very progressive, open-minded position regarding modern technologies and infrastructures. But it was about moderate modernizing, not unconditional. Nevertheless, this openness for progress reached such an extent that even icons of modern architecture, which were previously accused of being oblivious to local context and lacking in individuality (monotonous), were suddenly officially recognized, even if one, personally, advocated a traditional and cozier home style.

Peter Behrens, AEG Turbine Hall, Berlin.

Walter Gropius, The Fagus Factory, Alfeld.

Icons such as these include the AEG Turbine Hall by Peter Behrens, which was praised by Paul Schultze-Naumburg for how its entire beauty was designed by a simple good relationship of the clear and simple shape and omission of unnecessary 'embellishment' (Körner 2001, 329f.), or the Fagus Factory by Walter Gropius (see Lindner 1927, Fig. 530).—[3] Even modern building materials like reinforced concrete were recognized as progressive and practical (Schultze-Naumburg 1922, pp. 313–316). And ultimately, the aesthetic industrialization of entire areas such as the Ruhr District was more than welcomed. What normally would have been considered landscape destruction or disfiguration, as the "mighty rubble and waste dumps of the Ruhr District," belonged to architect Werner Lindner's "image of home" (Linder 1926, p. 92), because it was an expression of the industrial character of the area as a result of human use and power of creativity. This perhaps astonishing acceptance of modernity is due to the fact that in the new age, function became the general principle behind form and profoundly influenced architecture ("Functionalism").—[4] This attitude was shared in principle because, after all, every old farmhouse had already long been built in accordance with objective considerations. Why should it be different with modern artifacts? Hence, *Heimatstil* (traditional local style) indeed fed upon the criticism of new architecture, but ultimately wanted to establish a better modernity. Important was not only the characteristically objective design of the building itself, but also its site specificity and, hence, its cultural context. These together resulted in an individual character (*Eigenart*) that contrasted with the purely universal principles of technological progress.

3 It is no contradiction that societies for improving the appearance of the city or hometown were not always cutting edge in aesthetics and theory.

4 On Functionalism in landscape architecture in relation to the "Aesthetics of Pleasantness" see Körner 2010.

Although this may all seem very reasonable, heritage protection in Germany was discredited due to it its previously mentioned ethnic component, which the Nazis exploited in their propaganda. This is also why landscape architecture distanced itself (as did open space planning) from conventional notions of landscape. But it would be a mistake to think that heritage protection was just a hopelessly outdated mandate of the objectors of modernization, even if the fight against modern civilization was in fact its original driving force (see Rudorff 1897). Even for Ernst Rudorff, German composer, music teacher, and founder of the natural protection movement, it was obvious that heritage protection had to do more than conserve old traditions, because landscape was constantly evolving. For him, it was about establishing the right amount of change, and using the "work of our forefathers" as the model for one's own efforts (ibid., p. 24).

An attitude such as this was sorely needed, because at the end of the nineteenth, early twentieth century, modern progress led to a massive increase in a broad range of industrial uses. The associated construction of power plants, factories, power lines, villa neighborhoods, and finally the highways of the Third Reich made design absolutely imperative, if the image of the cultural landscape was not to be merely preserved, but made valid as a measure of development. It was undeniable that, to preserve the traditional landscape and, with that, cultural identity, an active landscape-appropriate balancing of modernization would be required in order to develop an "organic" balance between preservation and change. Hence, the "objectivity" of architecture was to be upheld, but its negative effects should be fought against: loss of quality craftsmanship, coldness of architecture, loss of the ability to age, the monotony of urban planning (see Körner, Trepl 2001).

Loading bridge as a modern, functional construction.

But this concept of design is way ahead of today's contemporary landscape architecture, at least in terms of one of its most prestigious projects in recent years. The supposed aim is to create contemporary, urban-industrial landscapes, but in fact at the moment in the Ruhr District—the largest area in Europe to be designed according to the urban landscape concept (Dettmar 2012)—what is being preserved is a picturesque, old industrial landscape, overgrown with vegetation.

Latz and Partner, Landscape Park Duisburg-Nord.

Another alternative is to crown slag heaps with art and picturesque views and declare them landmarks, as is common for instance with old gas holders. But this is not heritage protection. It treats the area more like a museum, which is ultimately preserving the economically obsolete remains of the industrial age for posterity.

Richard Serra, Slab for the Ruhr District, 1998, Schurenbachhalde Essen/Gelsenkirchen.

John Brinckerhoff Jackson's Concept of Landscape

Against the background of today's conservation-focused approach to nature preservation and the museum-like treatment of old industrial landscapes, the American landscape design writer and theorist, John Brinckerhoff Jackson (1909–1996), established a "progressive" landscape approach, according to his followers in German landscape architecture, when his examination of the urbanization of landscape and the emergence of new patterns of use since the nineteen-fifties led him to destroy the classic understanding of landscape. He believed it was no longer about rural and harmonious, "picturesque" scenes in the tradition of Arcadia, but about an open-minded, progressive, use-related landscape that was oriented toward modernity's dynamic transformations; in other words, an altogether pragmatic, progressive and social, democratic attitude to the world (see Prominski 2004). Therefore, landscape is "a system of man-made spaces" (ibid.). This definition has the advantage of merging the use-oriented tradition of open space planning with the design-oriented objectives of landscape architecture. However it is far too simplistic, and in this form does not do Jackson sufficient justice.

Jackson's position can only be understood when all of his writings, and, thus, his entire theoretical career have been taken into consideration. In the German debate, however, only some of his publications were studied and these were misinterpreted. By "man-made," Jackson is actually implying much more than humans simply structuring space according to use. A closer examination shows that he actually represents archetypal Christian-backed metaphysics and traditional design standards related to spatial individualism. Yet, at the same time, he positioned himself against the legitimacy of landscapes as materialized Arcadian visual images and, therefore, also against the Anglo-Saxon definition of the word landscape as "scenery." The pictorial character of landscape nevertheless remains crucial for him, because landscape expresses a cosmic order that can be designed by humans; and this cosmic order has the power to inspire awe, even worship. Jackson has no intention to defy this. Hence, landscape is, as such, an "image of Heaven" (Jackson 1952b, p. 5), an illustration of divine harmony. But the drawback here is that this harmony is lost in modernity. This problematic perspective Jackson shares with German heritage protection.

Landscape is designed by different factors, so that "[…] each element in the human landscape has perhaps been determined by natural conditions: climate and topography and soil; or perhaps each element is actually the expression of an economy: the availability of markets and labor and transportation; or finally the landscape may be what it is because a different race or a different period in history created it" (Jackson 1951, p. 4). In this way, cultural and spatial character (*Eigenart*) plus diversity are created, and developed in line with the forces of nature by the people inhabiting a space. In other words, nothing new.

In Jackson's theory, the landscape concept also contains a conservative-nationalist component. He presents it as purely American, which automatically means it will be associated with a specific ideal of progress. The traditional concept of landscape is thus combined with an unbridled enthusiasm for progress, and also possibly linked to an Anglo-Saxon ideology of white settlers. At least in this form, that is new. The essential characteristic of the white settlers who shaped the country is a pioneering spirit. They spread progress into world, because they came from a harsh northern European climate and were used to struggling with nature, yet were also able to develop an intense relationship to nature which is lacking in other groups: "That aggressive attitude is however only part of what earliest farmers in northern Europe bequeathed us. Since they created the human landscape themselves and under great difficulties, they had a deep affection for it." (Jackson 1951, p. 4).—5

Every culture makes an impact on the Earth's surface and displays its own character. The earth is thus the "home of the human race" (Johann Gottfried Herder, German philosopher, 1744–1803), based on the concept of a "home" that is settled by people from various nations. The cultural landscape "grows organically" from this settlement cell, and the earth is humanized and built into a "human landscape." Then it is an "image of heaven," so that the landscape design results in the implementation and perfection of divine order. Thus, it is "[...] the re-creation of Heaven on earth, just as the basic motive of his self-cultivation [of man] is the recreation of a Divine nature. [...] Man is the Product, the Child

5 This is what the National Socialists ascribed to the "Nordic Race," and used to justify their fight for *Lebensraum* (eng: habitat or literally living space). Jackson believed that a type of de-nazified geopolitics was ideal. The term "de-nazified geopolitics" is thus a "good working definition of the average contemporary writing on human geography" (Jackson 1952b, p. 4). Jackson did not really legitimize the colonization of Eastern Europe, but he did legitimize the conquest of America, if not the world, by the white race.

of God and that his work must therefore always betray, even in a distorted form, that identity. Man the Inhabitant reveals his origin in the habitat which he himself creates." (Jackson 1952b, p. 5)

Jackson is not propagating unrestrained capitalism or racial conflict; but he does, in fact, stringently follow a Christian worldview and then modifies it with an element of progressive ideology from the American pioneering spirit. It is about a social modernization that combines individual freedom with responsibility for oneself and for the environment, while creating a landscape in constant change and constant growth; that is, a landscape for entrepreneurial pioneers—"a landscape in the process of growth and development, a country for pioneers." (Jackson, 1952a, p. 4f.) In this manner, the rationally organized landscapes of the Midwest become the landscape manifestation of the classic functionalist ideal of expediency and simplicity, as an expression of American productivity and size. Heritage protection, when conveyed by the even older ideal of national beautification in terms of an identity of beauty and expediency (Däumel 1961), is basically able to tie into the modern age. Functionality yields a classic and clear beauty that is reduced to the bare minimum: "It is, to be sure, a landscape which conforms to Winckelmann's definition of Classical perfection: one of noble simplicity and quiet grandeur" (Jackson 1984, p. 153).

Jackson's American optimism, and especially his enthusiasm for progress, distinguishes him from the more skeptical, German tradition of heritage protection; which is why his theories seem new and modern to Germans and, hence, ideal for an approach that primarily rebels against their traditions, but does not ultimately want to change anything. On a practical level, accepting a constant transformation of landscape is a good prerequisite for the cultural appreciation of modern urban spaces as landscapes. In the nineteen-eighties, however, Jackson could not ignore the fact that the constant dynamics no longer created divine order but something rather like chaos. It is becoming increasingly difficult to interpret the "shabbiness" of the "scratched-up everyday," which should in fact be valued because it expresses that something has been well used, as the visual expression of singular classicism and as a noble reduction to the functional essentials.

Jackson's Attempt to Define a New Concept of Landscape

This led Jackson to embark on a search for an alternative concept of landscape. However, he regularly confused certain abstract levels, especially those of metaphysics and ideology, with the empirical description of real landscapes. This confusing of levels leads to a relatively simplistic cultural history and a woodcut-like division of the landscape concept into three subcategories, which are roughly based on historical periods: the landscape of tribal societies, "Landscape One"; the landscape after the Renaissance, "Landscape Two"; and the landscape of (American) modernity, "Landscape Three." But he confused his categories. He suggested that the mobility and "volatility" of tribal societies, which left behind few spatial artifacts but were very static in their traditionalism, were structurally identical to the mobility of a completely different era, that of modernity, an era known for overcoming traditions again and again.

Since landscape is to remain the result of an "organic, alive" and rich-in-character mediator of tradition and progress, but it does not really admit it, the concept of "Landscape Three" still subliminally positions itself along with the concept of "Landscape Two," which mainly represents the visual expression of landscape and the concept of perfect cosmological order. At the moment, landscape architects are assuming a central role now that the hubris of the human entitlement to design the earth becomes clear, because uses *per se* no longer alone produce simple, organic identity and harmony—if they in fact ever did—and because the "environmental issue" emerged on the scene. Because landscape architects should be able to ensure respect for regional natural potentials via "ecology." This is actually nothing new; it is only expressed in slightly different, less culturalistic terms.

This led Jackson to his "new" definition of landscape, which should be quoted at length: "My search for a definition has led me back to that old Anglo-Saxon meaning: landscape is not scenery, is not political unit; it is no more than a collection, a system of man-made spaces on the surface of the earth. What ever is shape or size it is *never* simply a natural space, a feature of the natural environment, it is *always* artificial, always synthetic, always subject to sudden or unpredictable change. We create them and need them because every landscape is the place where we establish our own human organization of space and time. It is where the slow, natural processes of growth and maturity and decay are deliberately set aside and history is substituted. A landscape is where we speed up to regard or divert the cosmic program and impose our own. 'By conquering nature', Mircea Eliade writes, 'man can become Nature's rival without being the slave of time […], Science and industry proclaim that man can achieve things better and faster than nature if he, by means of his intelligence, succeeds in penetrating to her secrets.' When we see how we have succeeded in imposing our own rhythm on nature in the agricultural landscape, how we have altered the life cycle of plants and animals and even transposed the seasons, we become aware of how dangerous a role we have assumed, and there are many who say that the salvation of Landscape Three depends on relinquishing this power to alter the flow of time and on our returning to a more natural order. But the new ordering of time should affect not only nature, it should affect ourselves. It promises us a new kind of history, a new, more responsive social order, and, ultimately a new landscape" (Jackson 1984, p. 156f.; emphasis in original).

Landscape should therefore not be scenery and not a political category—that would be "Landscape Two" for Jackson—yet it remains unclear as to why the political should not be apparent in the landscapes of modernity, where precisely highways, dams, power lines, and so on, as modern "American" infrastructures, are surely an expression of political will and, ultimately, of domination, as in Landscape Two. Landscape is a collection of man-made spaces on the earth's surface, thus not the result of (humanist) high culture and not an artistic product (landscape gardens), but also an everyday, sometimes overused, and thereby "shabby" looking artifact. The concept of the character of a culture or space, which is signified by the term Eigenart in German, and which is essential in Jackson's older texts,—[6] completely disappears. For Jackson, character (Eigenart) was originally a property of Landscape Two. But, because he will not and cannot abandon the element of classical landscape, this can also be attributed subliminally to Landscape Three because it will continue to be unconsciously evaluated in these terms. This is not surprising, since landscape is defined by the presence of regional character and diversity. It is just not said openly anymore, because firstly, modern spaces no longer seem to comply as readily, and because secondly, and for good reason, no one wants to denounce profane, day-to-day spaces as meaningless.—[7] Based on this growing deception and self-deception, the distinctions begin to blur with Jackson. Landscape (Three) then, is a poor imitation of the "old" landscape: the landscape architect becomes a small God, who should functionally and pictorially curtail the human hubris by providing uses and landscape harmony, and create representative order (see Körner 2010b).

6 For instance: "But no one is without character, no habitat of man is without the appeal of the existence which originally created it" (Jackson 1951, p. 4).

7 That it is not enough, to be simply pragmatic, useful spaces for most people. (See Tessin 2008).

Conclusion: The Modernity of Heritage Protection

This still very much resembles a heritage protection program, only now presented in American terms. One can also see how Jackson's optimism about progress breaks down, and how, from a design concern, the basic conditions were intellectually created for ecological planning, which in turn was accused in the nineteen-nineties of exaggerated naturalism and the abolition of design. This detour through the United States also shows that firstly the design practice of heritage protection was not as backward looking as claimed. Secondly, current landscape architectural projects, aimed at the overall design and spatial integration of technical infrastructures, confirm that the principles of heritage protection are applied over and over again, albeit with a slightly shifted accent. Again: it's about a contemporary, "sensible" landscape design through the integration of infrastructures.

We continue to proceed according to this design paradigm—even today in the Ruhr District, for instance with the redesign of the highway A 42 in the course of maintenance measures: the monotonous vegetation will be thinned out, and there will be no vistas of the Wartburg Castle or Chiemsee, as with the respective Munich–Salzburg Autobahn, but for example of the old stadium of the legendary Gelsenkirchen soccer team Schalke 04 or other landmarks.

View of Chiemsee from the highway Munich–Salzburg.

One also seeks to strengthen the local reference, by planting dawn redwood trees at regular intervals. Although these trees cannot be considered indigenous, they still serve as a symbolic reference to the early days of the coal industry, and thus to an important raw material of the industrial revolution and to the Ruhr District itself (see Dettmar 2012).Ultimately, referring to the history and thus the character of the place are design strategies that can individualize a profane area and emphasize its traditions, without giving the space museum-like treatment as was the case with the old industrial wastelands.

View of the old stadium of Schalke 04.

Hence, design not only enhances everyday practical contexts, but—this is especially and also clear with Jackson—is always a representation of an ideal, ordered, harmonious relationship between man and nature, in concrete locations by means of the organization of space.—8 If it is not possible to implement order on a consistent basis, then landmarks could be installed that have a visual effect on the whole. In the process, the concept of landscape still plays a role because there is no reasonable substitute. Its broad significance remains the basis for suggestions for improvement, especially in terms of identity.—9 What is happening in the Ruhr District today is proof of the fact that, even from the professional design perspective, the conceptual meaning of the landscape aesthetic continues to have an impact—10 even if attempts are being made on both the professional practice and theoretical level to still it.

At the same time, the Ruhr District, as one of the largest experiments in landscape architecture in recent years, shows that landscape images can be in fact created from a mix of intended and unintended, everyday-use-related designs, which might no longer be related to Arcadian harmonies on the superficial level, but nonetheless point to Eigenart and diversity, and hence, are full of character. If Tessin is still able to show that even the

8 Examined rationally, it is about improving the "soft location factors," in other words, location politics. This must, however, succeed as a design interest in a planning system that, in a fully differentiated society, breaks up into subdisciplines that all follow of their unique, more often than not purely functional logic. Therefore "events" are often used (IBA, European Capital of Culture).

9 Tessin explains the value of landscape, of landscape gardens, firstly through the fact that they became popular at a time where the building of parks was on the rise. Hence, it could be aesthetically influential alone or en masse. Secondly, different to standard architecture, it did not gain the stronghold due to destruction and reconstruction due to war, where people, for lack of alternatives, became accustomed to its sparse aesthetics and no longer expected architectural opulence. Tessin can also show that the landscape garden is astonishingly capable of assimilating to modern uses. According to his hypothesis, if landscape architecture in its current form simply continued with its aesthetic education—which was criticized by Tessin—of the public for another twenty to thirty years, then the public would also grow accustomed to a more sparse-looking "urban" style. But here, he leads his own argument in ad absurdum. His book would then not have been a criticism but a reinforcement of the current landscape architectural practice. However, the enduring significance of landscape patterns of perception can indeed be confirmed empirically, but not explained, because landscape is primarily an idea, and not a material object.→

open space user still strongly identifies with landscape-typical expectations of perception, then elite taste and laymen's aesthetics are obviously more closely related than design experts are willing to admit (Tessin 2008). That is a good prerequisite for accepting landscape architecture, when what you really want is open space.

Hence, the explanation can take the form of a kind of history of ideas. Tessin's statements are thus still somewhat speculative.

10 Yet it is not only about aesthetics, but always a specific conceptual construction.

Däumel, Gerd: *Über die Landesverschönerung*. Geisenheim 1961.
Dettmar, Jörg: "Die Parkautobahn A 42 im Emscher-Landschaftspark," in: *Landschaft und Verkehr*, eds. Stefan Körner, Helmut Holzapfel, and Florian Bellin-Harder. Kassel 2012.
Eisel, Ulrich: "Individualität als Einheit konkreter Natur. Das Kulturkonzept der Geographie," in: *Humanökologie und Kulturökologie. Grundlagen, Ansätze, Praxis*, eds. Bernhard Glaeser, Parto Teherani-Krönner, pp. 107–151. Opladen 1992.
Eisel, Ulrich: "Tabu Leitkultur," in: *Natur und Landschaft*, no. 9/10, pp. 409–417. 2003.
Eisel, Ulrich: "Orte als Individuen. Zur Rekonstruktion eines spatial turn in der Soziologie," in: *Raumproduktionen: Theorie & gesellschaftliche Praxis*, eds. Bernd Belina et al., vol. 5, pp. 226–279. Münster 2009.
Hard, Gerhard: "Zu Begriff und Geschichte von 'Natur' und 'Landschaft' in der Geographie des 19. und 20. Jahrhunderts" (1983), in: id.: *Landschaft und Raum. Aufsätze zur Theorie der Geographie*, vol. 1, Osnabrücker Studien zur Geographie 22, pp. 171–210. Osnabrück 2002.
Jackson, John Brinckerhoff: "The Need of Being Versed in Country Things," in: *Landscape*, vol. 1, no. 1, pp. 1–5. 1951.
Jackson, John Brinckerhoff: "What We Want," in: *Landscape*, vol. 1, no. 3, pp. 3–5. 1952a.
Jackson, John Brinckerhoff: "Human: All Too Human Geography," in: *Landscape*, vol. 2, no. 2, 2–7. 1952b.
Jackson, John Brinckerhoff: "Concluding with Landscapes," in: Id.: *Discovering the Vernacular Landscape*, 146–157. Westford/Mass. 1984.
Körner, Stefan: *Theorie und Methodologie der Landschaftsplanung, Landschaftsarchitektur und Sozialwissenschaftlichen Freiraumplanung vom Nationalsozialismus bis zur Gegenwart*. Berlin 2001.
Körner, Stefan, Ludwig, Trepl: "Bewahren durch Gestalten: Zur Geschichte der Landespflege als entwicklungsorientierter Natur- und Heimatschutz," in: *Handbuch Naturschutz und Landschaftspflege*, eds. Werner Konold et al. Landsberg 2001.
Körner, Stefan: *Natur in der urbanisierten Landschaft. Ökologie, Schutz und Gestaltung, Zwischenstadt*, vol. 4, Wuppertal 2005.
Körner, Stefan: "Funktionalismus in der Landschaftsarchitektur," in: *Stadt und Grün*, 59, 8, pp. 49–61. 2010a.
Körner, Stefan: *Amerikanische Landschaften. J. B. Jackson in der deutschen Rezeption*, Sozialgeographische Bibliothek, vol. 13. Stuttgart 2010b.
Lindner, Werner: *Ingenieurwerk und Naturschutz*. Berlin-Lichterfelde 1926.
Lindner, Werner: *Bauten der Technik. Ihre Form und Wirkung. Werkanlagen*. Berlin 1927.
Nagel, Annemarie: *Das Heilsversprechen der Natur. Die Auflösung der Aporie von künstlerischer Freiheit und Nachahmung der Natur im christlichen Humanismus am Beispiel der "Theorie der Gartenkunst" von C. C. L. Hirschfeld*. TU Berlin 1997.
Piepmeier, Rainer: "Das Ende der ästhetischen Kategorie Landschaft," in: *Westfälische Forschungen*, pp. 1–46, 30/1980.
Prominski, Martin: *Landschaft entwerfen. Zur Theorie aktueller Landschaftsarchitektur*. Berlin 2004.
Ritter, Joachim: "Landschaft—Zur Funktion des Ästhetischen in der modernen Gesellschaft" 1963, in: id.: *Subjektivität—Sechs Aufsätze*. pp. 141–163. Frankfurt am Main 1963.
Rudorff, Ernst: *Heimatschutz* (1897). St. Goar 1997.
Schultze-Naumburg, Paul: *Die Gestaltung der Landschaft durch den Menschen*. Munich 1922.
Sieverts, Tom: *Cities Without Cities. Between Place and World, Space and Time, Town and Country*. London/New York 2003.
Tessin, Wulf: *Ästhetik des Angenehmen. Städtische Freiräume zwischen professioneller Ästhetik und Laiengeschmack*. Wiesbaden 2008.
Trepl, Ludwig: *Die Idee der Landschaft. Eine Kulturgeschichte von der Aufklärung bis zur Ökologiebewegung*. Bielefeld 2012.
Vesting, Thomas: *Die Ambivalenz idealisierter Natur im Landschaftsgarten. Vom Garten des guten Feudalismus zum republikanischen Garten der Freiheit, Beiträge zur Kulturgeschichte der Natur*, vol. 8. Berlin 1998.

The Relationship between Plants and Landscape Architectural Design —An Attempt at Repositioning

Norbert Kühn

The loss of knowledge about plants among landscape architects has been lamented often and at length. However, there is a logical history behind this development, which has more to do with how the self-image of the profession and its mission have changed over time, and less about disrespect for plants as a resource.

When considering the status of landscape architecture today, the role of plants needs to be taken into account. The study of plants and their manifestations—or the images that vegetation creates, the ecological processes it triggers, and even the notion of nature itself—is the core driving force behind the development of this profession. The reasons why plants seem to have lost popularity over the last few decades therefore provide insights into how the discipline has developed in general.

Design and Plants—The History of a Complicated Relationship

The layman's idea of the landscape architect profession assumes that its practitioners somehow work with plants in gardens. This may make them popular, but it greatly diminishes the meaning and significance of the profession—nor does it do justice to the responsibility that landscape architects have for people and our living environment.

Hence, regular attempts are made to correct this misconception. Even avoiding the original term *Gartenkunst* (garden design) and replacing it with new ones—such as *Landschaftsarchitektur* (landscape architecture), *Freiraumplanung* (open space planning), or most recently *Urbanismus* (urbanism)—is proof of an endeavor to be understood either differently or in a completely different context.—[1] This is why it has been so difficult to form a discourse based on the core competences of the profession. For the most part, the discourse relies on distinguishing landscape architecture from other professions by identifying what tasks are specific to it and what benefits it can bring. In this context, plants are frequently considered as its nucleus. "The historical basis was and is the study of and about plants" (Neumann 2001, p. 16),—[2] as Klaus Neumann defined an education in landscape architecture in 2001.

1 This discussion was less vehement in English-speaking countries. New terms like landscape urbanism, urban design, landscape design, urban horticulture have appeared only recently and were mainly projected onto the profession from the outside.

2 At this time Klaus Neumann was chairman of the Hochschullehrerkonferenz Landschaft (HLK) (professor's conference on landscape).

This is an extremely reduced notion of our profession, still based on the nineteenth-century definition, and sheds light on how the profession was viewed in the beginning in Europe. The first landscape architects were architects and artists. According to Dezallier d'Argenville, in the first half of the eighteenth century, the professional profile of the new vocation of gardener, which emerged in the era of absolutism, was not limited to the mere increase, use, or care of plants. They also had to learn about the various elements of the garden and master surveying, soil movement, construction, and waterworks (Dezallier d'Argenville 1731).

Landscaped gardens gave us an unprecedented way of observing and working with plants. It may well seem that in these gardens everything is nature—design, layout, and technology appear to have been completely neglected. This is a popular yet misleading notion that we still advocate. It also significantly contributed to plants gaining overwhelming importance in our discipline. This notion was in turn reinforced when landscape garden design lost depth of meaning at the end of the nineteenth century, as an ossification of repetitive forms, which ultimately stifled the previously inherent intelligent examination of site and use—in other words the core substance that defines our profession. Form exhausting itself by constant repetition gave rise to mere ornament. Plants provided the lush, magnificent framework for eclectic productions and served as the perfect decoration within cut and paste designs. Marie Luise Gothein writes about this era as follows, "In this way, the garden gradually fell exclusively into the hands of the gardener, leaving the architect behind" (Gothein, p. 417).

This resulted in an educational program that upheld the garden components but brought the core purpose of the profession to a standstill. In 1909, Leberecht Migge described the typical graduates of the Königliche Gärtnerlehranstalt in Berlin, the most important educational institute for garden designers at that time, as follows: "[...] manually mediocre draftsmen, but in our opinion lacking sufficient development of rhythmical elements. The drawings are naïve yet pompous in presentation regarding content, and are completely devoid of the slightest artistic impulse, of any emotional or intuitive understanding of temporal qualities [...]" (Migge, p. 198).

Ultimately, a form of unity did develop, but not until the garden design reforms of 1900. Its duties were to extend far beyond the previous, long-established park planning for the governing princes. "In Germany, garden design has progressed and made astonishing advances over the last decades; what was once a hobby of art-loving princes and patriarchs has now become a *hygienic necessity* because of the massive increase of population in our cities" (Brügmann, p. 73). Still, plants were considered the most important material in this development. Landscape architects such as Erwin Barth, Hermann Mattern, or Karl Plomin worked closely with gardeners such as Karl Foerster. They used plants with great enthusiasm and created designs from the wealth of choice available, which is clearly reflected in their work. In the twentieth century, until the nineteen-seventies, plants were held

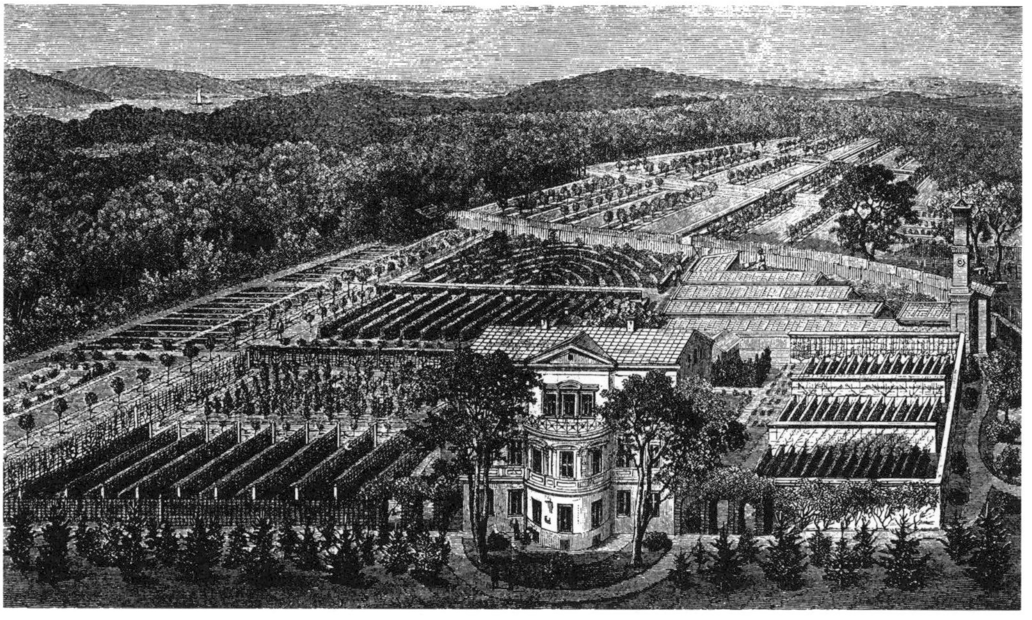

A starting point of academic training in "Gartenkunst" (garden design): the Königliche Gärtnerlehranstalt (Royal Gardener Academy). Founded by Peter Joseph Lenné in 1823, from 1824 with its own campus in the wildlife park in Potsdam.

in great esteem, even honored by those in the profession. Transformations brought on by ecological developments and open space planning influenced by sociology led to a general lack of confidence and raised long-avoided questions, shaking the foundations of previously established concepts.

Plants were important in ecology, for the purpose of nature conservation, as well as in open space planning, as an indication of usage. Yet, just as the need for design in general was dismissed as an aberration, planners also began doubting whether plants were necessary for a design. The profession needed artists, as well as sociologists, biologists, and planning technicians. Landscape architects trained in the use of plants embodied a subdued notion of the profession. This led to the development of various unrelated sectors: ecologists, for whom nature preservation was the priority; open space planners, for whom socially driven developments of open spaces were of the greatest importance; and landscape architects, who positioned themselves closer and closer to architects and artists. The fundamental aspects and substance of horticulture was disregarded because they were considered too traditional. This resulted not only in the previous common concept being dissolved; it also shattered the reciprocal relationship between landscape architecture and plants, which until then had been self-evident. A document from this period outlines the goals of the academic and research program of Department 14 at the Technical University Berlin; the word design had simply been removed from the list of objectives.

TABLE 1: Main Objectives of the Education and Research Program of Department 14 at the Technical University Berlin, 1979 (FB 14 1979, unpubl., translated):

1.	Landscape use and change, including the destruction of ecosystems by production and infrastructure
2.	Communal open space planning for reproduction and socialization
3.	Tourism and local recreation as elements of regional development
4.	Development policies in third world countries under the aspect of landscape development
5.	Landscape development theory

Over the following years, the use of plants continued to develop for the most part separately from and without relation to landscape architecture. Progress was made in particular in the use of herbaceous perennials, as Richard Hansen attempted to unite ecology and design with the theory of the habitats (see Hansen 1981) of plants. However, Richard Hansen complained in 1984 that the design aspect of plants was largely ignored. "Is it not strange that our terrains are for the most part *excellently modeled*, but that *the living ground vegetation is practically ignored?*" (Hansen Manuscript 1984). Furthermore, park authorities and garden owners were of course the main beneficiaries of the new herbaceous perennials (Kühn 2012).

Numerous professionals gradually added to this knowledge, as a rich spectrum of work for specialist plant planners eventually resulted from a system of garden shows that has grown steadily since the nineteen-eighties (in the form of international garden shows, regional garden shows, or county garden shows), and the increasing number of garden festivals. But their work was never considered to be part of a design process. They were seen as specialist planners, as experts called in at the last minute with the task of, at most, improving the basic design concept. Only some members of the group "Perennial Perspectives"—[3] managed to make a connection to aesthetics and design. Piet Oudolf, undoubtedly the most well-known representative of the group today, is even considered as an equal partner by designing landscape architects.

It thus remains to must be stated that plant use and landscape architecture have developed separately in recent years, indicated by the fact that plant designers are concerned almost exclusively with perennials, do not consider woody plants, and generally emphasize the ornamental. They often work within the niche of garden planner, a position rarely occupied by design bureaus today. Using plants on a large landscape scale is virtually non-existent now; the practice has been replaced by nature conservation planning. Hence, it is worth examining whether and how design and plant use can in fact be reunited in landscape architecture.

3 Perennial Perspective was an international group of gardeners, landscape architects, and lecturers who met regularly between 1992 and 2000. They attempted to bring together plants, aesthetics, and ecology, free of ideological constraints. The most significant influences came from the Dutch members Rob Leopold, Henk Gerritsen, and Piet Oudolf ("Dutch Wave") (see Kühn 2011).

Plants Are Old-fashioned—Which Is Why They Are So Urgently Needed

Plants are, in effect, extremely uncontemporary because they challenge our hope of a tamed or indeed tamable environment. Above all, they contradict the notions of spontaneity, flexibility, and mobility. They do not need or tolerate innovation—they require a stable environment in order to grow and develop, perhaps bloom, reproduce, become old, and finally die. In human-built open spaces, plants need people to care for them and remain committed to them for the duration of their lives. Hence it is currently very difficult for plants to establish themselves as an important material in open spaces.

TABLE 2: Theories on the Lack of Plants in Open Spaces

Theory 1:	It is not possible to create a final design using plants—and the client needs to trust the planner's competence. There is no place for trust in a world that is based on economics and a compensation culture. Charges cannot be brought against how a tree grows. Plants are always subject to a degree of uncertainty.
Theory 2:	Plants are comparatively inexpensive. They usually play a relatively insignificant role in construction budgets, do not add much to the landscape architect's fee, and could be replaced at any time. Hence, they are not considered economically valuable.
Theory 3:	Landscape architects are also a product of their times, and therefore also dislike working with a material that goes against all economic and social contexts—moreover, it fuels doubts about their own architectural and artistic competence. They no longer wish to be classified as gardeners.
Theory 4:	Plants need time to grow, ideally requiring long-term, competent care that is focused on a predefined goal. However, planning and construction processes are very different today. Plants suffer from repeated, uncoordinated and, as a rule, reckless construction activities. The obsession with the constant need for innovation is as true of open spaces as it is of other spectrums of society.

This may well all sound rather conservative, even reactionary. However, it inevitably leads us to a key conflict that shakes and divides the foundations of society today: human endeavor entails constant, far-reaching change that demands large amounts of energy and resources. On the other hand, we all want a stable, secure, and livable environment. With new concepts and notions such as sustainability, mindfulness, or resilience, we struggle to reconcile the irreconcilable—to continue the exploitation of resources and the basic foundations of life, while still ensuring wellbeing and security.

Applying this notion to current natural examples proves that our environment does in fact withstand changes and interventions—at the expense of other elements of the system being unintentionally set in motion. Just what impact this will have depends on the duration, intensity, and the properties of the system.—[4] Intervening in vegetation has a series of consequences, leading to an end product that is most likely quite different from how it started out and effecting many other elements along with the vegetation. Every intervention will thus have incalculable consequences.

4 There are several theoretical perspectives on the stability of ecosystems (see Holling 1973). At the moment, the concept of resilience seems to be best address sustainability theories.

Any notion of an immovable constancy, of stable living conditions, is as much an illusion as the hope of achieving better, happier conditions through persistent effort, appropriate intervention, and targeted change. This is because change as such is not the problem—it is even inherent in all natural systems. Landscape architect Hermann von Pückler-Muskau clearly brought this to a point when he spoke of the fundamentals of garden design: "For we are not in a position to deliver a permanent, final work in landscape garden design, as can painters, sculptors, or architects, because it is not dead, but alive, and like the images of nature and of ourselves, [...] will always be in motion and will never stand still [...]" (Pückler, p. 141f.). Thus, it is not about preventing change. On the contrary, we are obliged to accept and support design that brings about change, while adapting the degree of change to natural human conditions. For landscape architecture, this means that both courses of action are necessary, the conservative and the progressive, because recourse to reliable, familiar images and clear spatial situations will at least temporarily provide the security we need,—[5] while the search for innovative aesthetic challenges opens the path for new perspectives.

5 Regarding this point, landscape architecture and open space planning overlap, because the research into natural human living conditions as a starting point for design provides the findings that support this position. That may well be a simplification, but it provides an essential basis for establishing a true reference framework in terms of use (see Wulf Tessin's essay in this book).

Trust in change is something very familiar to gardeners. The knowledge that a plant will blossom next year, continue to grow, and perhaps develop magnificently in about ten years fosters a basic faith in positive change, in constant new transformation, and a certain degree of predictable development. It also has pseudo-religious connotations, which German gardener Karl Foerster identified in his concept of pantheism (see Dümpelmann 2001). Ultimately, it is the faith in a natural principle: the notion that growth under optimal conditions leads to a climax.—6 However, even the climax is not sustainable, because it is always subject to an element of decline and transience and therefore also something conciliatory—at least if one allows it. Czech writer Karel Čapek brought this to a point in a joke when he wrote that, "[a] gardener's autumn begins in March, with the first faded snowdrop" (Čapek, p. 76).

6 This concept of a predictability of natural developments is not sustainable in the face of ecological research. Nevertheless, gardeners believe in it and do everything in their power to ensure that it occurs. In reality, there are a number of influences (in some cases catastrophes) that can cause results different to those predicted. Chance plays an undeniable role.

Plants and vegetation—and horticulture as a caring treatment of the world—can serve as models for action. When Elisabeth Meyer wrote that landscape architecture provides more than "designed ecosystems" or "strategies for open-ended processes," but also "cultural products with distinct forms and experiences that provoke attitudes and feelings through space, sequence, and form," (Meyer, 2008, p. 10) the parallels become very clear. It also highlights the idea that horticulture pars pro toto could exemplify a sustainable, but design-oriented landscape architecture on a small scale. But are plants and vegetation also able to provide us with a new substantive point of reference for a more responsible handling of the basic requirements for life in open spaces?

Nature And How It Is Perceived in the Design Process

Adrian von Buttlar hoped as late as 1997 that modern landscape architecture would "reawaken the idea of an Arcadian-like paradise or cosmic, transcendental notion of nature within a new context" (von Buttlar, p. 114f.). This symbolic and exaggerated production of nature, which is reminiscent of the nineteen-nineties, has now taken a wide range of more tangible forms. The discussion about ways to secure the basic resources on which human lives depend leads beyond symbolic gestures to a real investigation of a wide variety of usages—often, however, devoid of any design ambitions. Approaches such as these are rooted in a new type of ecological ethics, namely that nature is not worth preserving in itself; instead merits preservation because of a moral obligation to humans that takes priority "in view of the ozone layer, climate, water, and soil" (Ott, p. 170)—and of course that includes all forms of plants and vegetation. This is where ethical obligation implies some form of action, if necessary, against economic constraints.

For landscape architecture, this moral obligation indicates a need to reposition itself. After being appropriated by ecology, the profession must first rediscover its original roots. "After years of ecologically influenced ideologization in the nineteen-seventies and nineteen-eighties and the one-sided emphasis on preservation and conservation, contemporary landscape architecture has declared itself free to design again" (Weilacher, p. 8). A new self-confidence in the profession emerged. At its core was renewed trust in its very specific method: design. Design can integrate data and knowledge into its decision-making processes, because it is able to abstract by means of artistic intervention and edit incoming information down to the absolutely essential. Hence, it is always open for action and is not blocked by the diversity and inconsistency of incoming information. The only aspects that need to be considered now are how much ecology, how much adherence to natural processes, and how many plants should be included in the design.

If we think we can just go back to the alleged starting point after the recent ecological upheaval, it means that we have completely misunderstood the facts. Ultimately, these "limits to growth" are precisely what we will be obliged to address from now on. However, how can we deal with ecological responsibility, which is a core duty of our profession? How can the mass of accumulated knowledge about natural resources and their finiteness be integrated into the design, in such a way as to ensure that human life might be improved or, at least, not worsened further?

Meyer emphasizes the need to understand sustainability beyond the rational perspective. "[It] will take more than ecologically regenerative design for culture to be

Successful example of integrating vegetation into the design process: Park on the grounds of the former Riem Airport (Planning: Luz Landschaftsarchitekten, Munich).

sustainable, what is needed are designed landscapes that provoke these, who experience them to become more aware of how their actions effect the environment, and to care enough to make chances" (Meyer, p. 6). She believes that, besides fulfilling an economic purpose, physical and psychological experience is equally essential, in order to arrive at "recognition, empathy, love, respect, and care for the environment" (Ibid., p. 7).

Consequently, ecology in landscape architecture cannot simply adopt unfiltered scientific knowledge. Its content needs to be analyzed and processed. The intended effects must be implemented as far as possible, but they should be easy to understand for the user. An emotional and sensual approach is often necessary.

Plants contribute on this level as well. Even if the notion of a concrete, tangible nature has been sentimentalized by the media and advertisement industry and abused for their own purposes, a sense of nature and its beauty is still a fundamental human need. Hansen also deliberately included this aspect by not only discussing the "living ground vegetation" as a necessary compensatory measure in cities—and hence supporting an ecological scientific argument—but also argued on an emotional level for its existence: "The different forms, the colors and scents of their blossoms […], the changing light that falls on them. I am also thinking of *all sorts of creatures*. Beetles, butterflies, insects of all kinds—and also of the people and their desire for life. I am also thinking about *the meaning behind plants*, as is testified by so many flower names" (Hansen 1984, no page).

Ecology in the Use of Plants

Ecology in landscape architecture does not necessarily go hand in hand with the use of plants. If they are to be included in a design, they should be considered as early as the conceptual phase. The formulation and development of the design process does, however, go hand in hand with images of plants, which means that the two are often closely related.

Ecology-related issues are a well-established aspect of the use of plants, often referred to as planting or vegetation techniques or biological engineering (see Florineth, and Hacker, Johannsen). Creating green rooftops and façades has been developing for years now. Trees along streets are credited for doing much to mitigate the effects of climate change, and water management provides solutions ranging from artificial wetlands for water purification and retention, to seepage wells and floating islands. There are also numerous positive examples of how design and ecology work collaboratively (see for instance the Dreiseitl office building). Nevertheless, what needs further development is the visual aspect, a design approach that not only unites the various built structures, but also lends them a formal quality.

Over recent years, the selection of plants used—in this case, specifically the use of herbaceous perennials—has been based on the natural vegetation stocks at hand. This is not due to ecological considerations, but rather to the tight budgets of municipalities that cannot afford high care and maintenance costs. Their way of thinking is that the more natural the design, the less need there is for intervention and, hence, the lower the cost. Then plant modules were designed in Germany and Switzerland (called mixed plantings) (Heinrich, Messer) that were based on a complex and labor-intensive exchange of soil, whereby the natural soil was replaced with skeleton-rich gravel and mineral substrate and could therefore be stabilized at least in the medium term. In England, various natural or semi-natural units of vegetation were used as established set models, such as the prairie, Highveld Grasslands, Central European meadows, coppices, perennial plants. They were produced by means of intensive cultivation and their botanical composition was modified, in order to create visual consistency (Hitchmough). Unfortunately, many of these new approaches merely served a decorative purpose and have not been exploited beyond their ornamental value. Searching for a link to the "spirit of the place" is futile. Examples where the use of plants led to a satisfactory design solution are rare, as in the park on the site of the former Riem Airport in Munich,—[7] or the High Line in New York.—[8]

7 Planning: Gilles Vexlard Latitude Nord, Paris; Vegetation: Luz Landschaftsarchitekten, Munich or Haase & Söhmisch, Freising.

8 Planning: James Corner Field Operations, New York; Vegetation: Piet Oudolf, Hummelo.

This confirms that there is only a limited relationship between contemporary plant use and design. Although there is, in fact, a strong basis for large-scale, atmospheric vegetation, it has yet to be applied to a design-related approach.

Plants and Vegetation Find Their Way Into Design Ideas

Being an expert in plants today is in fact a highly specialized field, because the sheer volume of material alone is overwhelming. Representatives of garden reform in the early twentieth century urged early on for a return to simplicity and convenience. "Just look at the beautiful Aquilegia and its many varieties. Does not double-flowered breeding merely create a caricature compared with the elegant, wonderful shape of the simple variety? The simplicity of the blossom is in many cases preferred to the 'double-flowered' variety, as is seen in examples such as the dahlia, hyacinth, narcissus, anemone, ranunculus, elatior begonia, cyclamen, violet, and many, many others" (Hoemann, p. 152).

"Classification" should serve precisely this purpose, but these efforts are yet to be truly successful. Only the varieties of woody plants and trees have stagnated for years and display almost no development. On the other hand, the profusion of available herbaceous perennials, bulbous plants, and annuals increases every year. Old varieties are preserved, new ones are bred, others newly introduced—for example from the prairies varieties—and this process is set to continue. Yet concluding that a comprehensive knowledge of plants alone means being able to design with them would be a great oversimplification.—[9]

9 Moreover, too much plant knowledge can even hamper the ability to design well with them, which can be seen in so-called collector's gardens.

As mentioned above, the use of plants is the only remaining connection to the original notion of the profession that is closely related to horticulture. This field covers a range of specific skills, from the breeding and production of plants to their planting, care and maintenance, as well as knowledge of fertilization, plant diseases, and plant protection. Such knowledge is anything but trivial for those wanting to design successfully using plants. Furthermore, it is important to place plants and vegetation in their ecological and environmental context. Hansen used the science of phytosociology in his approach to designing with plants. Knowledge about succession, natural vegetation, propagation, aging, and the life expectancy of plants is as necessary as studying the stability of ecosystems. This increased recourse to ecological theories is just beginning. Experts in the use of plants are now applying the strategies of John Philip Grime, the British ecologist and emeritus professor, in order to gain a better understanding of sustainable horticulture.

Ultimately, the task of creating long-term, or better, still sustainable planted designs is only possible if we start thinking inclusively. Often it is not recognized that it is not an end in itself, but is an aspect of critically important environmental design and therefore part of a larger context, and should in fact be guided by design.

So how can this be achieved? Possibly by referring to the spatial dimension of landscape and thinking in pictures again. A visual idea—if not just seen as a superficial backdrop but as one that rather permeates space—could well provide the necessary bridge between aesthetics, communities, ecological processes, detailed knowledge of horticulture, and human expectations of open space. Because images are as well a combination of reality and projection and, thus, inherently possess the dichotomy that is also intrinsic to landscape architecture. Visual ideas can come from vegetation ecology, culturally conditioned landscapes, or urban scenes. Their advantage lies in a consistent adherence to something holistic and integrative.

As part of a student research project at the Technical University Berlin, such images of vegetation were identified, described ecologically, and their atmospheric effect studied. In one scenario, they were applied to the new Tempelhofer Freiheit Park in Berlin. This project confirmed that it is possible to set a conceptual design process in motion, resulting in a predictable transformation while acknowledging the process-led aspect of natural development. The project also automatically raised issues such as expectations of open space, possibilities of use, atmospheres, and emotional worlds, of course leading eventually to the use of plants. It is certainly not the only design method, but it is geared to an open-minded approach that does not adhere to the superficial level, but considers a wide range of relevant factors.

The Return of the Use of Plants

Can landscape architecture or the use of plants return to "landscape"? From the nineteen-thirties, "open" landscape was increasingly seen as a planning task of nature conservation. Reinhold Tüxen propagated the potential of natural vegetation (PNV), a derivation of plant sociology, as a possible basis for future vegetation planning Pflanzengesellschaften als Gestaltungstoff (Plant Societies as Design Material) (Tüxen,1939). Beginning in the nineteen-seventies, the dominating paradigm prescribed that landscape—outside of urban agglomerations—should be reserved for environmental planning disciplines, such as Environmental Planning, and that landscape architecture should be restricted to urban areas.

This increasingly met with criticism. Yet it is not purely about the concept of landscape itself, but also about how the human environment is made up of both landscape and city. The massive changes in land use in recent decades have turned cities into landscape—in the shrinking cities in the West—and landscapes into cities (in the ever-expanding megacities). Conventional planning processes have not succeeded in giving these places either form or quality of life. Various ecological requirements have to be considered, such as water supply, climate control, and soil fertility—and, in addition, human habitats need to be created.

Once again, visual approaches based on pictures can be helpful. Our landscapes have always been shaped by use. Forest images, images of cultural landscapes, gardens, or the wilderness always provide information about different options for use. Developing them further to climate-related recreation landscapes or urban production environments requires knowledge about the possibilities and structures of such cause and effect structures. Once again, it is frequently images of vegetation that come to mind—or, rather, entire ecosystems that need to be developed in innovative and different ways.

Reapplying plant use to the landscape scale runs counter to the interests of nature conservation—or rather, to species conservation. While this should not present significant problems to true nature conservation, as it originated from the conservation of cultural heritage—a changing environment is devastating to species conservation. Established in the seventies as an anti-progressive trend, species conservation was thought to be practically obsolete and was gradually superseded by new concepts, such as process conservation, urban nature conservation, or ecosystem functions. However, the wheel of time was turned back by the "Convention on Biological Diversity in Rio." Anachronistic values and requirements resurfaced, which for some parts of the world were in fact new and important, but outdated for large parts of Europe. According to the Protocol of Rio, conservation should also apply to culturally induced biodiversity—thus attributing significance to the impact of human influence and the aspect of process. However, this gave rise to programs that were dedicated solely to the conservation of natural species, based on a very rigid interpretation of nature. This resulted in a stark black-and-white way of thinking: the species inventory of a particular landscape was to remain constant, any changes are as such unfavorable, and any non-native plants must be removed. However, negating the idea of the cultural landscape, wanting to prevent change and transformative procedures and halt any new developments, is a rather biased and extremely repressive approach.

But plant use has also distanced itself from the landscape level. This is quite apparent in the many theoretical approaches to the use of perennials, which do not apply to the use of woody plants or trees. However, woody plants and trees are precisely the elements that shape the essential basis of spatial design, atmosphere, and process-related developments. They are the core component needed to create a true design and a habitat from a mere decorative plant arrangement. There is a need for further theory here, a requirement which is yet to be met. Any attempts in this direction were swallowed up in the nineteen-seventies by the natural garden movement and its exclusive focus on (potentially) natural vegetation.

Ultimately, landscape provides the platform on which all forms of landscape architecture and designing with plants are based. And when Foerster writes "[my] inclination toward the world of perennials came from my experience with landscape" (Foerster, p. 84), he is certainly not alone.

Consequently, plant use must be considered holistically in relation to the landscape if it is to be understood as more than a planning detail and as vital to the actual design process. This is why it is so essential to preserve the environmental aspect, not in the analytical sense, but in terms of further developments based on design and the aspect of process.

Summary

Modern man is concerned on an unprecedented level about the limits of his ability to survive and about the resources on this planet. Awareness of nature has always been an integral part of the landscape architecture profession.

Working with vegetation and plants, in the case of ecological services, cannot merely directly improve the quality of the environment, which we urgently need in times of climate change. It must also address people's senses, give them a sense of security, and allow them the opportunity to feel like part of a natural environment. This relationship with the environment can be learned through and deepened by the study of plants. In the process, constructed nature assumes the role of mediator.

Nonetheless, the idea that the designer must also be an expert in plants is no longer sustainable today. The professional profile has changed too much. Yet, there will always be certain landscape architects who think along those lines. Other approaches are of course also possible, but an ignorance of the requirements of nature in open spaces is unforgivable. It is not about a superficial adherence to plant knowledge and the ability to apply it, but rather about landscape architecture being more involved with changing, process-led systems than architecture.

Ultimately, it is also an appeal to specialists in plant use: they have to abandon their focus on the ornamental function of plants and collaborate more consciously with designers on the plan. This requires that designers also accept that they no longer possess the necessary knowledge even about woody plants, and hence, no longer recognize or are able to utilize the possibilities this material provides.

Therefore, we need to modify the level of reference. The location of the detailed examination must not be abandoned, and certainly has great importance for the personal and individual well-being of some people. But only a discussion on the level of landscape will reveal the true possibilities of vegetation in landscape architecture.

"Just as the core usefulness of a garden design is to serve and comply with its practical purpose, namely people's convenience or benefit, there is as much beauty in the thoughtful selection of the individual, as there is in the arrangement of a diverse, perfect whole" (Meyer 1860, p. 6).

Brügmann, C. (1902): "Die Hochschule der Gartenkunst," in: *Die Gartenkunst*, 4, pp. 73–75.
Von Buttlar, A. (1997): "Revival des Landschaftsgartens? Zu aktuellen Tendenzen der Gartenkunst," in: Baumüller, B.; Kuder, U.; Zoglauer, T. (eds.): *Inszenierte Natur. Landschaftskunst im 19. und 20. Jahrhundert*. Stuttgart: Deutsche Verlagsanstalt, pp. 96–117.
Čapek, K. (1985): *Das Jahr des Gärtners*. Leipzig: Gustav Kiepenheuer Verlag.
Dezallier d'Argenville, A.-J. (1731): *Die Gärtnerey sowohl in ihrer Theorie oder Betrachtung als Praxis oder Übung*. Translated by Franz Anton Danreitter. Leipzig: Verlag Dr. Richter.
Dreiseitl, H.; Grau, D.; Ludwig, K. H. C. (2001): *Waterscapes–Planen, Bauen und Gestalten mit Wasser*. Basel: Birkhäuser.
Dümpelmann, S. (2001): *Vom großen Welt- und Gartenspiel*. Berlin: exhibition catalog.
Echtermeyer, T. (ed.) (1913): *Die Königliche Gärtnerlehranstalt Dahlem. Denkschrift zur Erinnerung an das zehnjährige Bestehen der Anstalt in Dahlem 1903–1913* Berlin: Verlagsbuchhandlung Paul Parey.
Florineth, F. (2012): *Pflanzen statt Beton*. Berlin: Patzer.
Foerster, K. (1986): *Es wird durchgeblüht. Thema mit Variationen*. Berlin: Union Verlag.
Gothein, M. L. (1926): *Geschichte der Gartenkunst, vol. 2, Von der Renaissance in Frankreich bis zur Gegenwart*. Jena: Diederichs.
Grime, J. P. (1979): *Plant strategies, vegetation processes, and ecosystem properties*. Chichester: John Wiley.
Hacker, E.; Johannsen, R. (2012): *Ingenieurbiologie*. Stuttgart: Ulmer.
Hansen, R.; Stahl, F. (1981): *Die Stauden und ihre Lebensbereiche in Gärten und Grünanlagen*. Stuttgart: Ulmer.
Hansen, R. (1984): *Lecture at the DGGL in Munich 1984*. Manuscript.
Heinrich, A.; Messer, U. J. (2012): *Staudenmischpflanzungen: Praxis, Beispiele, Tendenzen*. Stuttgart: Ulmer.
Hitchmough, J. (2004): "Naturalistic Herbaceous Vegetation for Urban Landscapes," in: Dunnett, N.; Hitchmough, J. (eds.): *The Dynamic Landscape. Design, Ecology and Management of Naturalistic Urban Planting*. London: Spon Press, pp. 172–245.
Hoemann, R. (1908): "Die Einfachheit in der Gartenkunst," in: *Die Gartenkunst*, 9, pp. 147–154.
Holling, C. S. (1973): *Resilience and stability of ecosystems. Annual Review of Ecology and Systematics*, 4, pp. 1–23.
Loidl, H.; Bernhard S. (2003): *Freiräume(n). Entwerfen als Landschaftsarchitektur*. Basel: Birkhäuser.
Meyer, G. (1860): *Lehrbuch der schönen Gartenkunst*. Berlin: Riegel.
Meyer, E. (2008): "Sustaining Beauty. The Performance of Appearance. A Manifesto in Three Parts," in: *JoLa*, Spring, pp. 6–23.
Migge, M. (1909): "Willy Lange—auch ein Erzieher," in: *Die Gartenkunst*, 11, pp. 198–199.
Neumann, K. (2001): "Bewusstes Vergessen systematisch lernen," in: *Garten+Landschaft*, 11/2001, pp. 16–18.
Ott, K. (1997): "Zum Stand der Diskussion in der Ökologischen Ethik," in: Baumüller, B.; Kuder, U.; Zoglauer, T. (eds.): *Inszenierte Natur. Landschaftskunst im 19. und 20. Jahrhundert*. Stuttgart: Deutsche Verlagsanstalt, pp. 162–178.
Tüxen, R. (1939): "Pflanzengesellschaften als Gestaltungsstoff," in: *Die Gartenkunst*, 11, pp. 209–216.
Weilacher, U. (2005): "Bilderwelten in Bewegung," in: Schöder, Th.; Joosten, H.: *Büro Kiefer. Rekombinationen–Recombinations*. Stuttgart: Verlag Eugen Ulmer, pp. 7–9.

"Landscapology"
Linking Natural Sciences, Humanities, and Aesthetics

Hansjörg Küster

Introduction

Landscapes are designed, painted, analyzed, presented, and planned. To specialists involved with all these activities, it can seem as if they are working with different items or objects; Gerhard Hard even argued that there exist two different concepts of "landscape." Painters are considered to be subjective, while geographers aim to be objective and science-based; some landscape planners think that they are working only on an aesthetically determined basis—however, they are all involved with the same topic of landscape. To clarify this, I proposed the new academic discipline of *Landschaftswissenschaft*, literally translated as "landscape science." In English this term may be inappropriate, as *Wissenschaft* in German does not have the same meaning as "science" in English, which is often overlooked. Science means "natural science" and is based on analytical methods and results. Science leads to objective conclusions, which are drawn after analyzing results. Wissenschaft in German includes both science and the humanities. It is not based only on analytical methods and results, but may encompass more essayistic aspects, as well as syntheses. Wissenschaft can be carried out by a physicist or a biologist, as well as by a historian, whereas in the English language "science" only includes physicists and biologists—a historian on the contrary works in the

Wilderness in the national park “Bayerischer Wald”.

Managed woodland.

field of the humanities. Landschaftswissenschaft should not be understood as a solely science-based academic subject, but as comprising the natural and cultural aspects of landscape.

Landscape: Nature and Culture

A natural landscape is characterized by mountains and hills, waterways, woodlands and individual trees. These elements are often regarded as being stable, but this is not the case: over the course of the Earth's history, continents have shifted, mountains, hills and islands have been formed and eroded, rivers have changed their courses, lakes have been formed by glaciers and later drained. These processes not only took place in the past, but are ongoing, mostly very gradually and on a large geological scale, but sometimes also abruptly: for instance, earthquakes, volcanic eruptions, and floods. Living beings reproduce, or are born, grow, and die. New individuals, populations, types of beings or species come into being and disappear. In nature, nothing is stable.

The culture of a landscape can mean two different things: firstly, landscape is always subject to interpretation, and therefore each landscape is a part of culture. This is one reason why "cultural landscapes" and "natural landscapes" are inappropriate terms. Every landscape is culturally determined, and therefore "cultural landscape" is a pleonasm. However, it often refers to specific cultural elements within a landscape, so the term should only be used in this sense and otherwise avoided, as landscape is cultural per se. Secondly, many landscapes feature cultural elements: buildings, fields, managed woodlands, roads, parks and gardens, also planted trees and factories, mines and wayside crosses, single barns and dismantled railway tracks. Cities or towns can also be important aspects of a landscape. These elements are often described as pertaining to a "cultural landscape," especially those

Hanover city center is subdued to natural change, if men are not caring for their houses: House façades are attacked by mechanisms of erosion—in the same way as rocks and mountains.

Gradient of vegetation on a woodland rim.

which are part of a "historic cultural landscape," including landscape elements that are not connected to land usage. Any aspect of the landscape formed by cultural influences is not stable either, despite man's intention, for the most part, to create stable structures. This not only refers to individual components of the landscape, but first and foremost to stable living conditions: the landscape should provide enough nutrition and ensure the conservation of aesthetic values, and hazards should be avoided. When people construct a house or design their garden, they are usually planning to create something stable that will hopefully never change in the future. Despite these intentions, one is forced to repair the house regularly and to care for the garden by removing weeds, cutting herbs after flowering, sowing seeds, and fertilizing soil.

People attempt to create stability in the face of natural change. They construct dikes to avoid flooding and to enable permanent agriculture in the polders behind the dikes. They build nets against avalanches, enabling secure settlement in locations which were previously often destroyed by rocks and snow. If the dike breaks and land is flooded, or the net is destroyed and the settlement is buried by an avalanche, one talks about a natural catastrophe. However, in fact it is nothing other than a consequence of natural dynamics, and these hazards show that ultimately man is not able to protect land and settlements against natural dynamics.

The Presentation of Landscape by Means of Maps

Natural and cultural landscape elements are presented by means of topographic or thematic maps. Geographers usually consider maps as an objective basis for their (natural) science and statistics, using them to present tables and structures, which they regard as objective landscape elements, such as the percentages of woodlands, of fields, or of settled areas of the Earth. Maps define precise

Coastlines are always shifting.

Low-lying areas within the Alps (Durance valley in the French Alps).

borderlines, for example between sea and land or between woodland and open land, but in reality the borderlines are very rarely located in the exact position where they are indicated on maps. This can be due to the existence of broad transition zones instead of abrupt borderlines, or due to permanent change, evident for instance on borderlines between land and sea: wind and tides are constantly and permanently changing the contours of the borders.

In historical geography, maps are often designed to reconstruct ancient landscapes, drawing the same borderlines between land and sea or the rims of woodland, suggesting that they had the same appearance as today. However, there is no evidence for this, and therefore such indications on a map can never be objective. Geographers tend to overlook the fact that maps are based on interpretations and ideas. Maps, in fact, can be compared to artists' works, such as painted landscapes. Interpretations in maps are based on definitions—but a definition is a part of culture, is based on an idea, and is not necessarily objective. Two important conclusions can be drawn from this: firstly, the character of a map is comparable to that of a pictorial landscape created by a painter. The drawn map and the painted landscape are both interpretations or are the result of interpretations. And secondly, it is not possible to pretend that a map can form a scientific basis. Perhaps the landscape picture designed by an artist is even more realistic than a map. This can be the case when the painter reflects on a specific landscape situation, while the geographer who designs a map only indicates an abstract type of landscape. A painter who depicts the Alps will present a typical view of these mountains, whereas the geographer will think primarily about where the borders of the Alps are. He can interpret these, but he will never describe a concrete situation as, for instance, there are gradients between high mountains and foreland plains, and there are also low-lying areas within the Alps such as the Valois or the Inn valley which are certainly not mountainous or even "alpine" landscapes. The Valais and other low-lying areas

A bog in Estonia included on a map as a woodland.

An oak woodland similar to the primeval woodlands which existed before the first clearing.

within the Alps can be presented as valleys or plains, which is also how they appear to visitors, but nevertheless the Valois is included in the area of the Alps by geographers.

Woodlands on Maps

A painter will depict a concrete woodland with its rims, whereas on a map one will always find the same generalizing borderline, which is not a true representation. It indicates the rim of a woodland, whether abrupt or a gradient, and it may also indicate nothing other than the edge of a forested area. This means that it is possible that the borderline of woodland on a map does not show the rim of a real patch of woodland, but only an area where a woodland plantation might be located in the future. In terms of forestry, this is also woodland area, but certainly not from the point of view of an ecologist or of any other person who is not involved with forestry. On the basis of exact lines on a map, it seems possible to indicate percentages of woodland within the landscapes at the point in time when the map was drawn, but one must take into account that the woodland surrounded by the borderline on a map could have had a very different character and possibly only indicates the area designated as future woodland.

Through the ages, woodlands had different characteristics, and consequently woodland edges differed in appearance, indicating a variety of usages. Primeval woodland was not used by man at all and natural processes alone determined its development. Later on, woodlands were cleared by mankind for agricultural purposes. Permanent crop growing and animal husbandry were not practiced for millennia. During prehistoric times, when stable political and economic infrastructures did not exist, settlements and their fields were abandoned after a number of decades, enabling the formation of secondary woodlands. The formation of secondary woodlands saw the proliferation not only of tree species that existed in the woodlands before

Beech woodland.

A grazed woodland.

clearance, but also of other tree species. In Central Europe not only could oak reestablish itself, but beech also proliferated. Consequently, woodlands changed their appearance significantly: primeval oak woodlands differ greatly from secondary beech woods, which are much denser and darker. Permanent villages and cities developed in some Central European areas from Roman times, in others from the Middle Ages. Patches of the landscape surrounding these settlements were utilized permanently for long-term purposes: fields were cultivated and woodlands were exploited for timber and wood production and also for livestock grazing. Rotation was necessary, but in principle crops were cultivated on the same patches of land for centuries. Other forms of cultivation emerged that required stability of landuse, such as gardening, growing vines and fruit trees, hops cultivation, and also meadow management. Meadows were irrigated to fertilize them and to melt the snow earlier, in order to increase the yields. In the woodlands, the percentages of beech decreased, as this tree species cannot withstand intensive utilization. This means that after an initial proliferation of beech in secondary woodlands, cultivation led to its decline. Oak and hornbeam proliferated, as these trees are able to sprout again after being felled. Woodlands once again changed in character.

Early modern times brought the realization that woodlands could be overexploited to such an extent that it was widely feared that they could be totally destroyed. Large areas of woodland were overgrazed and transformed to shrublands and heathlands, which were common land: anybody could use them as he pleased, for grazing, woodcutting, farming, hunting, etc. In the eighteenth and nineteenth centuries, land reforms were launched in many European countries to avoid land destruction and promote a sustainable development of woodlands, as well as of other landscape features. Common land was reclaimed by private landowners. Small plots were joined to form larger fields. Grazing was forbidden in woodlands, so that sustainable forest management could be established. Trees

A watered meadow: plant growth started earlier in irrigated sections.

Spruce forest.

were planted, in many cases conifers, so that woodlands once again changed in character. Conifers were preferred for several reasons. They grow faster than many broad-leaved trees such as oak, even in poor soil, and they are more appropriate for timber rafting: the specific weight of conifer wood is lower than that of broad-leaved trees.

Nowadays, fields have been joined again to form even larger acreages. Woodlands and forests are denser than one hundred years ago. In the late nineteenth and the early twentieth centuries, many forests had just been newly planted, so that small trees prevailed. Today, tall trees rise up in these same locations, which are now more than one hundred years old. On the map, woodlands from the early twentieth century are often indicated in the same way as present-day woodland, but they differ totally in character. It is only possible to compare woodlands that were established in equal or at least similar systemic conditions, but it is impossible to compare woodlands from different eras. Primeval woodland differs greatly from a piece of Neolithic woodland, and this in turn is totally different from medieval woodland and modern forests.

Fields

The same is true of fields. In early periods of agriculture, fields were created on changing plots of land and varied in size. In the Middle Ages, when permanent agriculture was established, narrow and long field strips were created, which were called acres. A field comprised a number of strips or acres. They belonged to different farmers, but all farmers were forced to cultivate the same crop on their field, because it was not possible to create pathways between the acres, and so the crops on the field strips had to be harvested at the same time. It was not possible to cultivate different crops within one field, as they would have to be harvested at different times. It is worth noting that the terms “acre” and “field” did not mean the same in the medieval land use system. During land reforms in early modern times, the strips were joined to form larger fields. This allowed more intensive land use, and farmers gained the freedom to cultivate whatever crops they chose autonomously. After the land reforms, the terms "field" and "acre" were used in the same way: a present-day field is also an acre, which was not the case during medieval times. This underlines the fact that medieval fields cannot be compared with those of early modern times and also not with present-day fields.

Systems of Land Use and the Respective Landscapes

All features of the landscape, not only woodlands and fields, but also grassland, settlements, gardens and so on, were integrated into systems of land use, which differed from era to era and were determined by man. A first land use system was that of hunters and gatherers in the late phase of the last Ice Age and the period shortly thereafter. Hunters had excellent living conditions in open grasslands, inhabited by many large herbivorous animals that could be hunted. Living conditions became harder when woodlands expanded after the warming of the climate at the end of the Ice Age. Large herbivorous animals did not inhabit woodlands, migrating instead to areas where woodlands had not yet proliferated. Hunters had to change their hunting methods and living conditions: smaller animals were hunted along coasts, rivers, and lakes. Fishing became important and hazel shrubs were planted, providing additional sources of nutrition. The inhabitants of Southwest Asia collected selected grains of wild grass species, which could be developed into crops. During this period, the character of the landscape was determined largely by natural developments. Over the last 8,000 years, more and more parts of Europe and also of other continents were dedicated to farming, which had developed first in the Middle East and also other genetic centers of cultivated plants in the world. Small agricultural areas, which were not used permanently, were created within woodlands. When such sites were abandoned new woodlands could develop.

A new land use system developed first of all in Mesopotamia and along large rivers, then on the Mediterranean coasts and later also in other parts of Europe, which was determined by state formation, historic tradition, economic infrastructure, and stability of settlements. Cities became the centers of this land use system, but they could not exist without rural settlements, whereas small villages could certainly exist without cities, a fact that is often overlooked. This land use system always leads to over-exploitation. Entire civilizations have broken down owing to increasing salinity, as a consequence of the long-term irrigation of fields or the over-exploitation of woodlands and the resulting increase in soil erosion. Another land use system was established by land reforms that took place from the eighteenth century, starting in various European countries, primarily England, France, and Germany. Larger fields were created, fertilization was improved, new land use techniques were introduced, and forests were managed sustainably. The formation of this land use system was greatly supported by industrialization: by using steam engines it became possible to mine coal and to distribute it by rail. This enabled the afforestation of many woodland areas.

Over a number of decades in the second half of the twentieth century, a new land use system evolved, leading to intensification and the formation of even larger fields than before, the formation of large settlements and conglomerations, but also the marginalization of remote areas, for instance in the mountains and on lonesome islands. Small settlements and former agrarian fields were abandoned.

A landscape of land reforms.

A vast present-day field.

Especially during periods when more modern land use systems superseded old-fashioned ones, it was noted that traditional structures were lost. Traditional structures were called "idyllic" or "Arcadian," or they were regarded as "nature." The first case of this was possibly when the Roman poet Virgil wrote his poems of the "Bucolica." He praised the living conditions of herdsmen in Arcadia. Arcadia is a historic landscape on the Peloponnese peninsula in ancient Greece, but Virgil translocated Arcadia to southern Italy. After Virgil, many poets and artists looked for "their" Arcadia in Italy—and not in Greece. Translocations of landscape names became common in later periods. Landscapes were regarded as being "English," "Swiss," or "Mediterranean" and they were considered as paradises, basically emphasizing the beauty attributed to these landscapes.

In Germany, it was acknowledged that the Roman writer Tacitus mentioned large woodlands as being characteristic of the land of Germanic tribes. Germanic tribes were regarded as indigenous to Central Europe and therefore were said to be best adapted to an environment characterized by large woodlands. It was not at all clear what these woodlands really looked like, except that they were large, dense, dark, and wild, and that they represented "German(ic) nature." During the Napoleonic wars forests were planted to ward off the French soldiers. Germans expected that French soldiers would not be able to operate in dense and large woodlands. They were compared to the Romans, who were said to be incapable of living in such woodlands; it was believed that the existence of dark woodlands in "Germania" was the reason the Romans were not able to conquer these lands 1,800 years previously. The French and the Romans were compared to each other, as they spoke Romanic languages. For this reason, a lot of dark conifer forests were planted in Germany during the nineteenth century, instead of the deciduous trees that had prevailed in Germany during the Roman age. It is hard to believe that some Germans really thought that French soldiers would get lost in dense woodlands, but it was clearly acknowledged that it was necessary to plant trees and dense forests as "German nature," especially after the Congress of Vienna, to safeguard the German identity and freedom.

Conclusions

To analyze landscape, it is necessary to examine natural and cultural aspects, and it is most important to deal with the ideas that are developed about landscapes. Although natural parameters and cultural elements can be analyzed more clearly than ideas about landscapes, the latter are most important to the public, therefore the formation and development of these ideas needs to be studied. This is only possible if the natural and cultural parameters of particular landscapes are analyzed closely and if there is an objective basis for the formation of an idea about a landscape: it should be clear as to why one particular landscape is called "paradise," another "Arcadia," "Tuscany," "nature," "Swiss," or "sublime." This is important for improving the basis for landscape planning, as the public will understand ideas better than natural and cultural facts. The public always wants the planning of a landscape to conserve its identity or central idea.

It is necessary to stress that landscape analysis and landscape planning are different activities: landscape analysis is the basis for landscape planning. Many landscape planners are nevertheless of the opinion that landscape analysis is not necessary as a separate preliminary professional step before planning, which may only be the case if a landscape planner also has the professional competence to analyze the landscape himself before planning it. However, it must be acknowledged that landscape analysis has such a wide scope that it is very unlikely that the majority of landscape planners have the necessary competence to do this job. It is also necessary to compile information about landscapes to educate the public, so that the public will gain a better understanding of the important aspects of a particular landscape.

To conclude this essay, the question arises as to what landscape analysis should be called as an academic discipline. “Landscape science” as a literal translation of the German “Landschaftswissenschaft” would not be appropriate. This was argued already at the beginning of this essay. Perhaps “landscapology” would be a suitable term? This can certainly be discussed in the context of a publication called “Landscript.” This title is not a traditional English term either. Perhaps it will be possible to find a better term for referring to professional landscape analysis, which encompasses all of its aspects: nature, culture, and ideas. It is not only geographers who are involved with all of these aspects. Landscapology, in the sense of landscape analysis and synthesis, is necessary as a representation of the concept of landscape as a whole. Then it will be clear to everyone that they are dealing with the same notion of landscape: the scientist, who not only analyzes but also interprets landscape, lay people who do the same on a more mundane level, or the painter and the planner, who play a central role in landscape development.

REFERENCES

Hard, Gerhard: *Die „Landschaft“ der Sprache und die „Landschaft“ der Geographen. Semantische und forschungslogische Studien*. Colloquium Geographicum 11, Bonn 1970.

Küster, Hansjörg: *Die Entdeckung der Landschaft. Einführung in eine neue Wissenschaft*, Munich 2012.

ÄSTHETIK
Topologische Strukturen III
Paneldiskussion: Stefan Körner, Lothar Schäfer,
Wulf Tessin, Jörg Zimmermann
Moderation: Albert Kirchengast

The City Is Not Landscape

Vittorio Magnago Lampugnani

The beginnings of urban development that led to today's agglomeration can be dated back to the mid-nineteenth century. Overly dense large European metropoles with their degrading poverty-stricken districts and unacceptable standards of hygiene led the search for radical alternatives. One idea that became established worldwide was the "Garden City" by Ebenezer Howard, which he first described theoretically at the end of the nineteenth century, and then realized in practical terms. He confronted the massive, nineteenth-century, urban "stone desert" with well-arranged settlements featuring plants and trees, and assumed these would become increasingly popular and eventually replace the large metropoles. The fundamental unit was a single- or multi-family cottage surrounded by green. It became the favored dwelling structure for all levels of society, gained more and more state subsidies, and as a corruption of the original garden city idea, eventually turned into the various forms of what we today call suburbia.

But this is only one of at least two instances of European urban expansion.

The other involves the expansion of the city into a new, more rational structure, which would maintain the compactness and density that was typical of the historical city. There are many models of this type of urban expansion. One of the most spectacular and impressive examples

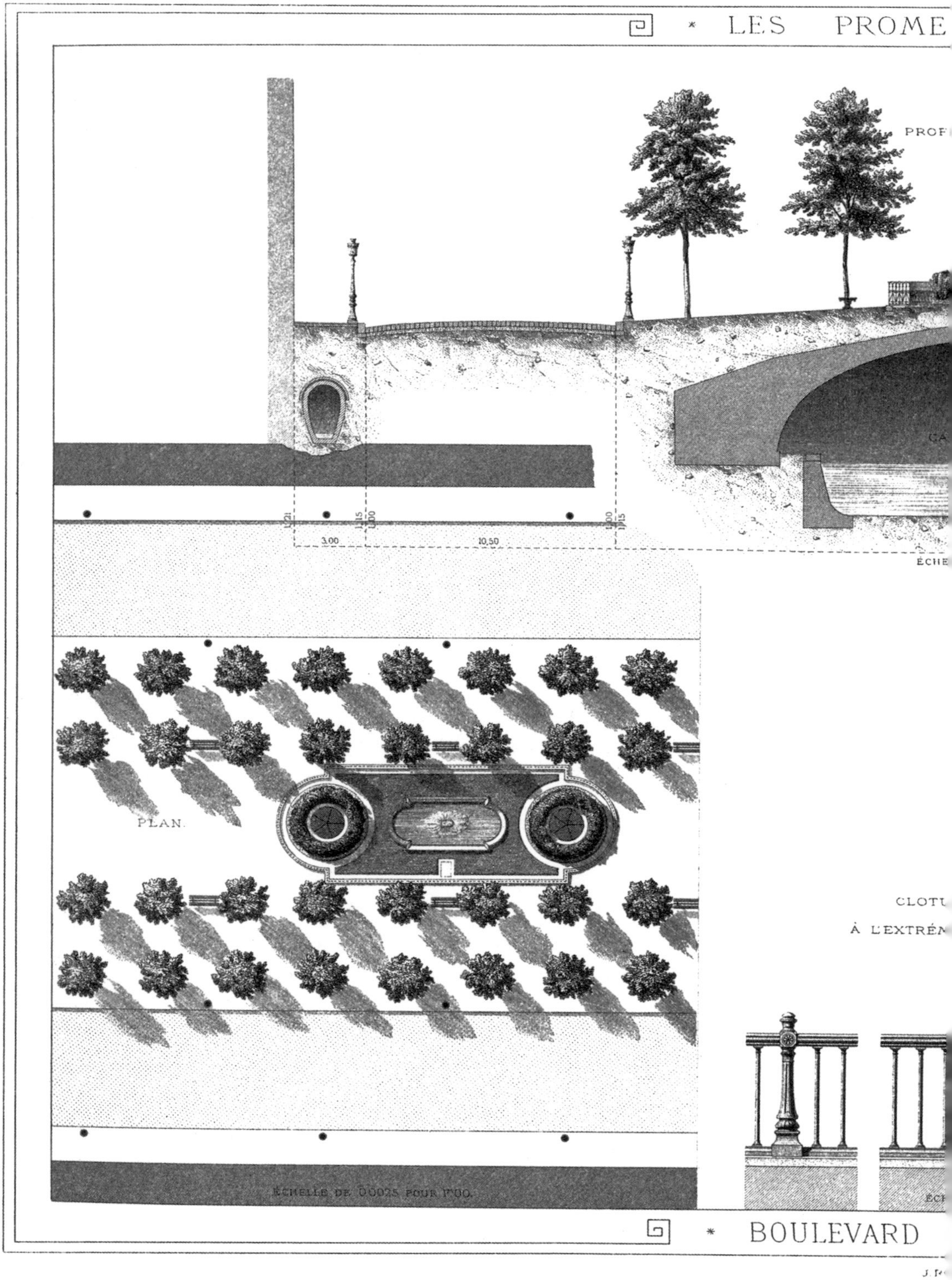
LES PROME
PROF
3.00
10.50
PLAN.
CLOTU
À L'EXTRÉM
ÉCHELLE DE 0.0025 POUR 1.00.
BOULEVARD

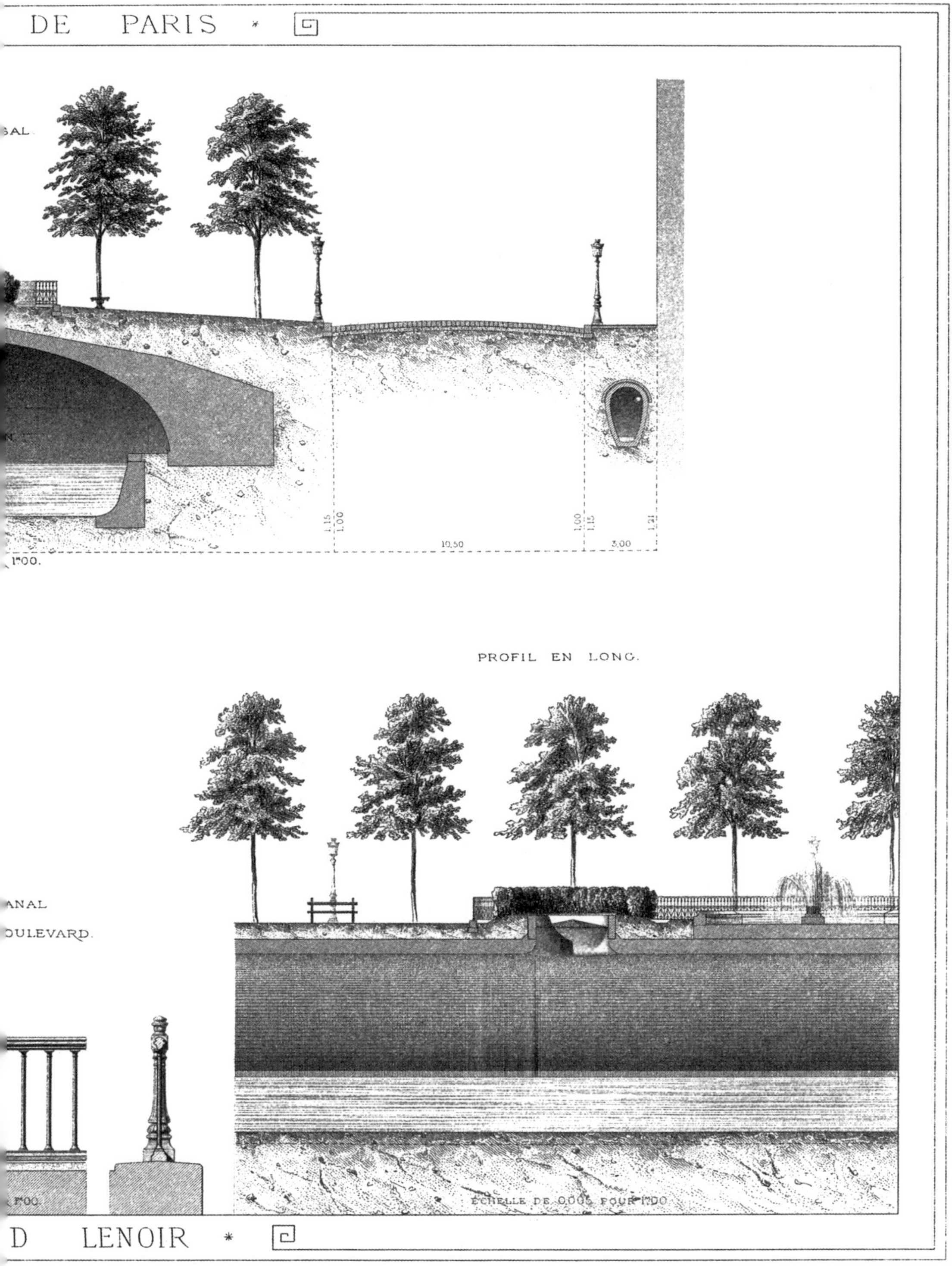
DE PARIS
SAL.
1,15
1,00
10,50
1,00
1,15
3,00
1,21
PROFIL EN LONG.
ANAL
OULEVARD.
ECHELLE DE 0,005 POUR 1m00
D LENOIR

R.

is the Ensanche area in Barcelona, planned by engineer Ildefonso Cerdà in 1859 and realized over the following years. It maintained the system of streets and squares that characterized the old Barcelona, but translated these into a more contemporary form and linked it with new technological achievements, such as the tram and the city train system. He retained the concept of density, but only as far as it would support better hygiene standards, sufficient green, and lighting. This concept resulted in a new city that boasted the same efficient use of spatial area as the older city, and immediately looked urban.

This second instance is the one we need to continue upon in contemporary urban design. And it is the original definition of city that we need to reexamine: one that sees it as an artifact that protects people, human interaction, as well as the possibility to identify with a place; hence, it sharply distinguishes itself from nature and is even in opposition to it.

In light of the situation today, this historical definition has become highly modern and contemporary. The destruction of landscape by city and village sprawl, but also by proliferating single buildings, has reached an extent that is more than threatening. At the moment in Switzerland, one square meter of land is consumed per second by construction, in Italy, eight. The landscape that we love and cherish, but also quite pragmatically need for food production and recreation, is soon at risk of being destroyed.

For this reason, we need a new, old city: dense and artificial, a dispositive for human life and interaction, a city that has no place for nature. If we want to preserve our nature, we should not bring it into the city, because this is ultimately nothing more than bringing the city recklessly into the landscape. On the contrary, the city needs to withdraw into itself, become dense, hard, and stone-like again. That might seem at odds with nature, but in reality, it is the only way of paying respect to nature.

This is not to say that the city has to be of stone and cement blocks—on the contrary, it has to make open spaces available, which should be designed carefully, in context, and be treated as a priority. This does not mean that nature should be completely banned from the city; but nature in the city is not real, it's a surrogate. Gardens and parks are not surviving parcels of landscape—as if they even could be biologically—they are artificial copies and metaphors of the landscape that they and the houses expelled. New York's Central Park might pretend to resemble the original, natural environment that typified Manhattan before it was constructed, but in truth it is the result of a complex reconstruction endeavor that produced a recreation machine from a piece of land, and then camouflaged it as a natural landscape. Even the trees that line our city streets have been mutated into architectural elements that look like columns, and are as artificially watered as the plants on our windowsills.

Should we therefore return the city portrayed by Ambrogio Lorenzetti in the Palazzo Pubblico Sienna in his fresco of *Buon Governo*? One that is compact and artificial, with walls sharply separating it from the surrounding countryside that provides its food and natural environment? No, because a modern city can never look like the Sienna of the fourteenth century. Yes, because it portrays, as does the Sienna of the past, an eminently artificial, and at best artistic dispositive for people to enjoy a comfortable and even happy coexistence.

In order to build a city such as this in the present day and age, we would need to rethink the disciple of urban design as much as the image of the city to which the discipline relates and from whence it came. Landscape architecture, which has penetrated the vacuum left behind by a negligent and exhausted urban design, cannot replace it, even if camouflaged as landscape urbanism.

We do not merely need to reinvent the city, but also the discipline that systemizes and collects knowledge about the city. Yet first, we must reflect on that, which has long been developed and tested but has fallen into frivolous, reckless, yes, even irresponsible oblivion.

Ambrogio Lorenzetti, Allegory of Good Government (detail), 1337–1340, Siena, Palazzo Pubblico.

ASTROLOGIA
PHILOSOPHIA

On The Freedom of Designing Nature and the Limitations of The Arbitrary

Lothar Schäfer

Nature untouched by humans is considered by many to be the epitome of the "beautiful" landscape, but in truth it has barely existed on this planet for a very long time, perhaps at most as an idea. However, in my opinion, not even the idea of untouched nature is a very good ideal for a "beautiful" landscape, and even less as the basis for a landscape design.

The Earth experienced a long history before humans were counted among its inhabitants, and any changes that occurred at that time did so without human intervention. But since humans have existed, they have also contributed to the restructuring of the earth's surface, as have all other life forms. In the beginning, these were insignificant interventions and changes compared to erosion, storms, volcano eruptions, and other natural forces, but meanwhile the intervention by human industrialized hands can no longer be ignored. Because environmentalists inform us that these interventions will have ruinous consequences for organic life on our planet, it is very tempting to see "nature untouched by man" as being the normative force for the creation of our environment. Human destructiveness is counteracted by the notion of nature that is alive and well. Nature should be the foundation on which we should base our actions if we are to avoid the ruinous effects of our interventions. Nature, not man, should provide the guidelines that establish which significant transformations are allowed or prohibited in nature.

This idea is as tempting as it is futile, because the opposing argument constructed here is rooted in misconceptions. In a certain sense, nature has always been nothing more than "understood" nature, and this understanding is reflected in our concept of nature. Throughout our history—and in various cultures throughout the world—very diverse concepts of nature have been formed, transformed, and even discarded. The epistemic status of these concepts of nature is uncertain. The only certainty is that not one of these concepts refers to invariant natural phenomena, or is the result of scientific research, because they are all based primarily on the human relationship to nature.

These basic notions of nature can best be interpreted as an expression of how humans see themselves in relation to their environment; they are an expression of the attitude with which we confront the world in terms of identification, evaluation, and action. Depending on whether the relationship humans feel they have with nature is conceived as more "exclusive" or "inclusive," whether they primarily understand nature to be an opposing force or see themselves as a part of nature, the understanding of the self and that of nature will assume an either "asymmetric" or "symmetric" form. These fundamental ideas about nature will depend in each case on how humans picture their purpose in the world. *The Human Place in the Cosmos* (*Die Stellung des Menschen im Kosmos*, Max Scheler) cannot be based on facts in the same way that the distance between Earth and the Moon can be measured. It is deeply rooted in the human self-concept. Therefore, the fundamental concepts of nature and its transformations will always remain an interesting datum for philosophical anthropology and—despite advances in knowledge—reflect the status of possible human self-representations.

The convictions that inspire us to learn more about nature are not based in true knowledge of nature, which would have to be a greater degree of knowledge because it precedes empirical knowledge. They are rather like the preliminary drafts of what we assume nature once was.

Analyzing them does not provide insight into nature itself, but rather into our own ideas of nature—and these are, as previously mentioned, reflections of ourselves: we only see our own reflection in the mirror of nature. We may well believe that consciousness is a "Mirror of Nature" (Richard Rorty), because it simply reflects that which surrounds us, but we also reflect ourselves in nature; human self-knowledge apparently needs a detour via external projections. David Hume thought it absolutely impossible to see anything other than oneself and that when exploring "the most distant corners of the universe we are moving in the universe of our imagination!" As useful as the mirror of nature is for the self-knowledge of man—especially for perceiving transformation in our self-image—it is nevertheless a great mistake to believe that our self-projections are true representations of nature.

It should be recalled that in the seventeenth century the outdated, Christian-influenced understanding of nature, which originated in ancient times, was replaced by the emerging modern natural sciences. The fundamental concept of the cosmos as the domain of divine and eternal order was superseded by the notion of an infinite universe, which has since become an open field for human research. What is new here is that the study of nature is no longer based on a method of pure *theoria*, but on empirical theories that are based on experimental activities. Knowledge of nature—its laws and conditions—cannot be obtained without interfering in the natural processes. This initially research-motivated intervention triggered the much broader idea of redirecting the purpose of nature research to the development of technologies in order to harness the forces and resources of nature on a grand scale. Nature becomes the *dominium hominis*, serving to alleviate human material needs. That was Francis Bacon's line of thinking; he recognized early on that large-scale industrial use would lead to a profound alteration of natural conditions.—[1]

From this perspective, we have the freedom to design nature, but it is widely known and much lamented that

1 See Lothar Schäfer: *Das Bacon-Projekt: Von der Erkenntnis, Nutzung und Schonung der Natur*, Frankfurt am Main 1993.

the aesthetic aspects of a design have played a far less significant role than the efficient utilization and better exploitation of nature.—[2] But from what model can we develop standards with which to impose constraints on unharnessed access? Nature has lost the charm (Max Weber) of its normative force. Those who attempt to derive standards for action from natural conditions are making a logical error: ought cannot be derived from an *is* ("naturalistic fallacy"). This criticism has been put forward so many times that it does not need to be repeated here. The limits of the arbitrary certainly arise from the use of the autonomous subject, meaning its obligation to physical wellbeing. Questions relating to the assessment of physical wellbeing lead us directly to the physical metabolism with our environment. In this sense, one can presuppose a "relationship with nature."

2 The following is a list of the results of the "ecological crisis": global temperature rise, ozone depletion, depletion of resources, destruction of landscapes, air and water pollution, species extinction in the animal and plant kingdoms, and much more.

The Body as an Indicator of an Intact or Impaired Metabolism in Nature

The human relationship with nature should be understood in a very concrete sense. As organisms, we exist in physiological interaction with our environment. This is the fundamental essence of organic life, and our well-being depends largely on the extent to which the exchange of energy and matter between the organism and the environment functions. It would be too narrow-minded to assess the viability of organisms purely in terms of how well they have conformed to the environment ("ecological niche"). Life and survival are a thoroughly dynamic process in which the environment also always experiences transformation. The flow of materials and energies that is indispensable for organisms and on which organismic metabolism depends, and that it in turn also influences, must be seen as a dynamic system of complex actions and reactions, whereby the cyclical processes in particular (food chains, cycles of water, phosphates and metals, etc.) are essential for life. They are presentable as cyclical processes only by including different life forms that contribute by means of absorption, distribution, transformation, or transportation.

This is an ancient and true insight, regardless of one's preferred philosophy or belief system. It is all the more astonishing how this truth has remained so unproductive in the context of the environmental reflections of philosophers, despite the fact that it is part of fundamental ecological thought. This may be due to the fact that metaphysical ideas in this context like to push to the fore, resulting at the same time in a normative overload for determining the human relationship to nature. As we ourselves are a part of nature, it should immediately follow suit that we feel a strong affinity to the elements of nature. However, it is not at all evident that we have to behave in a certain way, simply because we are a part of nature. Those who put forward such arguments have a very definite, normative conception of nature in mind: for instance, ancient animism or, the Christian notion of the equality of all creatures before God the Creator.

Given that I consider normative concepts of nature to be antiquated and incompatible with the scientific standards of the modern age,—[3] I advocate a human relationship to nature that is free from normative statements. I have also adopted the scientific concept of metabolism and the associated indicators of organic well-being or suffering purely as statements of fact. It is merely about cataloging circumstances that have no direct consequences as such. Only by associating these with acknowledged obligations do consequences result from our actions concerning nature. Physical well-being and health are indicators of how well we tolerate environmental conditions. These environmental conditions naturally consist of more than just factors that can be verified physically and chemically. We know, for instance, that psychosocial factors can lead to physical symptoms of illness. Architecture and housing, work and social structure are among the many factors

3 Lothar Schäfer: "Selbstbestimmung und Naturverhältnis des Menschen," in: Oswald Schwemmer (ed.): *Über Natur*, Frankfurt am Main, 1987, pp. 15–35.

that contribute to our well-being. Designed landscape belongs in the same category. However, the physically and chemically verifiable factors assume an essential role, since they are the factors that we influence directly through our technological interventions in natural processes. Due to our body's metabolic involvement in the cyclical processes of nature, we can regard our body as a sensorium for its compatibility with the external conditions in which we live. With the concept of metabolism, I am implying the physiological relationship of exchange between the human organism and its environment, in other words the passive external metabolism. My concern, however, is not primarily a quantitative balancing of accounts, but the qualitative assessment of the processes of exchange between organisms and nature that are expressed through physical wellbeing. Physical sensations express the overall balance, which is relevant for life, of this metabolic exchange with the environment. The state of the organism is an indication of whether the relationship with nature is intact or damaged. The wellbeing, which is manifested physically, functions as our ecological gauge of nature.

The Physiological Concept of Nature

Nature is thus not understood as the totality of that which exists under common law, meaning the concept of nature based on modern natural sciences, but rather it is the external things that relate to biological unit critically, in terms of beneficial and adverse, or wholesome and unwholesome. This central evaluation of the environment, environmental factors, substances, and all conditions is inevitably interconnected with the organism itself, and therefore also to us humans as organic beings. This evaluation also of course includes objects and conditions that have nothing to do with the metabolism, but they are not relevant to this essay. All that matters here is the real recorded material and energy levels—through nutrition, respiration, radiation, heat exchange, and so on—and the reaction of the organism in terms of its well-being or malaise. This hub of life, to which nature refers positively and negatively, gives rise to a very different concept of nature to the conventional one. I call the first concept, which implies that nature is the epitome of phenomena under general law, the "cosmological concept of nature." The concept that refers to the organism's metabolism with our environment, I call the "physiological concept of nature."

In the past discussion that, "in the name of nature," called for certain changes of behavior, the argument was based on the idea that the cosmological concept of nature was the basis of environmental considerations. However, since the concept of nature established by modern science was considered useless with regard to normative considerations, as I have previously stated, it seemed necessary to fall back on antiquated concepts of nature.—[4] It appears to me, however, that the discussion about a reasonable relationship to nature is generally not relevant to the cosmological concept—regardless of what version, ancient or modern (such as the Gaia hypothesis of James Lovelock)—but is in fact applicable to the physiological concept. This is because, the problems triggered by the ecological crisis deal primarily with different notions of nature and with identifying the kind of land use practices, with respect to nature, which allow us as organisms to assert our existence and thrive within our natural environment.

4 Hans Jonas, Robert Spaeman, and Vittorio Hösle work with the Aristotelian concept of natural teleology.

What can be said about the relationship between these two concepts of nature? How are they related? Is their relationship based on mutual exclusion, as the search for new and alternative notions of nature suggests, or do they complement each other? What constitutes the physiological concept of nature, in particular? These questions are of considerable urgency, because they raise issues that are at the core of current criticism of science and technology. In the search for an appropriate concept of nature, answers can be heard of affirmation and negation, or denial and justification of scientific knowledge "under ecological premises." I feel the proposal I put forward here is recommendable, because it frees us from an "either-or" situation; allowing acknowledgement of the strength and efficiency of the scientific methods of knowledge and culture without removing the sting from "ecological criticism."

The physiological concept of nature should take precedence in relation to the ecological problem, but cannot replace or eliminate the cosmological. The latter remains substantiated, because the natural sciences method of knowledge to which it is bound also remains the fundamental knowledge. It also remains the basis on which concept are formed. Because we gain the physiological concept of nature through exclusion on the basis of the cosmological. Consequently, the physiological notion of nature is not to be understood as identical to the concept of "environment", as developed by Jacob von Uexküll,—[5] because his hypothesis states that the "environment" is originally created through the organism and that it varies from species to species. The world of the tick, the world of the dog, the world of humans are all specifically constituted worlds and, according to Uexküll, there is no shared world in which (we) all live together. The universe of physics (cosmological nature) is little more than unsubstantiated fiction.

5 Jakob von Uexküll: *Umwelt und Innenwelt der Tiere*, Berlin 1908.

In contrast, the physiological concept of nature, as the term is understood here, is defined through distinguishing the real, reciprocal processes of metabolism between people and nature by drawing a border within the sphere of natural processes. Physiological nature is a segment of cosmological nature and yet has a peculiar unity. This segmentation of cosmological nature into physiological nature is not the product of territorial restriction—as was the case in ancient nature, when a differentiation was made between the "sublunar" and the "translunar" spheres. This differentiation does not correspond to the subdivision of the universe into our earth and the extraterrestrial realm, which is evident from the fact that the solar radiation necessary for the life of organisms on our planet is perhaps the most fundamental proof that physiological space extends far into cosmological space. It is possible to subdivide cosmological and physiological nature through a reference to the real metabolism that we maintain as organisms with our environment, including the conditions that metabolism is subject to.

This differentiation admittedly implies more than a containment of "cosmological nature" to "physiological nature" that relates to certain regions and specific procedures. What follows is primarily a new qualitative assessment and evaluation: there is no straightforward inventory for physiological reference, no neutrality of things that simply exist; instead everything is assessed and evaluated according to whether it is beneficial or detrimental, healthy or unhealthy. Living beings are central to the world, make it the space where they might thrive, or experience it as a threat to their existence. The concepts, in other words the units with which we describe or present this type of evaluated nature will be different to those typical of the natural sciences, and yet they will not make the latter obsolete.

This can be illustrated by the term "elements." We say that the health of an organism requires the purification of water and air, which we understand here as "elements of organic life." However, the term "pure" used in this case does not correspond to what natural scientists call "chemically" pure—(drinking Aqua Destilata would be as unhygienic as drinking "water" from the River Elbe today!). Nor does the term "elements," as used here, correspond to the periodic table of elements (air is a mixture of several, very different chemical elements, some in molecular form). However, the knowledge of chemists and their analytical detection methods are indispensable if we want to conclude something definite and accurate about the degree of contamination of the elements in the physiological sense. We have to weigh, count, and measure. Therefore the "physiological concept of nature" indeed presents its own viewpoints for consideration and articulates them in its own terms. Responding to these questions, however, remains dependent on the availability of solid, conventional natural sciences. Therefore, it is not a question of dismissing our present natural sciences in favor of a different way of thinking about nature, such as for example Aristotle's teleological nature, Paracelsus' Animism, or the romantic's sympathetic nature, as is often recommended. Nor is it about dismissing the "physical world" in favor of a biologically designed "environment," as attempted by Jacob von Uexküll. He placed a "sworn enmity" between these two worldviews and declared the cosmological nature a "phantom," an empty world that must be replaced by filled environments, each of which is specifically constituted by the different organisms.

The proposal being put forward here is attempting to take account of the ecological moment, while fully recognizing the scientific method of knowledge, which admittedly requires further explanation. It is always about critical qualifications, not however about making a case for replacement or about a process of elimination through strict, alternative approaches. The notion of physiological nature presented here cannot displace the cosmological concept; it is more a division within cosmological nature, which must make use of the validity of physical knowledge. In the environmental debate, it is almost always assumed that gaining a new understanding of nature will eventually mean that it should present an alternative to science, and that we should be concerned with displacing, replacing the latter. With the distinction suggested here between cosmological and physiological concepts of nature, an additional consideration ("the real metabolism") is brought into play, leading to a delineation of the organismically significant realm: the qualitative aspects of what is beneficial and detrimental to organic existence that emerge as a result are perhaps granted priority, but nevertheless allow the methods of modern natural sciences to remain in full force.

Compatibility of Real Metabolism as a Criterion of Planning Reason

Physicality does not have a normative function as such; it acts more as a pure indicator of an intact or disrupted external metabolism. Any normative claims would therefore need to be established on the principle of autonomy. Consequently, how might we imagine physicality and the principle of autonomy working collaboratively?

Self-determination and our relationship with nature exist in a flexible, mutual exchange of checks and balances. The autonomy of a subject's deep-rooted concepts of life on the one hand and, how our health is affected by a real metabolism with nature on the other, are independent and irreducible instances of cultural evaluation. The autonomous subject is capable of designing an unlimited number of different life forms. Francis Bacon's model, for instance, of a scientific and technological reconstruction of nature for the purpose of humanizing, does in fact present an attractive option for modernity. However, apart from the question of desirability within the framework of an ideal notion of humanity and its feasibility in technological terms, the question remains as to whether we as an organism would be able to tolerate a specific cultural design.

Our body has a right to reject engineered worlds and environments. We need to make designed utopias accountable for our physical and emotional health. It is precisely our physicality that binds us to this world and does not allow us to follow speculative flights into other "possible worlds." In recognition of our organismic existence, we need to protect and preserve nature's living conditions, as their existing evolutionary product. The "we ought to" sentences, formulated on the basis of a physiological concept of nature, are not accused of naturalism—that an ought is derived from an is—because this "oughtness" is not generated from a normative concept of our relationship to nature, but rather from the obligations we have to ourselves and, in this case in particular, from the obligation to protect and preserve our physical well-being.

Our physical integrity functions at the same time as a potential falsifier for the acceptance of planned interventions in the natural process. Changes to our environment are inadmissible if their consequences—that is, the sum of their intended and unintended effects—lead to a negative shift in the living conditions of our environment. Physical integrity marks only one necessary criterion for acceptability of cultivation forms, which requires a positive additive.

However, our future perspective would be truncated if the question of responsibility were answered in terms of our in fact having a responsibility to nature, but as it is *as such*. We would have to reduce the scope of our design and action to that of archiving and conserving. But this is not acceptable, because it excludes the human mode of existence, which is now intrinsically committed to the cultivation of nature and to the improvement of the forms of cultivation!

What Can Be Gained from These Considerations for Modern Landscape Architecture?

It seems clear to me that the aesthetic aspects of landscape architecture have to be supplemented by ecologically relevant factors, especially including those that cannot be captured by what looks pleasant. For traditional aesthetics, the reference to appearance and inspection were always significant factors. Green fields with loose groups of trees, hills, and mountains in the background, plus a river flowing through: what we consider to be a beautiful landscape has been illustrated countless times in painting. However, the appearance does not capture the extent to which our visual world is influenced by the things that our senses cannot register. The world of microorganisms forms a support layer for the macroorganisms and we need to include this layer in our environmental considerations.

To understand the ominous development that we have set in motion, we must turn our attention to the dimension of the invisible and the minimal: the world of microorganisms and substances that we cannot detect with our own senses. Changes at this level will ultimately influence, on a global scale, the type of life processes that are phenomenally accessible to us. It is highly likely that our climate and the proportional composition of our atmosphere also largely depend on the metabolic processes of microorganisms. Large animals are to microorganisms like the tip of an iceberg is to its submerged volume. We still know far too little about the physiological relationships between the life we learn about from behavior analysts, and the life of microorganisms that exist under the earth and in the depths of the ocean.

Over the course of billions of years, microorganisms have created the conditions on our planet that made existence possible for higher forms of life in the first place. They are subtly integrated as intermediate links into the food chain and as internal energy converters and enzyme producers in the lives of the large animals. In any case, the basic conditions of the biosphere, which are necessary for humans and other animal species known to us to thrive, are made up of factors we still do not know enough about.—6

6 See Daniel B. Botkin: *Discordant Harmonies: A New Ecology for the Twenty-first Century*, New York/Oxford 1990, pp. 133–151.

The seriousness of our interventions in natural processes is demonstrated by how difficult they are to undo. Many interventions are possible, as long as the basic conditions of life remain intact, as has been confirmed by the resettlement of some bird and wildlife species. However, if our manipulations affect the fundamental bases of life, then we affect the basic existential conditions on which life itself depends. Damage on this level is irreversible. What is environmentally “allowed” or “prohibited” can therefore be assessed by the impact of our actions on the sphere of microorganisms, which in turn form the fundamental basis for life on earth. In general, it provides a benchmark against which to measure the extent to which induced effects are reversible or irreversible. Our sensory organs, which are adapted to our surroundings and to our size, have caused us to eliminate or suppress states or conditions that disturb or offend us—the stench of a medieval town, the smoke from coal mining areas, and so on). After all, our sensory experience is undoubtedly a powerful motivation for our actions. Little is being done, because reason dictates that we are more disturbed by the smell of a dairy farm than by car exhaust fumes, and indeed there is a lot we are prepared to accept if our senses are not directly offended by what we would otherwise find disgusting. When the air in London became increasingly polluted by the many coal-fueled fireplaces and electricity plants located in the city, fireplaces were banned and the coal-fueled electricity plants were moved to the suburbs. This may have alleviated the unpleasant effects for citizens in cities—but by no means did it alleviate the pollution of the atmosphere with toxins, which continued to make a long-term negative impact on basic living conditions. The tons and tons of sulfur and nitrous oxides sent into the air by power plants, located far from the eyes and noses of urban citizens, are by no means insignificant. In fact, they represent alarming quantities. Yet, I am not speaking of observing the minimal in these terms. But rather only as far as our immediate perception does not register harmful effects and adverse consequences, because our senses connect us with what has emerged in the course of evolution as our perception's field of reference. The first are the things and events that we encounter in our ordinary experience and are immediately accessible. We need knowledge to free ourselves from this fixation on the immediate. We know that even if we do not smell CFCs, if they do not darken our skies, do not irritate our skin, they are still harmful because they contribute to the greenhouse effect and destroy our protective ozone layer in the upper stratosphere. However, knowledge can function as a watchdog here, and reason can halt us and make us remedy the damage. Whoever hoped to wait for the assault on the senses to trigger change is, as always, too late.

The emerging threats to the biosphere are caused, however, by the accumulation and combination of substances and effects that are initially considered minimal and unobtrusive and therefore appear negligible. Our carelessness with regard to the minimal does not correspond at all to its importance in the ecosystem. The dominance of aesthetics in our dealings with nature, which is associated with the fixation on what is immediately apparent, feeds the suppression of this dimension and can hinder rational action.

It would of course have even worse consequences to abandon the thought of design because it entails inevitable interventions in the "natural conditions." We must persevere with the project of designing landscape all the more, because our ruinous practice of exploiting nature does not mean will we abandon the idea of using nature. Aesthetic criteria will always be a priority and inspire the designs, but a landscape architectural project should only be executed if we can be sure that the fundamental ecological foundations of the area will not be destroyed by the project's associated interventions in nature.

The Sensuality of the Engineer

Joseph Schwartz

"The Sensuality of Engineering," or better, "The Sensual World of Engineers" seems far removed from common engineering topics. The world of engineering typically prioritizes the "rational" or even the "technocratic," which are concepts radically different from the idea of "sensuality." Furthermore, engineers are defined as "introverted" or, more flatteringly, as having a "natural urge to restrict and focus." The friction between these supposed contradictions is a productive place to begin a familiarization with some fundamental ideas.

As we know, humans were building—and yes, even extremely bold, beautiful, robust, and functional structures—thousands of years ago. Engineers were unnecessary at this point, because the builder was both engineer and designer. This was still the case in the seventeenth century when the Salti Bridge was erected in the Verzasca Valley in Tessin.

Ponte dei Salti, Lavertezzo.

It is interesting to note how using only locally available materials led the builder to focus on what was absolutely essential.—[1] The only obtainable building material was a local stone called gneiss. For the supporting arches, this stone was arranged in a radical manner along the arch line, and lined up horizontally for the arch trough. The builder chose to erect the bridge at a place in the river where it was easy to construct an intermediary support and, hence, to reduce the required span length. This is one reason the bridge blends in so well with the natural topographical conditions. To optimize the structural relationships even more, the arch trough was not raised to a constant level over the entire bridge length, but rather matched the form of the arches. This gave the top of the bridge a gentle, wave-like line, while reflecting the soft, formal language of the washed-out stone in the riverbed. Using local stone as the building material also encouraged the integration of the bridge into the landscape. The elegance of the structure is the product of simple and seemingly self-evident conditions. All decisions regarding the design were made intuitively on the basis of practical experience, as there were no theoretical methods of calculation at that time. The rational design of the bridge is guaranteed by clear sensual transparence, rigor, and the effortless nature of the construction.

1 Joseph Schwartz, Toni Kotnik: "Eleganz im Brückenbau," in: *werk, bauen + wohnen*, vol. 5, Zurich 2010, pp. 20–25.

The general concept of the engineer originated in the second half of the seventeenth century with Sébastien le Prestre de Vauban, the fortress builder of Louis XIV. He coined the term Génie militaire, whose main task was to build fortifications. The first engineer corps for street and bridge construction was established in 1720 in France, which was actually the birth of the Génie civil, the true profession of engineering. This is when the now irreversible division between "architect" and "engineer" began to evolve. The engineering profession experienced a great boost with the onset of industrialization in the second half of the eighteenth century. New building methods were developed, above all in wood and iron.

Le Viaduc de Garabit, St. Flour.

The Viaduct Gabarit in Auvergne by Maurice Koechlin and Gustave Eiffel, built at the end of the nineteenth century, is obviously a direct translation of existing forms from stone to steel structural supports. It is already characterized by influences resulting from simple calculation, such as abutment hinges taken from mechanical engineering. These analytical calculation methods, developed in the nineteenth century and based on the theory of elasticity, made it possible to design and realize increasingly complex structures. In the elasticity theory, engineers found a closed calculation method—developed by mathematicians and physicists—which mathematically formulated the relationship between load, stress, and strain for an idealized, linear elastic behavior. This gave engineers a powerful, scientific edge over the discipline of architecture. Adolf Loos wrote in 1898, "Are there still people today who work like the ancient Greeks? Oh yes! The English as a nation, the engineers as a profession. The English and the engineers are our Hellenes. Our culture originates from them; from them it has spread all over the globe. The English and the engineers are the quintessence of nineteenth-century man."—2

2 Adolf Loos: "Glas und Ton," in: id.: *Ins Leere gesprochen*, Paris/Zurich 1898, p. 66.

This perception could actually predict a promising basis for the further development of the engineering profession in the twentieth century. The impressive development of diverse new building methods points in this direction. The arched bridge built in 1890 over the Fabrikkanal of the Juracementwerke in Wildegg might have some formal

Juracementwerke bridge, Wildegg, 1890.

elements in common with the stone bridge over the Verzasca, yet, because a very different material was used, the bridge's design aspects and form are even more evident. A new construction method using concrete, based on the system monier, made it possible for the bridge to have one single span length of thirty-seven meters, with an elevation of three-and-a-half meters, and a minimal thickness of only twenty centimeters. It seems as if the bridge's arch is stretched to its limits, while the massive bridgeheads are resting tightly anchored on the shore. The low elevation of the bridge body integrates the structure into the surrounding environment, and the minimal appearance and restrained countenance works to link the two opposing shores. You sense the strong design drive in this attempt at the geometry of physical limitations. Important boundary conditons, such as the construction process and economic viability, served as the drivers of this reduction to only the most absolutely necessary elements. The elegance of this bridge's design is due to this urge to steadily rationalize the conditions.

It seems as though these engineers achieved a successful and very promising synthesis between design freedom and the necessity of physics in their works. All of the requirements were fulfilled, thanks to the technical, scientific process of creating architectural structures of outstanding quality. How wrong! In the twentieth century, the exact opposite became true. Engineer Christian Menn writes in 1996, approximately one hundred years after Adolf Loos, "Many so-called star architects have mutated into weightless designers and many engineers into technocrats without the least sense of form [...] and the number of statics or structural chin-ups is actually understood as a measure of design quality."—3

3 Christian Menn: "Acknowledgement," in: J. Hering (ed.): *Reden und Aufsätze*, Stuttgart 1996, p. 15.

The deep-lying division between the disciplines has had a very negative effect on the engineering profession. The grasp and sense of design has decreased over the last centuries to the point of neglect. Negative phrases like "sealing the landscape with cement" are evidence of the lack of awareness displayed by diverse branches of engineering.

Superstructure, Zurich City Highway.

Ducks paddle around concrete pillars and a gray heron circles over the eternally shaded waters under the Zurich City Highway—one of the most bizarre monuments and monstrosities left behind by the progress-thinkers of the nineteen-sixties, and a cause for reflection. In contrast: the vehicles stuck in traffic jams on the bridge above, and their bored occupants who never notice, and prefer to ignore, the morbid idyll that exists under the highway. This piece of highway symbolizes how we have surrendered to an utterly intolerable situation.—4 How is it possible that the aspects of aesthetics and our ethical responsibility to nature was so radically ignored by engineers, who are precisely the ones equipped with the perfect technical and scientific tools? In this context, engineer Stefan Polonyi states that, "The conventional procedure in science is deductive and thus analytical; measures of value are axioms. Due to this deductive method, scientific findings are often mixed with ethical postulations. This is why we expect science to make aesthetic decisions, which it cannot. An inductive understanding of science would clarify the battle lines. We have to revise our understanding of science!"—5

4 Richard Liechti: "Die Geister, die wir riefen," in: *Schweizer Ingenieur und Architekt*, vol. 43, Zurich 1999, p. 3.

5 Stefan Polónyi: "Wissenschaftsverständnis, Tragkonstruktion, Architektur," in: *Daidalos 18, Architektur und technisches Denken*, 1985, p. 36.

The widely spread notion of an abstract beauty that is based on mathematically described mechanical relationships falls short of the mark. The engineering sciences' typical system of validation is based on tangible numbers—span widths, slenderness ratio, or the structural support form resulting from the distribution of force—but this cannot be seen as the design criteria of an elegant structural support, nor as a means of evaluating it. Christian Menn's Bridge at Letziwald near Avers Cresta and the Bridge at Crestawald near Sufers both follow structural principles for arched

Bridge at Letziwald, Avers Cresta, 1960.

Bridge at Crestawald, Sufers, 1959.

bridges, but differ greatly in their formal language. The mathematics of natural law do not solve the hows or whys of design questions; they merely describe a network of causal relationships between different sizes, which are not concrete shapes until they have been through the design process by a designer.

This is particularly evident in the two bridges by Menn: both are stabilized by the same principle of the interplay between arches and track supports. The Bridge at Letziwald is braced by the arch, which is designed to be sturdy looking and, based on Robert Maillart's Salginatobel Bridge, has a variable elevation and merges monolithically with the more slender supports. The lower pillar height this allows for lends the construction an extraordinary dynamic, which is emphasized by the form of the arch. The upward swelling curves makes the bridge look tensely focused, as though the Bridge at Letziwald triumphs over the steep canyon like a wild cat in mid-jump. The arch's structural and visual dominance emphasizes the truly courageous design of this bridge in such topographically difficult terrain. In comparison, the Bridge at Crestawald is braced by the track support, which relieves the load from the arch, allowing the connecting supports to remain slender. The end result is a highly transparent structure that emphasizes the "opening of the valley." The generosity of the arch's lines make the bridge appear relaxed, as though it is reclining over the surrounding landscape.

Both examples demonstrate how vital a designing engineer is to the construction of an elegant bridge. In other words, a person with a synthesizing mind, with the solid technical expertise and strong creative drive necessary to ensure both rational and sensual aesthetics. As Menn has stressed, "a real bridge is a sophisticated structure." An engineer is, therefore, not only accountable to budgetary considerations, "because what remains is not the invoice, but the bridge in its relation to time and to the landscape into which it was built."—[6] An intuitive understanding of the internal forces is a clear prerequisite for designing structures, such as the cable structures for the Braga Municipal Stadium by Eduardo Souto Moura completed in 2003.

6 Menn, op. cit., p. 9.

Eduardo Souto de Moura: Municipal Stadium, Braga, 2002.

We believe that merging form and internal forces is a requirement for the creative design of structures. This is also the philosophy we follow in training architecture students in the Institute of Structural Design at the ETH Zürich, by focusing purely on the graphical structural design and completely dispensing with analytical statics.

International School at ETH Zürich 2012.

Álvaro Siza: Expo-Pavillon in Lisbon, 1998.

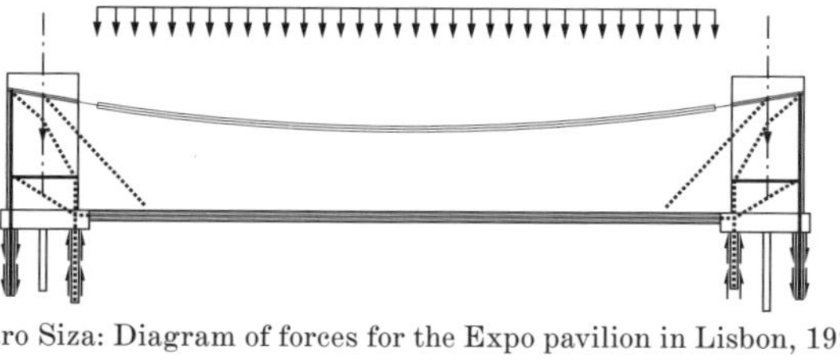

Álvaro Siza: Diagram of forces for the Expo pavilion in Lisbon, 1998.

We strive to convey a physical sense of the internal forces, and to establish a methodology for structural design in which the design parameters are varied in certain ways. This is what makes it possible to go beyond the conventional, rational approach of structural engineers, who build using data about the structural safety and usability of support structures. We have succeeded in finding ways in which aesthetic issues can be incorporated into the design of structures, using intuitive procedures.—[7]

7 Joseph Schwartz: "Structural Theory and Structural Design," in: Aita Flury (ed.): *Cooperation: The Engineer and the Architect*, Basel 2011, pp. 243–247.

As a practicing engineer, I have long been aware of the limits to the technical and scientific tools of my profession. Theories are never more than a mere description of reality—regardless of how sophisticated they are mathematically and physically—and the results, which are conveyed through a model, are only as strong or as weak as the assumptions on which they are based. And, here is a sore point in the conventional training of engineers: analytical tools are greatly overestimated. They detract from a holistic design process, but also give structural engineers the reputation for being technocratic specialists. This is not very attractive to creative thinking, technically talented high school students, which means that too few of them study structural engineering. But examining the ground-breaking work by the great engineers of the past centuries proves that they always thought and acted differently to the norm. On this note, engineer Eugène Freyssinet, the inventor of prestressed concrete, writes:

"There exist, to my mind, only two sources of information: direct perception of the facts and the intuition through which I perceive the expression and the synthesis of all the experience accumulated throughout life. [...] Of course, intuition must be controlled by experience. However, when it happens to contradict the result of a calculation, I have the calculation checked, and my colleagues confirm that, when all is said and done, it is the calculation that is always wrong".—[8] And yes, there have been structures based on faulty calculations. The Malpasset Dam was located in the Provence in the southern foothills of the Esterel, about nine kilometers northeast of Fréjus, a city on the Mediterranean Côte d'Azur.

8 Eugène Freyssinet: "Die Entstehung des Spannbetons," in: *Revue Travaux*, vol. 236, Paris 1954, p. 463.

Barrage de Malpasset, Fréjus, 1958.

The dam was completed in 1954 and its reservoir supplied water and irrigation to the nearby town of Fréjus. But in 1959, it breached due to heavy rains and a tectonic fault in the soil.

Ruine Barrage de Malpasset, Fréjus, 2003.

The flood wave at the onset was said to be as high as forty meters and to travel at up to seventy kilometers per hour. It first reached the small villages of Malpasset and Bozon, which were completely destroyed. Roughly twenty minutes after the wall collapsed, the wave reached Fréjus at a height of three meters, burying much of the city under mud.

The back of the hangar Caquot, B.A.N. de Saint-Raphaële-Fréjus, 1959.

Over 400 people were killed and the total financial damages amounted to just under 70 million US dollars.

A gap on the left side of the wall was found to be the cause. Water seeped under the wall, collected underground, and was unable to escape because the weight of the dam had made the rock impermeable. This caused water pressure to develop and push diagonally upward against the abutment of the dam wall, making it slip away at the gap. This problem was not discovered initially because it was not directly under the wall, but a little further downstream. The engineer responsible was so devastated by the catastrophe that he died almost six months later. After a lengthy trial, a court of cassation decided in 1967 that there would be no criminal charges brought against any responsible parties.

With a center span length of 853 meters, the first Tacoma Narrows Bridge in the US state of Washington possessed, at the time of its completion, the third-longest span of suspension bridges worldwide. After nineteen months of construction, it was opened on July 1, 1940 and collapsed spectacularly after only four months of operation on November 7, 1940, as a result of aeroelastic flutter.

Tacoma Narrows Bridge, Washington USA, 1940.

The most significant consequence of the disaster was that it made designers and engineers consider dynamics in addition to statics in the design of bridges. Furthermore, before a large bridge is constructed, a model of it is tested in a wind tunnel, which, for instance, also led to the development of aerodynamic forms for roadway cross sections. These dramatic events, which the responsible engineer cannot ignore, make successful structures all the more fascinating when they are observed in nature.

Kölnbrein Dam in Malta, Austria, 1978.

This even more intense, the more visible their sheer power becomes and the more successfully the structure interacts with its surroundings, which could surreptitiously trigger feelings in an engineer that might be described as sublime, awe, even dizzying. When climbing around a slope under a spectacular bridge construction, this feeling is enhanced

Christian Menn, Ganter Bridge in Ried-Brig, 1980.

by the belief that technology certainly has its place in nature. And, of course, by the great respect for the builder who succeeded in taking the ethical component of his or her mission in relation to humans and nature uniquely seriously.

Yet everything is always pervaded by the formidable question of the engineer's responsibility, which at least in the past was why the profession was held in such high regard. As the responsible party for the structure at the Leutschenbach Schoolhouse in Zurich, I remember all

Christian Kerez & Joseph Schwartz, Leutschenbach Schoolhouse, 2002–2009.

too well the emotions I experienced when the struts in the floating ground floor were removed during construction. These feelings can hardly be described in words, but perhaps: massive excitement combined with a deep anxiety—feelings that cannot be explained or influenced by rationally.

Robert Maillart is one of the most important engineers of the last century. In 1940, Mirko Roš wrote in tribute to his friend, who is said to have made bridge calculations on the back of old envelopes, “Robert Maillart was an engineer in the truest sense of the word. He gave equal priority to experience and scientific knowledge. He saw clearly that the ultimate secrets of matter would always remain a mystery to engineers who struggle with the natural forces—and thus their work will always express an awe of nature and its laws.”—9

We have now come full circle; this is where the rational and the irrational indeed begin to touch upon physics and, perhaps, even metaphysics. And where the responsible engineer is tempted to abandon everything technical so he or she can finally fulfill the job's creative, political, social, cultural, human aspects, as well as all the other dimensions that go beyond. “Because,” to repeat the words of Christian Menn, “what remains is not the invoice, but the bridge in its relation to time and to the landscape into which it was built.”—10

9 Mirko Roš: “Robert Maillart zum Gedächtnis,” in: *Schweizer Bauzeitung*, Zurich, Nr. 19, 11. May 1940, pp. 224–226.

10 Menn, op. cit., p. 9.

Landscapes of Nature and Art

Martin Seel

Nature

A famous statement by Theodor W. Adorno may be altered to say that it has become self-evident that nothing that concerns nature is any longer self-evident. For a long time now, popular awareness has realized that we are living in an era of increasingly frequent and severe ecological crises. But this awareness has a peculiar characteristic. With each menacing report, it flares up anew; only thereafter to soon subside into a restless dozing. Yet there are more than enough disquieting circumstances that would be suitable for taking an unblinking look at the uncertain future of non-human as well as human nature.

The most sobering and obdurate fact is that "nature" cannot be destroyed. Human beings are not the center, crown, or guarantor of nature. They may nourish or exploit it, but they cannot take over its direction. If mankind were to fully destroy its living conditions, what would remain would be nature, which wins every competition with it. A second, concomitant fact is that alterations "in nature" belong to its very nature. The developments of industrial culture bring about changes in these alterations, accelerating them or imparting another direction to them, but they remain subject to its dynamic. We are a factor in the history of nature, even where we set out to modify our genetic program. The third fact consists of the recognition that under current conditions, local effects have a global impact in many cases. The emissions increasing throughout the world, the melting of the polar icecaps, the flooding of coastal areas, the wasteful use of water, the pollution of the oceans, the cutting down of atrophying forests, the erosion of soil—all these factors add up to an alteration of the landscape that no nation-state can slow down on its own, not to mention offer a cure. Social, political, and military confrontations over the distribution of land, air, and resources are the foreseeable consequence. The politics of nature has become the domestic politics of the world.

A fourth circumstance, especially widely repressed from awareness, consists of the fact that the appearances of nature often continue to maintain their aesthetic fascination there where their impact has become threatening or overwhelming. Our sensory grasp is unable to measure sufficiently the quality of external nature. It could be that we perish in a theatrical display of cruel beauty. This recalls the fifth and, from a practical point of view, pivotal fact that an objective, solely decisive indicator with regard to the treatment of nature does not exist. Our relationship to outer and inner nature is dependent upon a complex elucidation of what we *intend* to undertake with our knowledge about the condition of the earth—and accordingly, how the further shaping of the human life form is supposed to look.

Clear-sighted policies with regard to nature will have to be concerned less with *physical* nature, in spite of the importance of the investigations that provide us with information about the ecology of the planet. The challenge lies much more in the protection of a *physiological* nature that sustains our own bodily organism just as it does those of animal and vegetable life forms, with which we are required to live in symbiosis and synergy for good or for evil. Precisely because it is a matter of our survival, this is not a matter of only our own survival. What matters is the preservation of the climatic, geological, and geographical preconditions for life on earth. The nature on which this depends is not an object that we can dominate to a greater or lesser extent, not a counterpart to which we can more or less correspond, not even an environment where we have allowed much to become wrecked and which we are now desperately trying to repair, but instead the global *space* in which cultures and societies will remain capable of development or will stiffen in agony. For this space, humanity—represented above all by the rich industrial nations—has a responsibility it is presently failing to meet, because it manages its economies without giving consideration to losses. The protection of nature is a protection from us ourselves, for the sake of us ourselves: from the neglect and dissipation with which we disregard our own living sphere.

Art

But what these uncomfortable reminders have to do with art? A great deal—because they have to do with *its* discomforting powers. There, where the more and most recent visual art concerns itself with the phenomena of nature, it fathoms the manifold disturbances of the modern relationship to and understanding of nature by means of unsettling presentations. Art experiments with its forms in order to investigate those of nature. It attains its beauty out of the power of unadorned views of the eerie foundations of physical life. It establishes a reference to nature while being constantly overcome by doubt as to what it is in fact referring to.

This becomes especially clear with the digitally modified photography of our era. The appearance of fulfilled referentiality belongs to the photographic image even where the picture no longer corresponds with this gesture. It is only the stubbornness of this assumption that can explain the uncertainty, for instance, that emanates from many of the monumental photographs of Andreas Gursky.

Created out of digitally edited and assembled shots with a large-format camera, they offer to the normal human perspective views that are irreally shifted and often surreally modified. At the same time, however, they present a plethora of details that are often recognizable only at close range, and definitely depict an abundance, and sometimes an overabundance, of what was present at the respective setting at the moment of the exposures. These pictures are, and yet are not, realistic photographs—particularly where they summon up to view seemingly distant or apparently familiar landscapes. They manifest doubt, as it were, concerning the photographic view as whose outcome they present themselves—not in the sense of a mere "as if," however, but rather as an elaborate combination of realistic gesture and imaginative composition inquiring into the possibilities of photographic vision and with which, at the same time, the impenetrability of many living conditions under the sign of globalization is summoned into view.

The question of how much fortuitousness or arbitrariness is involved remains uncertain. Often, one cannot recognize with the naked eye whether it is a single shot or a montage of shots that gives rise to the depicted scene. Furthermore, it is sometimes not even clear the degree to which the picture presents only one scene. As soon as one varies the distance to the pictorial surface, quite different views become apparent. The picture *Beelitz* from 2007, created from a montage of photographs, has an agricultural landscape as its subject. But this is not recognizable at a first glance, because when viewed from a greater distance, the photograph has a quite different appearance than when examined up close. At a distance, one sees a gigantic roller blind damaged here and there, an abstract linear construction, or a strange painterly ornament. Only upon closer inspection does one recognize a field of asparagus, which is mostly covered by black sheeting, and the bent-over, seasonal laborers who, from a retreating perspective, appear like pawns in the grim game of a bone-hard agrarian economy. An agriculturally utilized nature, familiar from the local surroundings, is staged here as the object of an anonymous labor relationship that is subject to a calculation involving the efficient production of commodities. The abstract organization of the picture, which from a distance seems almost playful, gives rise to the concrete violence of an instrumentalized appropriation of nature, which presents itself to the viewer in a break with the formal elegance of the composition.

The photographic landscapes of Beate Gütschow are constructed images in a quite different manner. To be seen in a mild light on her picture *LS#7* from 1999 is a well-tempered scene of Central European provenance. From a raised position, the viewer looks down into a hollow, which is framed by a towering group of trees on the right and by a hill on the left, and limited in the middle by a gentle upward slope, behind which a bright sky opens. The idyllic atmosphere is enhanced by a group of four people who are sitting on the grass at the front edge of the hollow and who, for their part, gaze into the expanse of land. This group already imparts a staged quality to the scene. But it is much more than this. As may be recognized through the disproportion of the various parts of the picture, the overall situation has been compiled from different photographs. This landscape exists only in the picture, although its individual sections were photographed in authentic landscapes. It is literally a view from nowhere, which is forced upon the viewer of this scene, representing an instance of painting by means of photography. It leads to an ironic dialogue with the classic motifs of pictorial art. The four people who may be seen in the foreground are not enjoying an erotic repast in nature. These are commonplace people clothed like tourists, who possibly can only see what the phantasmagoria of traditional painting has placed before their eyes. They gaze upon their own reproduction synthesized from many paintings, which Gütschow's composition presents to the viewers outside the picture. This photographic montage brings to light a mode of vision that unconsciously guides the perception of landscape. At the same time, it brings to

Andreas Gursky, Beelitz, 2007.

perception the invisibility of the cultural impressions tacitly at work in our encounters with natural situations. Built into the close-up onto nature is a distance with regard to it, which presents itself to us through the artistic image.

Similar effects, however, occur not only where works of art depict views of objects or landscapes in an altered visibility, but also where no definite shapes of a natural and/or artificial space are represented. A mode of painting operating in a more or less "non-representative" manner is capable, through the play of its energies, to fathom the energies of nature. Gerhard Richter's *Abstraktes Bild* (*Abstract Picture*, Sprengel Museum Hanover, 1992) belongs to a series, begun in 1976, of often large-scale, colored compositions, which signaled at that time a clear turning point in his artistic output. The picture presents a dense and inhomogeneous color-surface that is dominated by green and above all by brown tones, and endowed with unbroken horizontal and vertical structures through the use of long wooden bars. The still-wet paint was brushed smooth with these large scrapers into narrow segments of an irregular width fluctuating between five and twenty centimeters. The traces of this design are apparent everywhere. Thus, one recognizes that the vertical rhythm of the picture's body was added subsequently to the horizontal pattern, because the vertical strips of color clearly dominate the horizontal ones. In this way, the picture creates a tension between the underlying waves of color and the treatment that shapes them. Furthermore, it displays traces of the time of its production, which influences the dynamic of the perusal of the picture, whose vestiges of vertical treatment demand a greater attentiveness than do the horizontal ones. Through this tension, the nominally "abstract" picture proves to be a highly concrete image. In its pastose, almost relief-like structure, it brings to the fore an almost physical working with the paint, in which there is an equilibrium between the energies of the modestly luminous pictorial background and its rhythmic organization.

At the same time, however, it is still possible to view this picture, not simply as a depiction of its own energies, but additionally as the representation of extra-pictorial configurations. The vertical lines, for instance, may be seen as a close-up of tree trunks, so that the picture also looks like a photograph from within a jungle—admittedly a jungle that overgrows each of its aggregate states. Shapes only flash forth here before subsiding within the occurrence that gave rise to them. Vibrating in the metamorphoses of the picture are those of nature. It belongs to the fundamental gestures of this picture, laconically and ironically entitled "Abstract Picture," that it makes one aware of the often chameleon-like nature of artistic pictures—and perhaps of artworks in general. In its own oscillation between shape and event, it evinces a deep affinity with the processes of nature.

Nature and Art

"It has become self-evident that nothing concerning art is any longer self-evident"—this is the first sentence, slightly altered at the beginning of this essay, of Adorno's *Ästhetische Theorie* from 1970.—[1] These two sentences, however—the original and its alteration—belong together. But the insight that they are interrelated is for its part anything other than self-evident. Instead, it indicates the outcome of a long historical process. For it was only in the final third of the twentieth century that the recognition of an inner, yet always delicate and dynamic, complicity between art and nature fully asserted itself—impelled by diverse developments in artistic production and accompanied by an increasingly sensitive theoretical reflection.

From antiquity well into modern times, thinking about the interconnection between art and nature was defined by hierarchical concepts. First nature was the model, then it became a replica of art—thus one could summarize the history of their relationship in a single sentence.—[2]

1 Theodor W. Adorno: *Ästhetische Theorie*, Frankfurt am Main 1973, p. 9.—In the second half of the sentence, Adorno adds: "neither in itself nor in its relationship to the whole, not even in the justification of its existence."

2 See Martin Seel: *Eine Ästhetik der Natur*, Frankfurt am Main 1991, esp. pp. 11–33 and 163–178.

In both phases of this development, the theorem of imitation remained crucially formative. At first, it was the role of the artist involved in shaping his work to orient himself with regard to the masterful works of nature, and hence with regard to the laws of an overarching cosmic order, or the genius of a divine creator. Ever since the Renaissance, but especially since the end of the eighteenth century, an anthropocentric reversal of this normative order was initiated, which was completed with verve in the nineteenth century. Oscar Wilde gave striking expression to this turnaround when he laconically observed that "life imitates art much more than art imitates life." Connected to this was a direct reversal of the traditional doctrine of imitation. For Wilde asserted, "that external nature also imitates art. The only effects that she can show us are effects that we have already seen through poetry, or in paintings. This is the secret of nature's charm, as well as the explanation of nature's weakness."—[3]

3 Oscar Wilde: "The Decay of Lying," in: *The Collected Works of Oscar Wilde*, Wordsworth Library Collection, Ware 2007, p. 943.

From a contemporary perspective, one must take note of these statements in order to recognize that this reversal of the imitation topos falls short of the dialectic between natural becoming and artistic creating to no less a degree than does its original version. Misleading oppositions of this type nonetheless continue to be mirrored in many theoretical debates concerning what is actually to be understood with the term "nature." Ultimately, everything is nature—so runs the naturalistic thesis. Everything is basically culture—so runs the culturalist riposte. But however these extreme positions are formulated and substantiated in individual instances, they miss the mark of the correlation they grandly claim to explain. For the relationship between nature and culture cannot be understood by someone who is not capable of comprehending their infinite interweavings. All comprehension of nature is a cultural product, just as all cultural production is also always dependent upon a performance of natural forces. Moreover, the difference between nature and culture—including the fascination, strangeness, and endangerment contained within their coexistence—arises out of this complex connectedness. It is precisely the visual arts, perhaps more than any theory, which are qualified to plumb the depths of these interrelationships. One could almost say that it is one of their fundamental missions to issue a reminder that we cannot allow ourselves to take things too lightly or too easily with regard to our cultural nature.

Its recent history offers extensive evidence for an underlying adaptation of art to nature, such as has also left enduring traces in Gerhard Richter's series of *Abstrakte Bilder*. The emergence of pictorial works emancipates itself from the fixation on an unambiguous image of familiar figures from the external world. "The more strictly artworks abstain from rank natural growth and the replication of nature, the more the successful ones approach nature."—[4] This sentence by Adorno could be used as a motto for the uncovering of a central thread running through the visual arts of the last two centuries. Gottfried Boehm has demonstrated in the case of painting how little the provisional end of landscape painting at the close of the nineteenth century signifies an end of the artistic image of nature.—[5] What comes to completion during this period is namely an orientation, less towards a *natura naturata*, than towards a *natura naturans*—the transition from a summoning up of nature's creations to an investigation of its processes. With Monet and Cézanne, for instance, the theme of the pictures is not a space of nature lying opposite the viewer, but rather a process of nature that includes the position of the viewer. This is what Adorno's aphorism is aiming at. With a view to Kandinsky, Mondrian, and Pollock, Boehm sketches out a few further steps in this development. The dignity of art comes to consist, even while maintaining a distance from all thematization of nature, in nonetheless creating "equivalents of nature."—[6] If one were to follow this development into the present, it would indeed be necessary to shift the accent of the representation once more. For in no way has recent art developed along a straight path of ever-progressing abstraction, which would

4 Adorno, op. cit., p. 120.

5 Gottfried Boehm: "Das neue Bild der Natur. Nach dem Ende der Landschaftsmalerei," in: Manfred Smuda (ed.): *Landschaft*, Frankfurt am Main 1986, pp. 87–110, here p. 92.

6 Ibid., p. 104.

Beate Gütschow, LS#7, 1999.

only allow a non-representative relationship to nature. The actual practice of art has long broken with this taboo of modern theories of art. Only now—through the artistic development of the past decades—have the old hierarchies been completely dismantled. The faith in a normative precedence in artistic production—whether the imitation of nature through art, the imitation of art through nature, the representation of a *natura naturata*, or the dramatization of a *natura naturans*—these instances of one-sidedness scarcely continue to play a role in what contemporary artists do. Their conquest engenders the possibility of a new liaison between art and nature, which has its roots in an interest on the part of art-making in the non-produced richness as well as the non-controllable changeability of natural phenomena.

And yet—this development is not to be equated with an end of the concept of imitation. (As is well known, there are far fewer ends of the line in art than is believed by its theoreticians.) Adorno, for example, uses this theorem once again in his *Ästhetische Theorie* in order to unhinge traditional thinking with regard to naturalness and artificiality. "As indeterminate, as antithetical to definitions, natural beauty is indefinable, and in this it is related to music, which drew the deepest effects in Schubert from such nonobjective similarity with nature. Just as in music what is beautiful flashes up in nature only to disappear in the instant one tries to grasp it. Art does not imitate nature, not even individual instances of natural beauty, but natural beauty itself."—[7] This "natural beauty itself" stands here for the quality of never-being-the-same evinced by the phenomenal world in mockery of conceptual discourse; it indicates the particularity of things and situations of which the aesthetic perception of nature issues repeated reminders. Accordingly, Adorno also writes, "The purpose of the work of art is the definiteness of the indefinite."—[8] Its configurations can give rise to that which must remain invisible in both the quotidian and the scientific knowledge of the world—namely, the inextricable

7 Adorno, op. cit., p. 113.

8 Ibid., p. 188.

interweaving of attachments and desires that determine and motivate us in the background of our superficial certainties and habits.

However, the classical formulation of the reciprocal relationship between aesthetic nature and aesthetic art had already been found nearly two hundred years earlier. In § 45 of his *Kritik der Urteilskraft* from 1790, Immanuel Kant wrote: "Nature was beautiful when it simultaneously resembled art; and art can only be deemed to be beautiful when we are aware of the fact that it is art and yet appears to us like nature."—[9] What Kant is concerned with here—already back then—is the resolution of the question as to which serves as the model for aesthetic perception and production: free nature or free art. Kant's solution lies in the thesis of a double exemplariness of nature for art and of art for nature. The presence of aesthetically perceived nature is a model for the inner vitality of the work of art; the imagination of the work of art, on the other hand, is the model for an intensive perception of nature. The reciprocal fecundation of aesthetic art and aesthetic nature arises only when nature, among other things, can be perceived *as* successful art and when art, among other things, can be perceived *as* free nature, without the difference between art and nature being extinguished in the process. It is neither nature perceived in the appearance of art, nor art perceived in the appearance of nature, which Kant elevates to the norm of an unrestrained aesthetic consciousness, but rather the *dialogue* between art and nature. But this is always *our* dialogue. It is accomplished in both the production and the contemplation of art, as soon as we open our sensitivity to the realization of how scarcely self-evident our own nature actually is to us.

9 Immanuel Kant: "Kritik der Urteilskraft," in: *Werke in zwölf Bänden*, edited by W. Weischedel, Frankfurt am Main 1968, vols. IX and XI, pp. 235–620, here p. 405.

The Model of the Landscape

The visual arts participate in this dialogue in an outstanding manner. In the diversity of their genres and forms, they give rise to quite different reactions to our reactions with regard to nature. Whether it is a matter of painting, photography, video, or sculpture, however these categories are inclined to make subliminal or explicit deals with each other, or whether it is installations that integrate some of their relatives into their own structures—they all allow themselves to become uneasy at the uncertain and vulnerable relationship, endangered from both within and without, which is maintained by contemporary societies and cultures to the natural aspect of their existence. This relationship, however, affects to no less a degree the individuals who are part of a highly cultivated life form that nourishes and destroys its natural foundations to an unbalanced degree. What impels the encounter between art and its counterpart is accordingly both the individual and the collective self-relationship of contemporary mankind which, at every random corner of the world and in the contemplation of each individual artificial or untreated object, knows itself—or can know itself—to be situated in the middle of the global play of comprehensive social and natural forces. Where artistic shaping stages, so to speak, this play of forces in one way or another, it uses its techniques to investigate the landscape character of our relationships to nature—aspects of the circumstance that, in our various activities, we move in realms that we know constantly exceed the horizon of our perceptual capabilities.

In the classical conception, the landscape is the zone that brings the culmination of the experience of natural beauty. But the experience of landscape is in no way limited to natural settings predominantly untouched or staged in the manner of parks: it can open itself frequently to an envisioning of domesticated and urban districts. In any case, the reminder must be issued that almost all landscapes today, even those on the fringes of civilization, are never purely nature but always also, even if to quite different degrees, *alloys* of nature and culture. At the same time, however, the structure of every landscape, even of those in the space of a large city, is also always a state and event of nature, simply through the influence of wind and weather. Each one, regardless of how it may be marked and altered by the works of mankind, offers to the aesthetic sense an essentially unguided play of abundance and transformation—just as in predominantly untouched nature.—[10] It is precisely this reciprocal fecundation of nature by culture and of culture by nature in the configuration of landscape-areas, which transforms the experience of them into a theoretical model for the dialogue between nature and art conducted in the visual arts. The dislocations of the landscape offer a paradigmatic insight precisely into the tectonic tensions of individual structures in which the mutual penetration of culture and nature becomes concrete.

10 Therefore one can say bluntly that nature is the nature of landscape. See Seel, op. cit., pp. 220–233, esp. p. 233.

The space of a landscape exists, like almost every space, together with a variety of objects *in* this space. What is fundamental for the experience of a space as landscape, however, is not the phenomenal encounter of individual or multiple objects, but instead the experience of being *right in the middle* of these objects: in their proximity and distance, in their constricting or liberating, eloquent or dumb presence. Whoever finds himself to be right in the middle of an abundance of appearances, for him there is *no middle* from which a fixed order could be discerned for these appearances. The space of the landscape *surrounds* the perceiving persons; it *reshapes* their location. And these are in no way simply observers concerned with a distanced overview or panorama (which is a common form of blindness to landscapes), but instead they are corporeal subjects who sense themselves to be receptive and vulnerable beings amid a spatial occurrence. Thus, the perception of landscape is not solely the experiencing of the existence and transformation of many things in a space, it is the experience of a *happening space*: the experience of what it is to be under and amid a multiform processual appearance of spatial shapes.

This occurrence can only take place in an extensive space. Its reality begins where a space steps *out of its*

Gerhard Richter, Abstraktes Bild, 1992.

dimension, in the sense that its measurements cannot be comprehended by those who find themselves within it. The space of a landscape has neither edge nor border, it ends at a horizon: where the contours, forms, and delimitations become diffuse; or in the case of a labyrinthine city, where it palpably extends further, without it being possible to comprehend these extensions from one's own standpoint. Landscapes are thus spaces that—from the perspective of those who perceive this space as a landscape—can be neither surveyed nor measured. In the shiftings of their horizons, they go past our own horizon. A park *landscape* is distinguished from a smaller urban park, for instance, in that it is not always possible to see through it, in that one can "lose" oneself in it, can give oneself over to the occurrence of an unbounded site. *Unüberschaubar* ("vaster than the eye can see") is also the applicable attribute for the landscape of a desert in which nothing presents itself to view. For whoever stands in the middle of a desert finds himself surrounded on all sides by a vastness that he cannot measure by seeing or hearing, cannot classify, cannot integrate into an overview.

It is only with this vertical and horizontal incompleteness that the space of a landscape opens up. This incompleteness always means an openness for a subject who conducts himself in a certain manner with regard to the space of his surroundings. Ultimately, the entire sense of a perceiving entry into landscapes lies in the fact that in them we arrive *outside*: into a simultaneously real and metaphorical outside. This outside is real because we depart from our own four walls, in fact from all clear and straightforward spatial coordinates. We go outside. However, this is only a necessary, but in itself not sufficient precondition for the experience of landscape. For an expansive space extending in all directions is, in its own terms, simply a *potential* site for the presence of an aesthetic landscape. There only occurs an *actual* experience of landscape when, in the real exterior, we also attain a *metaphorical exterior*: when we loosen the attachment to the pragmatic orientations that define our normal behavior in space; when we no longer move through this space with specified goals, but instead maintain an openness for the irregular presence of the more extensive space itself. However we attempt to make such presences *possible*—through forms of architecture and of the design and preservation of landscape in city and nature—the process of its presence exceeds all acts of doing.

Against Blindness

In the experience of landscape, in other words, wherever it may occur, there resonates a feeling of the connectedness with nature in all cultural practice, in all social organization and with it, in all technology. Inherent in this experience is a seed of the affirmation of the borders of all culture and thereby at least a trace of ecological humility. For short moments, it ushers us out of our imprisonment within the conviction that, for the sake of our welfare, we ought to be increasingly able to dominate our inner and outer natures. Furthermore, where its counterpart is not primarily a natural landscape, it guides us towards the open aspect of our nature-bound, historical world.

For reasons such as this, Adorno contradicted the "cult of grandiose landscape," calling it an "a non-artistic (*amusisch*) behavior" in which the human spirit once again celebrates only its own grandiosity.—[11] The abstract grandeur of nature here becomes a "reflex of bourgeois megalomania, a preoccupation with setting new records, quantification, and bourgeois cult of the hero worship. [...] Thereby it is neglected, that this critique, however, fails to perceive that natural grandeur reveals another aspect to its beholder: that aspect in which human domination has its limits and that calls to mind the powerlessness of human bustle."—[12] Adorno counters a narcissistic enthusiasm for nature with an objection that suffocates the experience of landscape in its own gesture of domination. This sort

11 Adorno, op. cit., p. 109ff.

12 Ibid., p. 110.

of celebration of the magnificent and mighty must be repudiated by the theory of the naturally beautiful as well as by the artistic investigation of nature. "This skepticism toward natural grandeur clearly originates in the artistic sensorium."—13

13 Ibid., p. 109.

This sort of distancing from all self-celebration of its and our capabilities characterizes the current encounter of art with nature. Herein, it unfolds its power and enchantment. It transforms the cultural interior into a metaphorical exterior, and the natural exterior into a metaphorical interior. It brings distance to proximity and proximity to distance. It causes the familiar to become foreign, and the foreign to remain foreign. With its constructions, it examines the contingencies, with its technology the displacements, and with its processuality the ongoing decay of nature and of life. It continuously causes the sublime to revert to the beautiful and vice versa—and thereby demonstrates how artificial the opposition is between the two. To experience the world in clear proportion *or* in clear disproportion to one's own possibilities—it is not this that is compelling, but rather listening to the disharmonious in the harmonious and to the harmonious in the disharmonious. According to the sound-mix, one may tend to designate the inducement in this regard as "beautiful" or "sublime", or to employ another aesthetic attribute. But the one or the other quality remains non-vital without the component of the other. Beauty that soothes without irritation is none; sublimity that unsettles without freeing cannot hold our gaze in avid fascination. The land of the aesthetic knows no borders. And that is the essence of the aesthetic: to impose no borders upon the capabilities of our perception.

This makes it possible for art to arrive in diverse ways at the borders of its and our nature. In the interior space of its surfaces, painting brings into view relationships that tacitly correspond to the exterior space—both of the picture itself and of the pictorial motifs. Furthermore, photography proposes a riddle as to what was lying beyond the croppings of its exposures. The artistic video repudiates the settling down into a narrated world. Sculpture and object-art do not permit an unambiguous standpoint with regard to their shaped forms. In its realm, the art of installation redirects the countenance of the outer world to the inside, and that of the inner world to the outside. All of these arts present that which withdraws itself from us. They create sites with a lack of location with regard to the places that we seem to know so well. In their appearance, they bring to light the invisible aspects of the human relationship to the world. Herein lies their fundamental reminiscence of mankind's non-transparent position in and towards the diverse dimensions of "nature". Because often enough with nature, one does not realize how it affects us and how we are affecting it.

It is this fundamentally social relationship to which the artistic policy of the image reacts with regard to nature. Along the path of a pictorial disturbance, it interrupts all self-certain handling of the difference between nature and culture. Just as in the unchained experience of landscape, it presents to view the fact that all far-sightedness, no matter how extensive, succumbs to a blurriness that is only the reverse side of our clarity. It refuses an overview most emphatically where we deem ourselves to have an overview. It entices us to peer into the *claire-obscure* of our knowledge. It endeavors to awaken us from the dogmatic slumber with which the comfort of the industrialized world repeatedly lulls its prosperous inhabitants. Not only nature proceeds past our horizon; art as well can transcend it. In the best cases, it allows us to see our own blindness.

First published as "Das Unsichtbare sichtbar machen. Zur aktuellen Lage des Austauschs von Kunst und Natur" ("Ushering the Insivible into View. On the Current Exchange between Art and Nature"), in: *Ferne Nähe. 'Natur' in der Kunst der Gegenwart*, exhibition-catalogue, Bonn 2009, pp. 161–181.

"The Impact and Power of the Example" of the Whole and in Detail: Some Selected Observations on the Work of Garden Designer, Landscape Architect, and Urban Planner Peter Joseph Lenné

Michael Seiler

Carl Joseph Begas, portrait of P. J. Lenné from ca. 1850.

Why is the Lenné quote, "The most important thing we may hope for is the impact and power of the example,"—1 chosen by Harri Günther for the title of a chapter in his Lenné book, so indispensible when I try to give a modest idea of Peter Joseph Lenné's formidable contribution to garden design and landscape architecture? As impressive and as seductive as Lenné's plan drawings may have been for his clients, and as formative as they were for his school, he nevertheless invested his entire energy, his entire organizational talent, and untiring perseverance

1 Quoted from the "Einladung zur Zeichnung von Aktien bei der zu Potsdam errichteten Landes-Baumschule" (invitation to subscribe for shares in the country built to Potsdam nursery) from August 1, 1824. Published in the *Proceedings of the Society for the Promotion of Horticulture in the Royal Prussian States*, vol. 2, Berlin 1826, p. 165.

in realizing his ideas for gardens and landscapes, while hoping and trusting in his motto about the impact and power of the example. His contemporaries and followers all confirm the great success of this attitude. However, setting these priorities left little time for theory. If you want to understand the significance and impact of his work, you need to read his very few surviving and, hence, very valuable writings, because this is where he developed in full the gardens and landscapes he realized as outstanding "examples." This is the only way to come close to understanding his impact, which reaches from garden design to land improvement and urban planning.

Lenné's roots lie in the garden world of the French Enlightenment. His father, electoral court gardener and, during the French administration (1794–1813), Inspector of the Botanical Garden at Bonn, was employed in Koblenz from 1812 onward. He was also acquainted with André Thouin, Director of the Jardin des Plantes in Paris, where he arranged for his son to study from April 1811 until the summer of 1812. Here, the young student not only pursued his love of the botanical and began to develop his plan drawing style, but also his signature method of closely interrelating the modeling of the ground surface with the network of pathways.

After years of traveling through southern Germany and a long stay in Vienna where he designed a large, unrealized plan for Laxenburg, he returned to Koblenz at his father's request to serve as Imperial Garden Engineer. In 1816 at the age of 26, he was called to Potsdam to restore and modernize the Prussian gardens, which had been neglected during the Napoleonic Wars, in line with the latest developments from France and England.

During his fifty years of Prussian service, he maintained a liberal and confident attitude, which he played down to powerful parties using the alleged naivety of the gardener. André Le Nôtre before him had also used such tactics to successfully manage the difficult job of dealing with Ludwig XIV, otherwise known as the "Sun King."

Lenné, a child of the Enlightenment, was deeply convinced by the mission of garden design. On January 17, 1849, he wrote to Franz Kugler, the Cultural Administrator of the Prussian Ministry of Culture, regarding the debate on the status of garden design in relation to the visual arts: "[...] that it is the specific task of garden design to creatively demonstrate, in its cultivation of the great, noble, and exalted in nature, imbued with the individual spirit of the artist, how to awaken the sense of beauty, as do the other arts, and, and like them, to serve as an educational resource for the people."—[2] In his only partially surviving draft of a *Lehrbuch der Landschaftsgärtnerei* (Textbook of Landscape Design), we read: "Your true strength is first revealed in eliminating the unbeautiful by rejuvenation, in evoking the beautiful, refining the fundamental existing forms; in enriching one form by adding another, facilitating the enjoyment of the beautiful; but above all in providing each particular use (the ornamental square, the garden, the park, and so on) with a corresponding whole, an organization that is structured and coherent in itself, such as a human figure, or a chorus of song, and always emanating life that moves the soul."—[3]

2 Quoted by Wimmer in von Buttlar 1989, p. 65.

3 Mack, L. L.Wittmack: "Lenné's Entwurf zu einem Lehrbuch der Landschaftsgärtnerei," in: *GartenFlora*, 38, Berlin 1889, p. 541.

Pleasureground in Glienicke Park, 1862.

The first garden to be realized by Lenné was commissioned by his patron, the State Chancellor Prince Hardenberg, father-in-law of Hermann von Pückler-Muskau. In autumn 1816, Lenné created a pleasure ground on the prince's Glienicke property. The principle and method of design that became visible here would be characteristic of his life's work in Prussia, which began with this project. The landscape design Lenné created for this approximately 250 × 150-meter-large triangle of terrain between the Havel, the road from Berlin to Potsdam, and the manor house garden attracted much attention. It also exemplified his design concept in the interplay of pathways, soil modeling, and deep views into the landscape through natural-looking terrain with valleys, soft mounds of earth, and a remarkable hill. This hill, and a path that leads through a right-hand curve to its crest, form the stage for the magnificent and surprising approach to a four-kilometer-deep view of the Havel waters, which are framed by more hills. The remarkable design element here is the transition from the plant-lined curve of the pathway to the rise of the hill. Approaching this on foot makes one feel as though tension is being released step by step by the way the horizon gradually opens to the viewer. In 1872, Lenné's successor, Ferdinand Jühlke, said that "Lenné had a masterful and rare understanding of how to individualize soil formations and, with a sweeping, picturesque concept based on the local physiognomy, lend the groupings in form and color an expression, to which all his many creations in the Fatherland bear eloquent testimony!"—[4]

4 Jühlke 1872, p. 22.

In the garden administration, the young garden engineer from Bonn was initially occupied with comprehensive planning. The king was not satisfied with the development between 1787 and 1793 of the small-scale, densely planted New Garden designed by Johann August Eyserbeck from Wörlitz, and had the court gardener, Morsch, rework parts of it in 1814 and 1816. But he still found the results unsatisfactory. The *Hofmarschall* and *Gartenintendant* von Maltzahn immediately commissioned Lenné to submit a plan to redesign the section in the New Garden between Heiliger See and Jungfernsee and requested the king to approve the "realization of this plan in the coming spring [...] in order to see whether this gardener, who has been so highly recommended to me, is talented in reality."—[5] The king found the plan too expensive, but he did approve work to be done between the pyramids and the Red House based on Lenné's plan, which was then realized between 1817 and 1818. By 1830, the New Garden had been redesigned with dynamic pathways created by Lenné and extensive views, mostly towards Heiliger See.

5 Hinz, p. 37.

In his first year in Potsdam in 1816, Lenné had prepared several plans for the Sanssouci Park, using the French-influenced drawing style he had previously introduced. These sophisticatedly depicted woodlands and bird's eye views. One of the most impressive among these is the 89 × 193-centimeter-large, carefully drawn "Plan of Sanssouci and its surroundings, along with the project to introduce flowing and bubbling water, as well as redesigning the promenade." He made a bold demonstration of his abilities, and could hardly wait for the plan to be approved and financed. In the plan, he picks up the nearly two-mile main avenue from the eastern entrance of the park to the new palace, and replaces it with a thirty-four-meter-wide vista, crossed by many pathways. In this way, he preserved the actual function of the main avenue, namely to serve visitors as a visual point of reference while successfully preventing them from mistakably misusing it as a dreary promenade. In this context, it should be recalled that in his six versions of "Manière de montrer Versailles," Louis XIV never actually strolled along the Allée Royale, but repeatedly crossed its axis and paused, in order to use it as a visual point of reference.

The fifty-year course of Lenné's highly successful work in Prussia and beyond was based on his ability to merge his artistic talents with his excellent organizational skills. Very early on, he created a threefold material and conceptual foundation that enabled him to realize his garden designs. In December 1821, he submitted a "promemoria" on the establishment of a national nursery to the Hofmarschall Department and the Government. When this was refused, he turned to the "Society for the Promotion of Horticulture in the Royal Prussian States," which he himself had co-founded. During their second session in the following year, he presented the first treatise entitled "Principles for the Establishment of a National Nursery in Potsdam." It also included a proposal to link the national nursery to schoolteacher training. This idea gave birth to the concept of the horticultural school. The national nursery and horticultural school were launched by the highest cabinet order on August 20, 1823. Lenné was appointed director of both institutions in October of the same year.—6

6 The horticulture school did not begin its lessons until the spring of 1824.

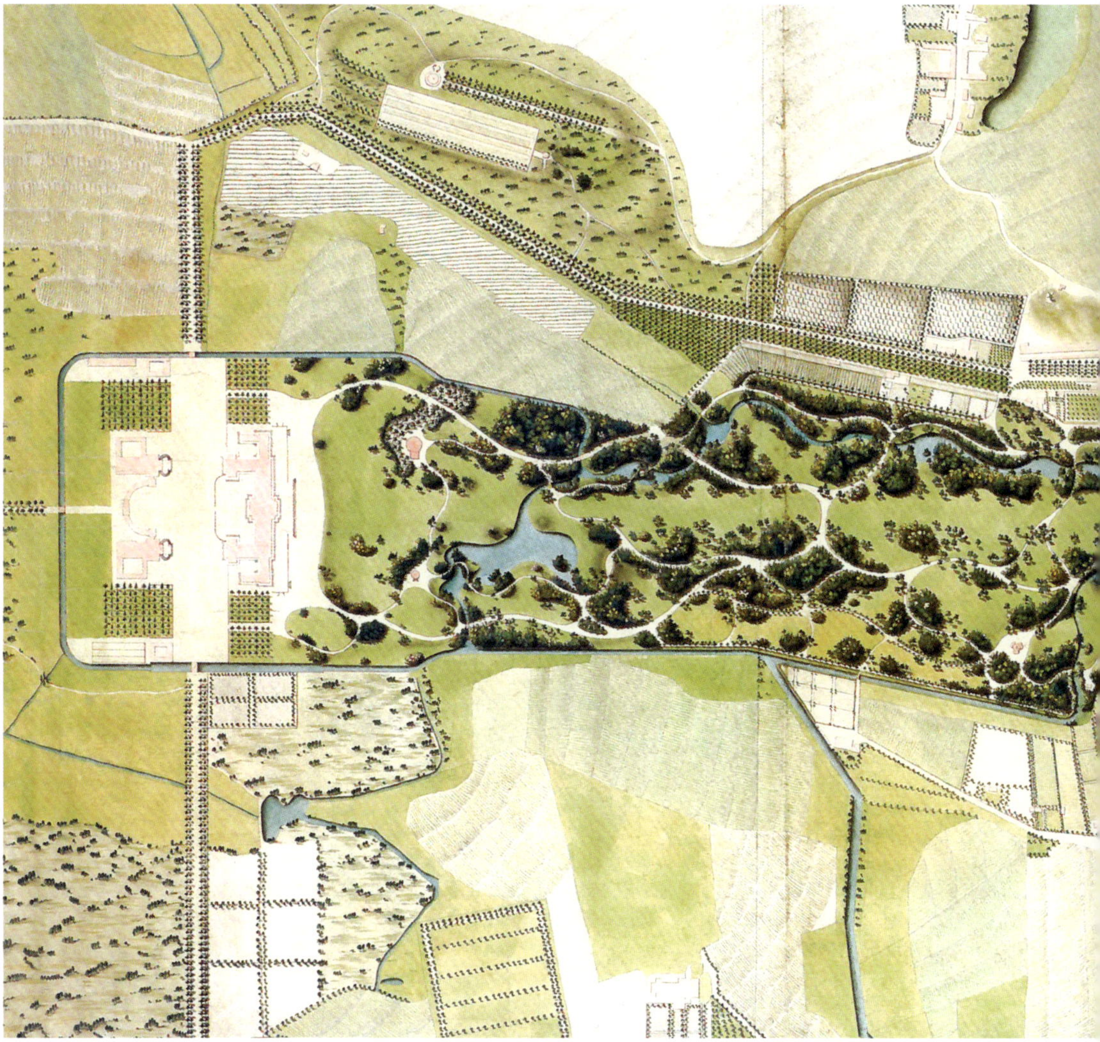

P. J. Lenné, plan of Sanssouci, 1816.

PLAN
von
SANS SOUCJ
UND DESSEN UMGEBUNGEN,
nebst
PROJECT
fliessendes und springendes Wasser dahinzubringen,
so wie auch die Promenaden zu verschönern.
Entworfen und Gezeichnet von P. J. Lenné. 1816.

Insights from Lenné's Trip to England in 1822

In response to an accusation made by Prince Hermann von Pückler-Muskau—a direct competitor of Lenné's—stating that the latter had never viewed an English Garden personally, the King of Prussia approved Lenné's appeal to visit England from August to October 1822, about which he reported to the Horticultural Society in May 1823.

He discovered both model and reprehensible examples of garden design, as well as inspiration for a spatial planning concept for the area between Berlin and Potsdam. Encouraged by the landscaped route between the city of Chester and the Eaton Hall estate, Lenné wrote: "[...] that a similar decoration is worthy in that sense for the most traveled roads near the royal residences in Berlin and Potsdam, though not in the least based exactly on those ideas. For instance, as pleasant as the planting of the road is between Berlin and Zehlendorf, with its straight line of cottonwood poplars, this kind of design is unfortunate because its monotony eventually becomes tiresome, and it does not grant the wanderer cooling shade during hot summer days. Uniformity of this kind is all the more noticeable here because there are few decorative elements and no trees in the surrounding countryside. Decorative planting would be very useful here, and could be accomplished by introducing groups of trees along the Pappel Allee (especially hardwoods that create gaps in the forest canopy). Such larger, sometimes smaller, and variously shaped groups, which change at each curve of the path, would lend the landscape a more attractive foreground; the large areas divided into smaller sections and interrupted, will allow the traveler's eye to be pleasantly distracted and entertained. Between Zehlendorf and Potsdam, this beautification could be achieved with little difficulty and at a low cost. Here, travelers are constantly wrapped in walls of dense pine, which, because they obscure all views, produce the same feeling of monotony and boredom that, earlier in the opposite manner, was caused by a total lack of trees. This part of the road would be given a new and unanticipated charm by introducing entire groups of such hardwoods that thrive in the local soil; by thinning the dense forests in areas that present beautiful, landscape painting-like vistas; by opening the tree masses that otherwise veil the picturesque, green grounds between Zehlendorf and Wannsee; and by making space for individual, old oak trees that are suppressed and hidden in several places by the pines."—[7]

7 *Debates of the Society for the Promotion of Horticulture in the Royal Prussian States*, vol. 1, Berlin 1825, p. 87f.

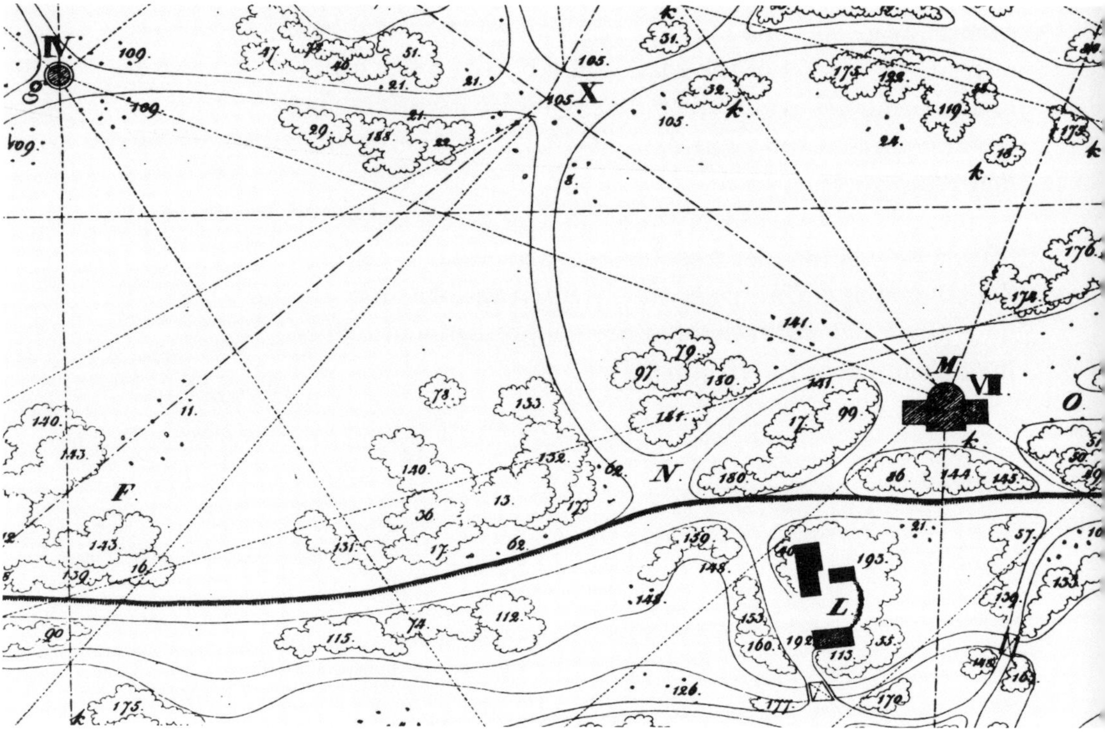

P. J. Lenné, design for the Volksgarten in Magdeburg, two details from the graphic plan and the planting scheme, showing the grounds around the social events house.

Volksgarten Magdeburg

On January 9, 1825, Lenné submitted his three plans for the construction of a public garden in the city of Magdeburg to the "Society for the Promotion of Horticulture" and provided detailed written explanation. It states: "Invited by the same (Mayor Franke) to design a plan for the new site, I had the permission of my supervisor (the Gartenintendant) to commit myself to this task during this summer (1824)." Then: "Moreover, due to the internal arrangement of the main area of the site, the surface of the soil is in need of a diverse enhancement. The pleasant wave-like form of the soil surface is as essential to the beauty of a site as the various curves and contours of the pathways and surrounding vegetation. The main contours of the terrain are quite fortunate. But they should be refined by lines drawn over the structural shape of the leveling." Toward the end of the explanatory notes Lenné writes, "While I have heard of princes and wealthy private individuals collaborating on the fine art of garden design, this is the first enterprise of this kind that I have encountered in my professional life, being undertaken by a town government, which according to preliminary estimates, and excluding the buildings, will cost no less than 18,000 Reichsthaler."—[8] The royal patron and the princely and royal members of the horticultural society might have been impressed by such an enthusiastic commitment.

8 Ibid., vol. 2, Berlin 1826, pp. 148–160.

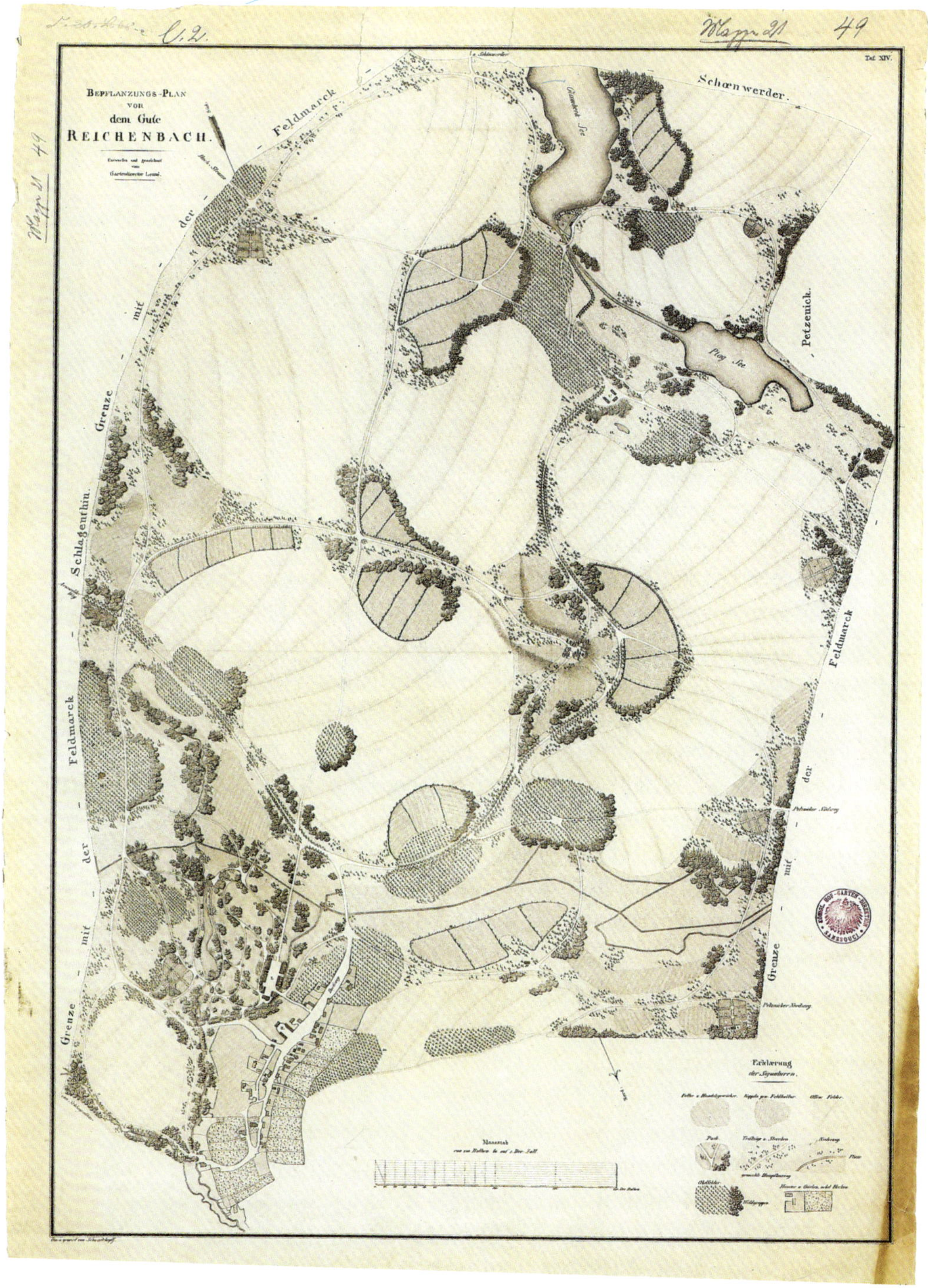

P. J. Lenné, Planting Scheme of Gute Reichenbach, lithography.

The Example of The Reichenbach Estate

When on January 5, 1823, Lenné spoke at the Garden Design Society on the "Principles for the Establishment of a National Nursery in Potsdam," he was thinking about both the economic optimization and aesthetic improvement of the *Feldflur* (the open corridors of fields throughout Potsdam), which he undertook two years later in a project aimed at economically improving the design of the Reichenbach Estate, and eighteen years later, starting in 1841, with the Bornstedt-Bornim-Nedlitzer Feldflur north of Sanssouci. In the introduction, he wrote, "One should not envisage the poor vegetation in the private gardens of our compatriots, but rather the pictures of those districts and towns where the most is done to create country roads lined with fruit trees, plantations on common grazing lands, entire fruit orchards, and field lots, which are harvested twice, once directly from the soil and then again from a terrace above the same soil, from the branches of fruit trees spread over the field."—9

9 Ibid., vol. 1, Berlin 1825, p. 27.

The horticultural society, certainly inspired by its member Lenné, announced several prizes in June 1824 for the year 1824/25, including, a "Guide to an Economically Advantageous Design of Whole Marked Fields." The two submitted disquisitions were judged by Lenné and not deemed worthy of an award. In his review of the first work, presented to the assembly in May 1825, Lenné wrote, "There is hardly a landscape conceivable, let alone a marked field, which would be incapable of aesthetic adornment and economic optimization through cultivation by the organizing hand of the artist. Even the most fortunate landscape, possessing all the rich formations of nature, can be cultivated aesthetically and optimized economically through proper use of garden design and the many resources available to it. The same is true, although to an unequal lesser extent and with more difficulty, of those areas that nature has neglected. The sad pine forest will take the hiker with more kindness if its dark colors are enhanced, by planting light-colored hardwoods before them. Variety, life, and fertility are all given to barren, flat land, wherever garden design comes to the aid with its formations."—[10]

10 Ibid., vol. 2, Berlin 1826, pp. 241, 242.

The then director of the Horticultural Society, Carl Gottlieb Bethe, professional senior councilor of the Agricultural Department in the Ministry of Interior Affairs, submitted at the same meeting his disquisition "written with the participation of Mr. Lenné" on the "Adornment of Whole Marked Fields" (suitable for local areas and some neighboring provinces of comparable agricultural conditions). The eighty-page disquisition entitled "On Pasture and Field Plantings" was presented to the society together with Lenné's designed and sketched "Planting Scheme of the Reichenbach Estate" in Pomerania—known today as Radaczewo in Poland—which was owned by Bethe. It was also published in 1826 in the second volume of the negotiations.—[11] The work is divided into two main sections: "A. Development and Defense of the Plan in Relation to Economics" and "B. Further Development of the Plan in Relation to Aesthetics." The disquisition is written in the we-form, in accordance with Bethe's statement that it was written with the participation of Lenné. The statements that focus on garden and landscape design in section B distinctly differ linguistically from the text that cites agricultural authorities. The choice of words here corresponds to Lenné's in the written

11 Ibid., pp. 270–349.

statements, which can be clearly attributed to him. I am convinced that the verbal contributions are in fact Lenné's, and have assembled a selection relevant to his design ideas elsewhere. In this essay however, I will limit myself to two of those statements,which are related to the topic of my presentation:

"Landscape is only made complete through its relationship to people. The traces of human existence will always offer a pleasant addition to inspired feelings and thoughts, regardless of how powerfully nature might act on our minds in its original forms, and how many of these actually still exist in landscape. The more the shape of the landscape differs from its original form and the more this is appropriated by culture, the closer the relationship of the artistic forms must be to those of the areas of dwelling, and the stronger these should be emphasized as the central point of the whole."

"The clearer and more powerfully the forms of a given landscape are expressed, the more pleasant and lively are our memories of the repeated pleasure they bring; and the main difference between the enjoyment of a well-ordered park and a landscape composed of mere natural formations or random additions is precisely that, in the notion of the latter, as beautiful as it may be, everything fluctuates in indefinite shapes and contours; but in the notion of a park, certain basic principles are presented that facilitate the perception and regeneration of the mind's eye. Within the mighty rush of all of landscape's flowing forms, there is indeed a need for our soul to hold on to certain lines in order to find its way and to wander there with a certain reassurance."—12

12 Seiler 1999, pp. 13–27.

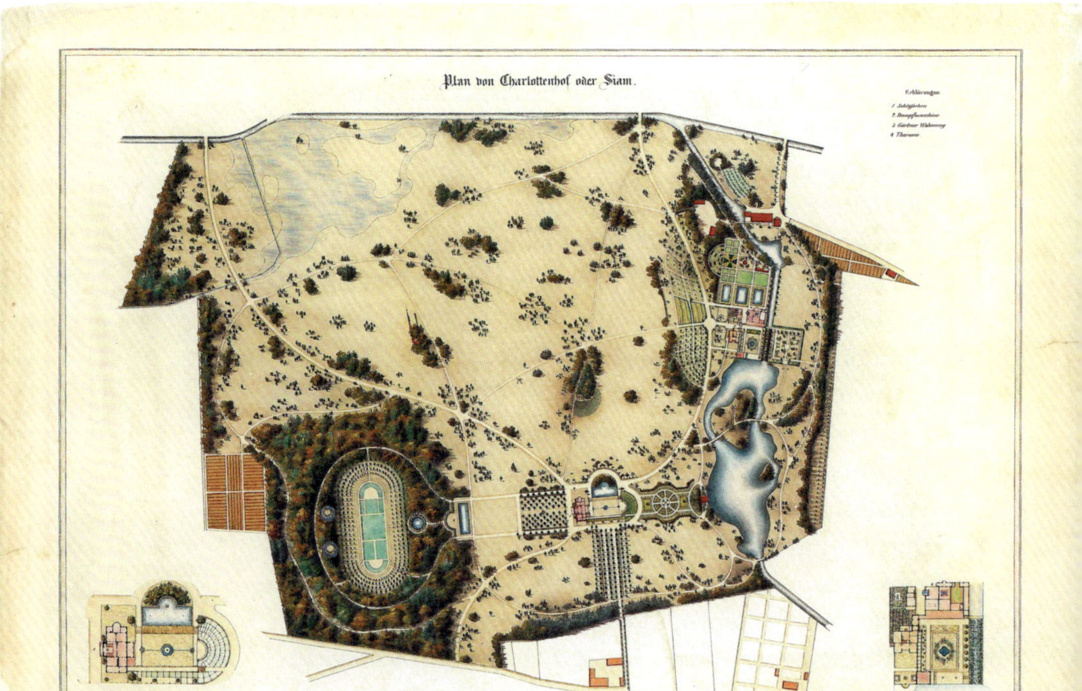

Plan of Charlottenhof or Siam, color lithography, 1839, draughtsman G. Koeber.

Charlottenhof

On Christmas Day 1825, the later King Frederick William IV of Prussia obtained the Charlottenhof Vorwerk, which was adjacent to the south side of Sanssouci's Rehgarten. The site was flat as a table and inherently unattractive. The grace of the modeled soil and the water surfaces had to be created artistically and artificially, as did the garden- and forest-like spaces by grouping trees. Karl Friedrich Schinkel was commissioned to transform the existing manor house into a Roman villa for the Crown Prince and, on another site, to build a residence for the gardener. According to his letters, Schinkel's task to theoretically reconstruct the Villa of Pliny the Younger was to include its gardens. The Crown Prince's interest in the results was so great that he wished to realize this model world not only architecturally, but regarding the gardens as well. The collaboration between Lenné and Schinkel in Charlottenhof inspired the garden director, who had previously been occupied purely with landscape design, to integrate geometric shapes in the landscape garden. After Charlottenhof, his work displays geometric gardens that serve either as historical references or as separate forms. With this dialog, Lenné opened up an entirely new world, for which his interest had previously been awakened by Jean-Nicolas Durand's lectures in Paris 1811. In the process, he demonstrated how he adopted and further developed the essential qualities, ideas, and changes.

In 1839, he published the park, which had been developing for fourteen years, as a color lithograph by one of his employees, Gerhard Koeber. In the south, Schinkel and Lenné developed an east-west oriented geometric architectural and garden axis from the original north-south facing manor house. To adorn the level that extends northwards, soil obtained from excavating the picturesque, contoured *Maschinenteich* (engine pond) was used to create eight small hills and groups of trees placed at spatial intervals. Unlike the case of Marly Garden, the new spatial structures here link up with those of the old Rehgarten—through the palace trenches that had previously marked the property's border but no longer exist today—ultimately merging both parks. The initial plans involved an idea that could not be realized, namely to place a large lake in front of the palace that would act as a mirror. The funds that had been provided for this plan, after Frederick William IV's accession to the throne in 1841, were used for a different, equally daunting project: the Ruinenberg.

The architectural and horticultural axis begins on Maschinenteich—at the steam engine house, which was originally built as a lookout but unfortunately demolished in 1923—and runs through the rose garden, the terrace, the castle, the dark grove of 192 chestnut trees, and the (now filled) pond, to the Hippodrome hidden in the forest. Not only do Greco-Roman models experience a new birth here, but the east to west view to the gardener's residence, the vineyard, and to the dome of the Neues Palais is also an analogy of human history and of individual human life.—[13] Over the vast grounds of the park lying to the north of Rehgarten, Lenné distributed grove-like tree groupings in the shape of islands, so that interlacing spaces and views would open and close to the visitor strolling along wide arched pathways. As soon as one meadow unfolds through the swaying tops of the surrounding trees, there is the sense that the next is

13 Schönemann 1997, pp. 12–20.

just beyond. Planted groups of bushes conceal the strict geometry of the axis, which offers only partial, diagonal picturesque glimpses of the individual buildings. The effect of the geometry of architecture and garden is thus all the more powerful and surprising when one enters the field of their lines of force: Charlottenhof Park is a finely tuned, symbolic composition in every elevation, in every path's curve, and in every group of bushes and trees.

Sanssouci, Charlottenhof, view from the island to the castle.

P. J. Lenné, G. Koeber (drawing), Beautification Plan for Potsdam and its Surroundings, 1833, draughtsman G. Koeber.

Beautification Plan for the Area of Potsdam

In the résumé he formulated for being selected as an honorary member of the Academy of Arts on June 13, 1853, Lenné wrote the following, truthfully and not without pride: "Lenné's attention is forever dedicated to regional culture and regional beautification."—[14] He always tried to convince his clients to realize large-scale, far-reaching plans, and he was very often successful in convincing them to purchase land outside of the actual plan, in order to secure sightlines and future expansion. In the cited résumé we read further: "It was very tempting to connect the many older and newer designed parks in and around Potsdam in a landscape manner, for which Lenné had drafted a plan in 1833 that had already been honored by the approval of the now ruling King (then Crown Prince), under whose reign the construction began and continued. The main idea was to surround the Havel as a lake with a large park of an area of almost two German miles (7.42 kilometers) from the Karlsberge near Baumgartenbrück to the Pfaueninsel."—[15] In 1834, his opponent, Prince Pückler, wrote in this regard in his famous *Andeutungen über Landschaftsgärtnerei* (Notes on Landscape Design): "But may we hope that the royal parks, under the supervision of their well-deserving director Lene [sic!], which are to enclose and surround all of Potsdam with one vast park, will certainly set such a pattern."—[16]

14 Quoted by Wimmer in von Buttlar 1989, p. 14.

15 Ibid., p. 13f.

16 Quoted from the reprint of 1977, p. 15.

Area of the Bornstedt-Bornim-Nedlitzer open fields from Map of the Potsdam Peninsula, 1869.

Potsdam's Feldflur

From the height of the Norman Tower, which was adjoined to the Frederician-Era *Kolosseumswand* (Colosseum Wall) in 1845, the view is to the west and north of the Bornstedt-Bornim-Nedlitzer Feldflur, which is called today the "Lenné Feldflur." Lenné was particularly interested, as we learned from his work for the national nursery and the project of decorating the Reichenbach Estate, in the combination of economic, aesthetic, and—in today's terminology—ecological concerns.

With the accession of Frederick William IV in 1840, the vision of an "Adornment of the Island of Potsdam"—[17] could begin. The precondition for a reorganization of the Feldflur was a "separation," meaning dividing and privatizing the properties that were held collectively. In 1848, the reorganization and enhancement of the Bornim Estate was completed according to Lenné's proposals. The estate had been relocated from the village and, according to plans by Ludwig Persius, rebuilt on a gentle hill in an imposing position near Lake Fahrlander. Lenné surrounded it with mulberry and fruit orchards planted at regular intervals, and built a Lindenallee with a soft curve that led up to and through Bornstedt. Its curve refers to the natural modeling of the soil surface and from the left curve directs the eye from Nedlitzer Kirchberg

17 Formulation of the State Minister of Ladenberg in his letter dated July, 3, 1842. See Seiler 1994, p. 125.

to the extensive waters of Lake Fahrlander, which, due to the tillering of the bank with trees, can unfortunately no longer be experienced today. Additional avenues lined with hardwood trees, many of them fruit trees, brighten up the sequence of agricultural fields. Lines of hedges run between them in a north-south direction. Thus, an "agricultural Arcadia" was created against great odds, where Karl Förster would later establish his world-famous perennials nursery. After 1945, rationalization efforts destroyed almost all hedges and many of the avenues, while the remaining avenues suffered heavy damage through ruthless cultivation. The pressure to create settlements threatened to destroy everything. However, through a consolidation of land, based on the cultural and historical value of the property, and as a supplement to the Bundesgartenschau Potsdam (Potsdam National Garden Festival) in 2001, a plan to restore most of the Feldflur was completed in 2002. The imagery of this "agrarian Avecsouci" is the timeless addition to the artistic gardens of Sanssouci. It gives the city, which is surrounded by a wreath of landscaped gardens, an utterly unique charm, which can be found nowhere else in the world.

Sanssouci, Marlygarten, view from the garden administration building to the Friedenskirche.

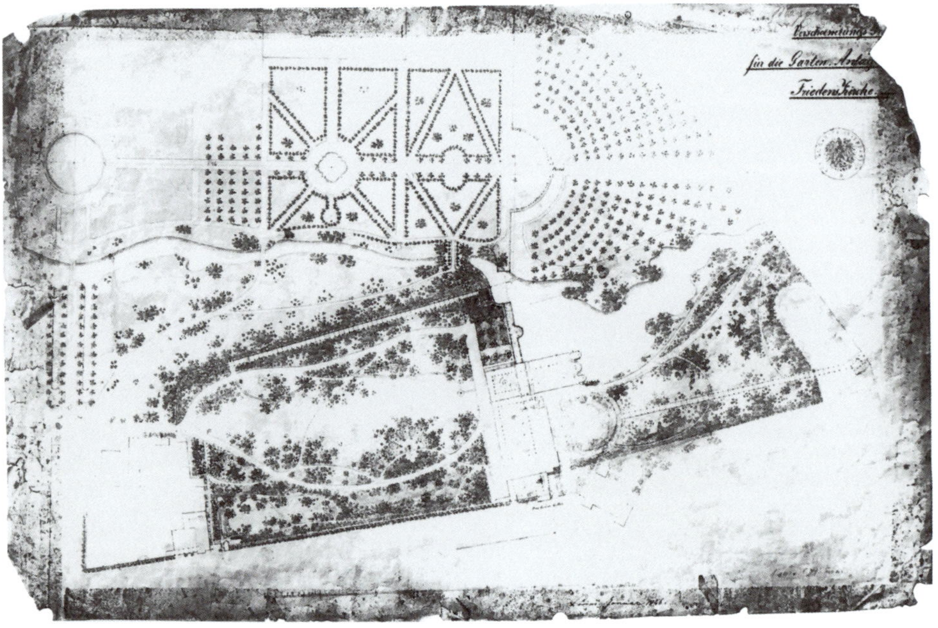

Decoration Plan for the Garden Facilities of the Friedenskirche, signed: "Lenné January 1846," draughtsman G. Meyer. The deliberate juxtaposition of the restored formal garden in the upper section of the plan, compared with the landscape facilities designed one hundred years later in the lower part plan is vividly clear.

Plan of the Marlygarten in Sanssouci, ca. 1855, draughtsman G. Meyer.

The Marly Garden at Sanssouci

King Frederick William I of Prussia, known as the "Soldier King," had the decorative gardens of his predecessor converted into training grounds or kitchen gardens. He also had a kitchen garden planted before the gates of Potsdam and gave it the mocking name of "Marly"—the same name of the French Sun King's luxurious palaces and gardens. Besides growing fruit and vegetables, the kitchen garden also served as a location for target practice. In addition, there was a modest *Lusthaus* (summerhouse), which was demolished when his son and successor, Frederick II, began construction in 1744 on the palace and gardens of Sanssouci, which was in the immediate vicinity. The kitchen garden was maintained for one hundred years. However, on the palace and gardens of Sanssouci, which was the creation of an atheistic king, there was no church. Frederick William IV, on the other hand, was a pious man and had already found this lacking when he was Crown Prince. He subsequently commissioned a church to be constructed on the east side of the kitchen garden, which would serve the court and three Potsdam suburbs. The foundation stone for this place of worship, called the Friedenskirche, was deliberately set on April 14, 1845—exactly 100 years after the foundation stone was laid for Sanssouci Palace. Now the former kitchen garden would need a suitable design. The history-conscious King wanted to preserve the historical name of Marly, adding, "Let us make the garden more beautiful, we do no wrong." For an entire year, beginning in 1846, Lenné developed the 200 × 120-meter-large flat kitchen garden, which was situated directly in front of his official residence, into a much-admired decorative landscape park with subtle ground modeling. The King himself called it "the pearl of the landscape garden." Moreover, because the partially remaining hedge garden remaining from the Frederician-era Lustgarten was deliberately restored, something very groundbreaking developed in garden design: an intentional contrast of one hundred years of garden design history set intentionally next to each other. The kitchen garden walls remained. Old and new was not blended together, but deliberately juxtaposed. In Marly Garden, with its artificial, subtle ground modeling and projecting and receding woodland scenery, a unique spatial diversity unfolds when the visitor strolls along the narrow side paths,making the garden seem at least as wide as it is long. This essay cannot go into the many religious allusions of this garden composition, but references to the appropriate scientific papers for further reading have been included below.—[18] The garden became the unrivaled model for many private gardens of the second half of the century.

18 Michael Seiler: "Marly Garden and Peace Garden," in: Karg, Dreger, pp. 218–227.

My presentation has highlighted only a few aspects of Lenné's work, but I hope to have shown that he was a liberal, yes, almost democratic child of the Enlightenment. He derived a sense of esteem and self-awareness for his professional duty from his deep conviction that garden designers and landscape architects ultimately have a philanthropic mission. His trademark was perseverance in the pursuit of this duty, in small steps if necessary, without ever losing sight of the goal. His success depended on his organizational skills, extraordinary diligence and ambition, his energetic commitment to educating future garden designers (horticultural school), and—in modern terms—"lobbying," as it was manifested in the Society for the Promotion of Horticulture. That which is created from the spirit of a place proves to be greatly sustainable, even today. Landscape designers today have to test and apply a variety of new methods in order to meet the challenge of redesigning agricultural, energy, and transport wastelands in an ever-shrinking world, so that people can use them as sites of recreation, enjoyment, and identification. Lenné's deep belief in a mission, and his successful perseverance when realizing that mission, should be a source of strength and enthusiasm for those who have taken up the task.

Bornstedt-Bornim-Nedlitzer open fields, view from the Lindenallee to Nedlitzer Kirchberg.

Given the abundance of relevant literature, the author has limited the list to the examples cited in his essay.

Von Buttlar, Florian (ed.): *Peter Joseph Lenné, Volkspark und Arkadien*, exhibition catalog, Berlin 1989.

Gröning, Gert: "Das Gut Reichenbach (Radaczewo), Pommern—eine musterhaft verschönerte Feldflur?" in: *Die "ornamental farm." Gartenkunst und Landwirtschaft*, Muskauer Schriften vol. 7, Zittau 2010.

Günther, Harri: *Peter Joseph Lenné. Gärten Parke, Landschaften*, Berlin 1985.

Günther, Harri, Harksen, Sibylle: *Peter Joseph Lenné. Katalog der Zeichnungen*, Stuttgart/Tübingen/Berlin 1993.

Habrok-Henrich, Petra et al. (eds.): *Peter Joseph Lenné. Eine Gartenreise im Rheinland*, Publication for the occasion of the homonymous exhibition in Koblenz/Regensburg 2011.

Hinz, Gerhard: *Peter Joseph Lenné. Das Gesamtkunstwerk des Gartenarchitekten und Städteplaners*, Hildesheim/Zurich/New York 1989.

Jühlke, Ferdinand: *Die Königliche Landesbaumschule und Gärtnerlehranstalt zu Potsdam*, Berlin 1872.

Karg, Detlef, Dreger, Hans-Joachim (eds.): *Peter Joseph Lenné, Gartenkunst im 19. Jahrhundert*, Beiträge zur Lenné-Forschung, Berlin 1992.

Karg, Detlef, Dreger, Hans-Joachim (eds.): *Peter Joseph Lenné. Parks und Gärten im Land Brandenburg, Werkverzeichnis*. Forschungen und Beiträge zur Denkmalpflege im Land Brandenburg, vol. 7, Worms 2005.

Reinisch, Ulrich: "Peter Joseph Lennés Wirken als Stadtplaner von Berlin," in: Karg, Detlef, Dreger, Hans-Joachim (eds.): *Peter Joseph Lenné, Gartenkunst im 19.Jahrhundert*, Beiträge zur Lenné-Forschung, Berlin 1992.

Schönemann, Heinz: *Karl Friedrich Schinkel. Charlottenhof, Potsdam Sanssouci, Opus 12*, Stuttgart/London 1997.

Seiler, Michael: "Die Verschönerungs-Anlagen in der Umgegend von Potsdam. Die hindernisreiche Schöpfung der Lennéschen Kulturlandschaft im Spiegel der Akten," in: Schmidt, Erika, Hansmann, Wilfried, Gamer, Gamer (eds.): *Garten, Kunst, Geschichte. Festschrift für Dieter Hennebo zum 70. Geburtstag*, Worms 1994.

Seiler, Michael, Hamm, Manfred: *Inszenierte Landschaften, Blicke ins Preußische Arkadien*, Berlin 1999.

Wimmer, Clemens Alexander: "Äußerungen Lennés zur Gartentheorie," in: von Buttlar, Florian (ed.): *Peter Joseph Lenné, Volkspark und Arkadien*, Berlin 1989.

On Designing Infrastructure Systems as Landscape

Antje Stokman

New energy policies, climate change, and increasingly rapid urbanization: landscape architects are faced with a situation that makes their profession more necessary, yet more critically questioned, than ever before. There is an increasing urgency to define and design new forms of coexistence between architecture, infrastructure, and nature. Landscape architects can contribute significantly to the cultural-aesthetic development of landscape by means of systematic interventions in infrastructure systems. New approaches to understanding, designing, and creating landscape as a topological system are an important precondition. They enable landscape architects to collaborate in interdisciplinary teams, developing new conceptual ideas, designing and organizing infrastructural spaces in landscape.

Searching for a New Scope of Duties

In the context of the exhibition curated by Donata Valentien and Anna Viader entitled “Wiederkehr der Landschaft” (The Return to Landscape) at the Akademie der Künste (Academy of the Arts) in Berlin in 2010, Joan Roig, of the Spanish firm Battle i Roig in Barcelona, spoke of a typical situation in a professional landscape architect’s day-to-day practice: “When the engineer was building the highway, he called us and said, 'do something.'" The relationship between landscape and infrastructure and between other disciplines involved in its design is a hot subject at the moment. What role do landscape architects play in the design of infrastructure in landscape, or, how can that role be altered?

Traffic systems, energy networks, and water systems that are planned by engineers largely determine the large-scale development of landscape. These infrastructure systems, which are vital to the development of our society, are integrated into the landscape and greatly change the way they are perceived. Up until the nineteenth and twentieth centuries, designing infrastructure facilities was one of classic architecture's central tasks. Yet, in modern times, the increasing complexity and pure scale of infrastructure projects led to the emergence of many new specialist disciplines and hence, to the loss of an interdisciplinary understanding of the interlinked systems of natural landscape, urban space, and infrastructure (Heidenreich 2004, Graham, Marvin 2001). Today, infrastructural systems are typically planned in sectoral, highly regulated planning processes based on economic and technological perspectives, and then spatialized. In the process, ecological and aesthetic aspects play a secondary role.

In this respect, landscape architects have largely been seen as subordinate specialist planners. They are called in after the technical part of infrastructure planning is mostly finished and facts have already been established. The conflict of how the profession deals with this divides it into two contrary roles. The design-oriented members of the profession are usually considered as decorators, who put plants around an infrastructure facilities' unused grounds (tellingly called "roadside greenery"). The ecology-oriented members of the profession on the other hand, are usually seen as nature preservers who fight to avoid, compensate for, or at least minimize so-called interventions in nature, made by engineers, architects, and even their own colleagues (and here once again, the name for this is telling enough:

"supplementary planning for landscape conservation"). One creates a supplementary landscape deco whenever the budget allows or where it will not disturb or disrupt. The other struggles to conserve specific landscape fragments and instrumentalizes rare animal and plant species for the fight against large-scale infrastructure projects. The cohesion within the discipline of Landscape Architecture is threatened by a possible division into two different fields: that of design-based project planning that mainly focuses on small-scale schemes, and the large-scale landscape planning that focuses on legislative instruments.

However Landscape Architecture, in all its professional complexity, does in fact possess specific expertise that enables the discipline to play an integrative role in fundamental decision-making regarding infrastructure, spatial design approaches, and ecological landscape development strategies:

— Landscape architects are able to link the knowledge gained from both the natural sciences and the engineering sciences by means of artistic and architectural strategies, and hence, can create an exciting relationship between natural landscape elements, technical systems, and the human environment.

— Landscape architects are typically used to thinking across the board, and to recognizing and conceptually including the correlation between the large-scale, systematic level of landscape (meaning the interaction between ground, water, topography, vegetation, climate, and the built urban space), and the small-scale project (for instance, park or town square).

— Landscape architects are knowledgeable about the specifics of different disciplines (such as ecology, water management, soil science, urban planning, agriculture, transport planning), and therefore are able to communicate with very different disciplines, work closely with them, and integrate different discipline-specific notions of space into their projects.

How can landscape architects develop these specific abilities further and apply them to designing infrastructure systems in landscape? And what role would topology play in that respect?

Topological Understanding of Space and Design

Studio urbane Landschaften a trans-disciplinary network for education, research, and practice developed a specific approach to designing urban landscapes and infrastructure systems as—in the words of Hille von Seggern—a "multi-dimensional performative process" (von Seggern et. al. 2008). Their approach particularly looks to identify the changing dynamics of the respective space and then to develop potentials and practical approaches, in order to contribute to the space's development and design.

This approach is rooted in a notion of space called topology. This concept is different to a purely geometric or topographical understanding of space, which reduces a site's visible spatial form to the Euclidian concept of a concrete spatial entity based on three dimensions (height, length, width). The definition of space as "surface area and three-dimensional borders" (Loidl, Bernard 2003, p. 48) is widespread among landscape architects. Representations of landscape as Euclidian space—in the form of maps, sections, models, or pictures—may well describe what landscape looks like formally, but they only represent a type of snapshot, which, due to various factors, changes constantly. Landscape is characterized by growth and cultivation, by the change of season, droughts, and floods, as well as its use and alterations by humans.

Cartographic representations of water in landscape are good examples of how limited purely geometric descriptions of space are in expressing landscape. They usually display clearly defined, fixed borders between water and land—which also greatly influences how we imagine them to be. But how can a shoreline be pictorially represented when it constantly fluctuates due to varying water levels, shifts in time and space? In his book, *The Conquest of Nature* (Blackbourn 2006), David Blackbourn asserts the theory that Johann Gottfried Tulla's "Rhine-rectification" was largely motivated by the fact that the dynamics of the River Rhine conflicted with permanently demarking its shores. Maps can only be drawn and borders defined if the waters' shorelines are fixed—human rationale triumphs over dynamic, landscape-changing natural processes. Even today, the floor plans, sections, renderings, and the various forms of models that we use to present and sell our designs are still predominantly based on a Euclidian understanding of space. Yet, they are very limited in their ability to integrate and communicate the dynamic forces that alter space.

Studio Urbane Landschaften developed a topological understanding of space and design, which relates the appearance of space to the spatial processes that shape and continuously change it. In this sense, space is not a fixed, defined form, but is continuously generated by the natural and social processes of spatial alteration and the corresponding socially and culturally influenced perception of space. Space is an expression of the interaction between human intervention and natural processes—and hence, more an "perfomative process" than a "form." From a topological perspective, the geometric concreteness of space plays a lesser role than the perception and description of the processes by which it is generated and altered. "Topologies do not consider spatial conditions, they examine the basic structural alternatives of spatial organization. [...] They abstract concrete, factual characteristics in order to recognize their underlying, basic topological patterns" (Sick 2012, p. 9).

The large-scale view of landscape in particular needs new approaches and design methods, in order to reveal the correlations that produce landscape, and to be able to work with and design them. Urban landscapes are characterized by complex processes and abiotic, biotic, and cultural factors that overlap in various, dynamic ways and are constantly generating unforeseen, diverse new spatial types. These spatial types are influenced by various, reciprocally influential urban and natural challenges, such as: the simultaneous processes of shrinking and growing cities, rising spatial disparities, increasing informal and uncontrollable dynamics of global change, escalating influences of weather-related problems due to climate change, infrastructure's inability to adapt to or function with unanticipated developments, or the increasing influence of urban material flows on the ecosystem. In order to develop large-scale landscapes in the face of this great complexity, it is necessary to manage the complex relationships between natural spatial factors, spatial development trends, and human needs and to design their interaction. In other words, in our understanding we landscape architects do not form landscapes, but rather design their emergence as a "multidimensional performative process" (von Seggern, Werner 2008, p. 35).

The Euclidian, measurable, static understanding of space is beginning to make way for a more dynamic, processual, relational concept in other disciplines as well. In mathematics, Gottfried Wilhelm von Leibniz was the first to develop the topology theory to characterize properties of mathematical structures that are under continuous deformation. Meaning, this is not a geometrical description of spatial structures in terms of metric calculations, but rather the description of spatial points in relation to their continuous and flexible positions as a network. Even in the humanities, the "spatial turn" led to a more dynamic understanding of space: away from the "localization thinking of representation" and toward a "changeable,

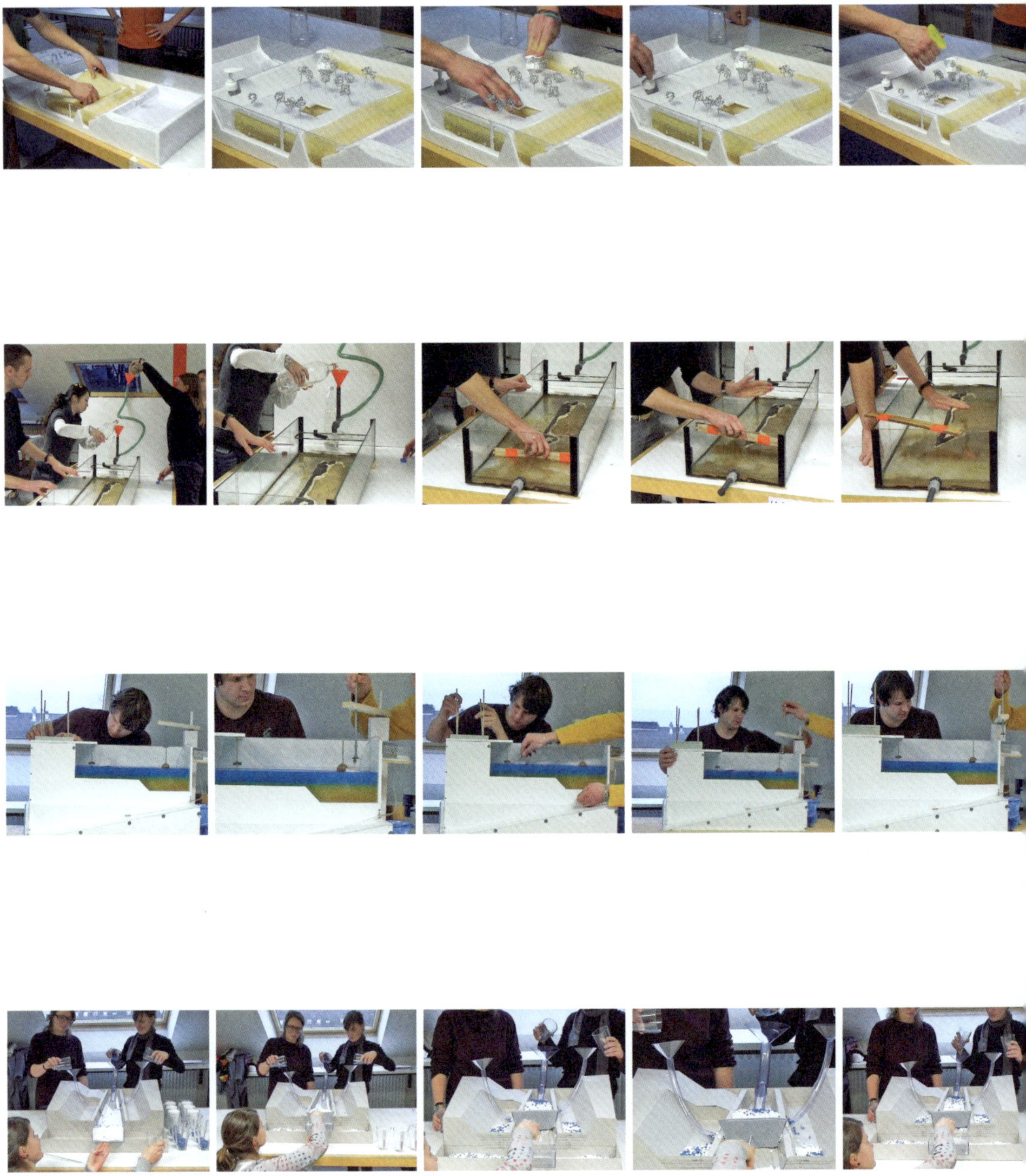

Models as “landscape machines”: representation of landscape as a performative process, including the influences of natural and human processes on spatial change.

time-based field of relation"—termed "emplacement" by Foucault (Dünne 2009, p. 5). In the field of ecology, Canadian C.S. Holling developed a hypothesis, which diverged from the ideal climax theory of ecological systems based on equilibrium, of ecological systems' continuous, sometimes sudden change on different scales of space and time—not as an exception to be prevented, but as the foundation of the resilience of ecosystems (Kaufmann, Blum 2013, p. 101).

Understanding and Designing Landscape as Infrastructure

Studio Urbane Landschaften's topological understanding of space and design is an important foundation, from which landscape architects may contribute to a large-scale development and design of landscape as infrastructure.

Natural spaces, their specific qualities, and different time-based dynamics are the "basis" for human use and change of space through infrastructure. A landscape's natural spatial components—meaning its geography, topography, hydrology, climate, and vegetation—also exist and change independent of human intervention. Moreover, natural spaces have very diverse physical characteristics and a variety of dynamics that also affect their spatial and physical qualities. It is up to us to recognize the specific dynamics of ecosystems, to control them by means of design and forms of cultivation, and to optimize them for human needs—as well as to communicate the resulting strategies to the respective clients and cooperation partners. Natural systems such as soil, water, vegetation, or microorganisms have an autonomous ability to form structures, and an innate function that can be used and even improved within a design context. We need to show that the value of a designed landscape is not purely in its formal, aesthetic experience of colors, shapes and forms. The beauty of landscapes is based on a performative aesthetic that results from our interpretation

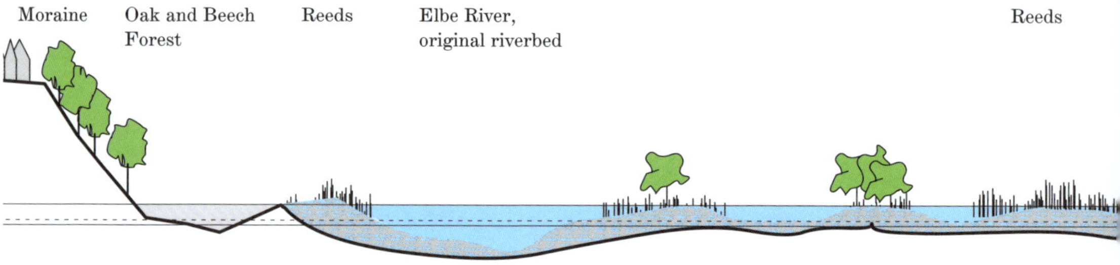

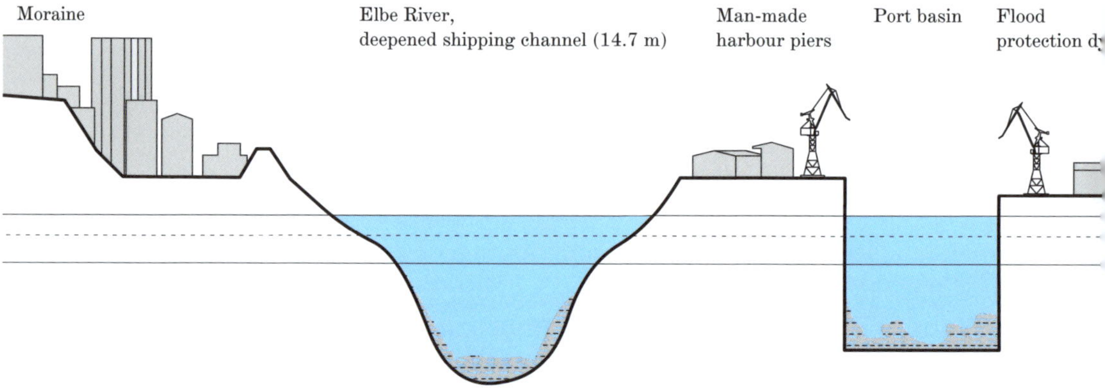

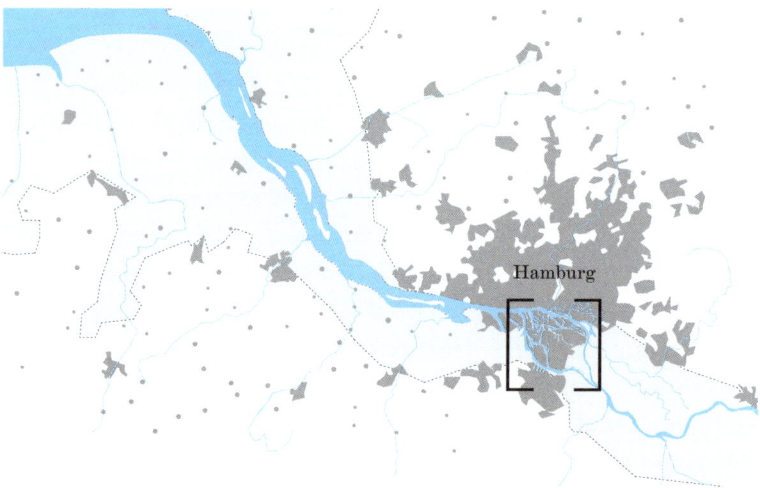

The transformation of the Elbe Islands from archipelago to flood-protected harbor and hamlet landscape: The intense remodeling, through deepening the Elbe and reducing floodable areas by elevating the land mass and building dikes, led to a problematic increase of the tidal range and sedimentation process.

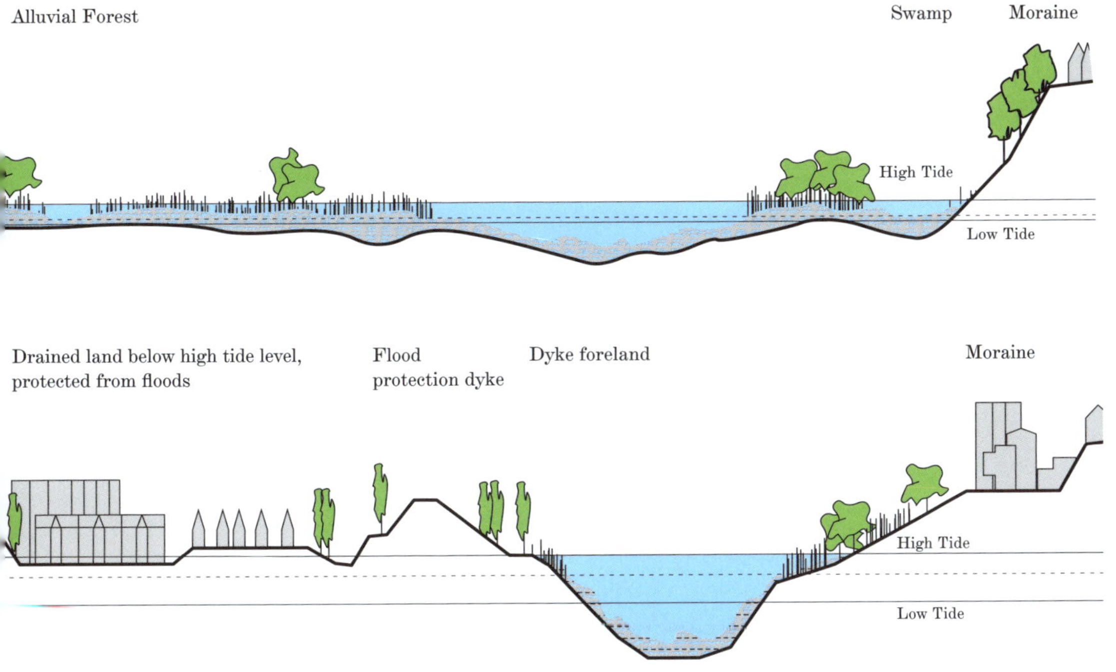

Principle sections through the area of the Elbe island where the river branches.
Top: state after the last ice age about 20,000 years ago.

of the interplay with other systems such as city, society, water cycles, infrastructure, or biodiversity.

This way of looking at landscape allows the perspective to change from seeing infrastructure as an isolated layer and system separate from landscape, to a holistic vision for a completely new landscape: one that integrates infrastructure systems and becomes infrastructure in itself. Designing landscape as infrastructure or designing infrastructure in landscape is always an expression of the dynamic interplay of culture and nature. Their different forces have to be intertwined in such a way as to develop at best a synergetic productivity that results from merging rather than opposing specific qualities. There is a great need for action, as evidenced by the lack of acceptance and increasing social conflict regarding diverse types of large-scale infrastructure projects. How can landscape architects position themselves to actively contribute to designing infrastructural changes in our landscape, by applying a topological understanding of landscape and design?

The results of two research projects by *Studio Urbane Landschaften* aim to support landscape architects in their collaboration with other disciplines in understanding and designing water landscapes and urban rivers as possible topological spaces.

Wasseratlas (Water Atlas) IBA Hamburg—WaterLand Topologies for the Elbe Island in Hamburg

The Internationale Bauausstellung (IBA) theme of "Stadt im Klimawandel" (Cities and Climate Change) is dedicated to prospective ways of dealing with the qualities and dangers of urban development in water landscape zones. Worldwide, two-thirds of all large metropolises with over five million inhabitants are located in low-lying estuaries, and are especially threatened by a climate-induced rise in sea levels and the frequent, increased danger of flooding. The Water Atlas is a project by *Studio Urbane Landschaften* commissioned by the IBA (2008). It is a means to provide a new view of the complex water-related relationships of the Elbe Island and to enable the development prospects that arise as a result. It served as a guideline for the further development and qualification of different IBA projects in relation to relevant water issues, as well as a future point of reference and basis for design for the planners and architects on the Elbe Islands.

The first part of Water Atlas presents the extremely dynamic and changing topographical relationship between water and land as a decisive criterion for the Elbe Islands. Despite the 110-kilometer distance to the North Sea, its tidal effect pushes ocean water against the directional flow into the River Elbe twice a day, causing the water level near Hamburg to fluctuate as much as three-and-a-half meters. Due to the need to protect people from flooding and to keep reclaimed land dry, raised linear areas (dikes/walls) or surface areas (landfill/polders) were built onto the originally flat, alluvial land. This decreased the surface areas into which water could potentially spread during high tide and heavy flood events. This means that increased intensity of human intervention has caused water levels and tide amplitudes to rise considerably over the last century. Consequently, the dikes and landfills were raised higher and higher while the River Elbe was made deeper and deeper for harbors and ships, making the difference in height between land and water even more extreme. The dramatic changes in the Elbe Islands' water-land dynamics are reflected in a permanent and fluctuating topographical reshaping: onshore, land-raising in the form of bollards and dikes, and in the water, deepening of the navigational routes and harbor basins.

The highly dynamic water-land topographies form the basis of a topological starting point for future interpretations of the Elbe Islands, which is open to new designed forms. This topological understanding of space developed for Water Atlas describes the Elbe Islands in terms of the

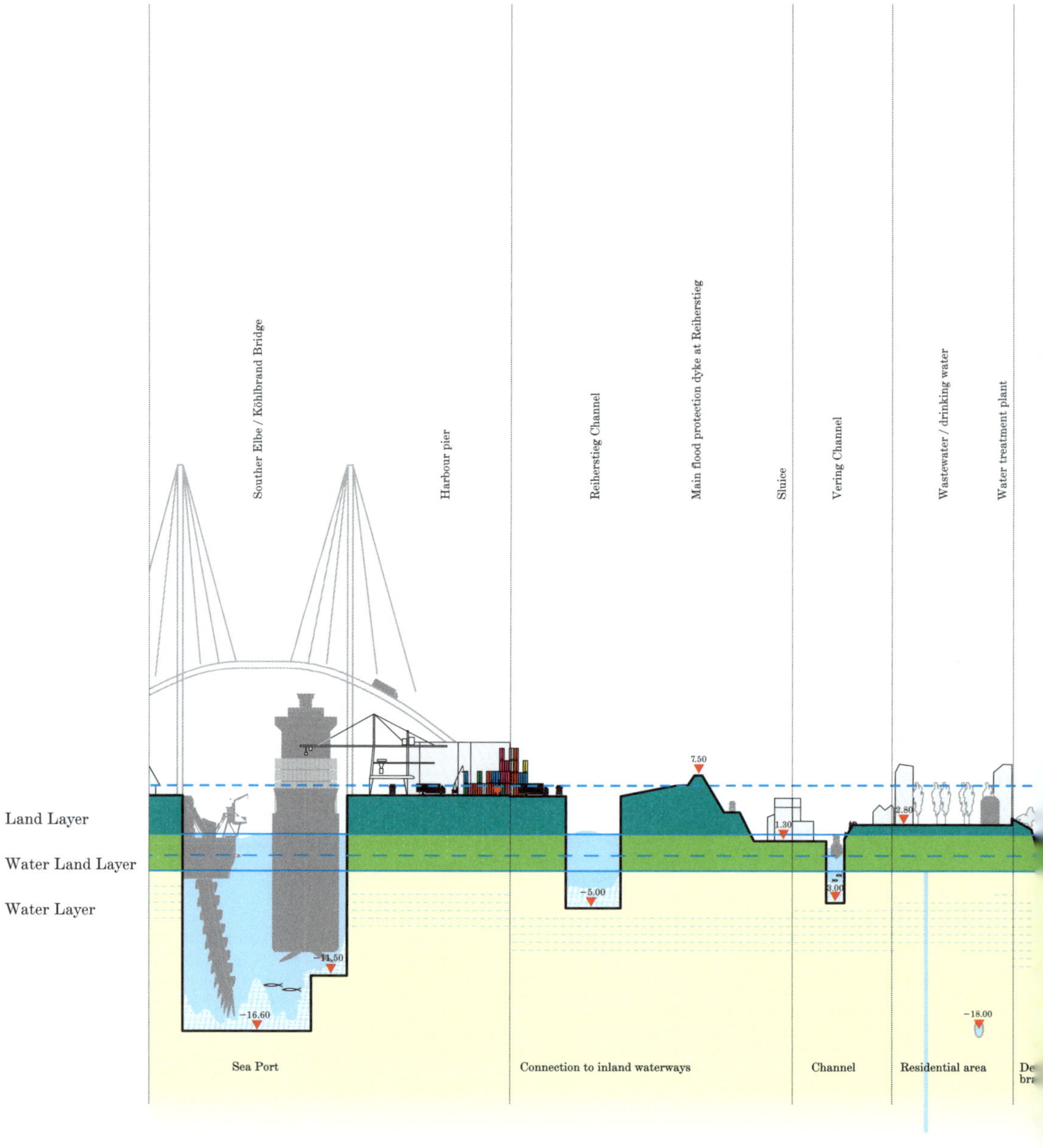

This principle section shows the relationship between the three areas of process, spatial typologies, and the infrastructure systems that shape them, such as dikes, sluices, weirs, and pumping stations. These technical elements represent boundaries as well as transitions between the different process areas—they are the foundation for the appearance and use of space.

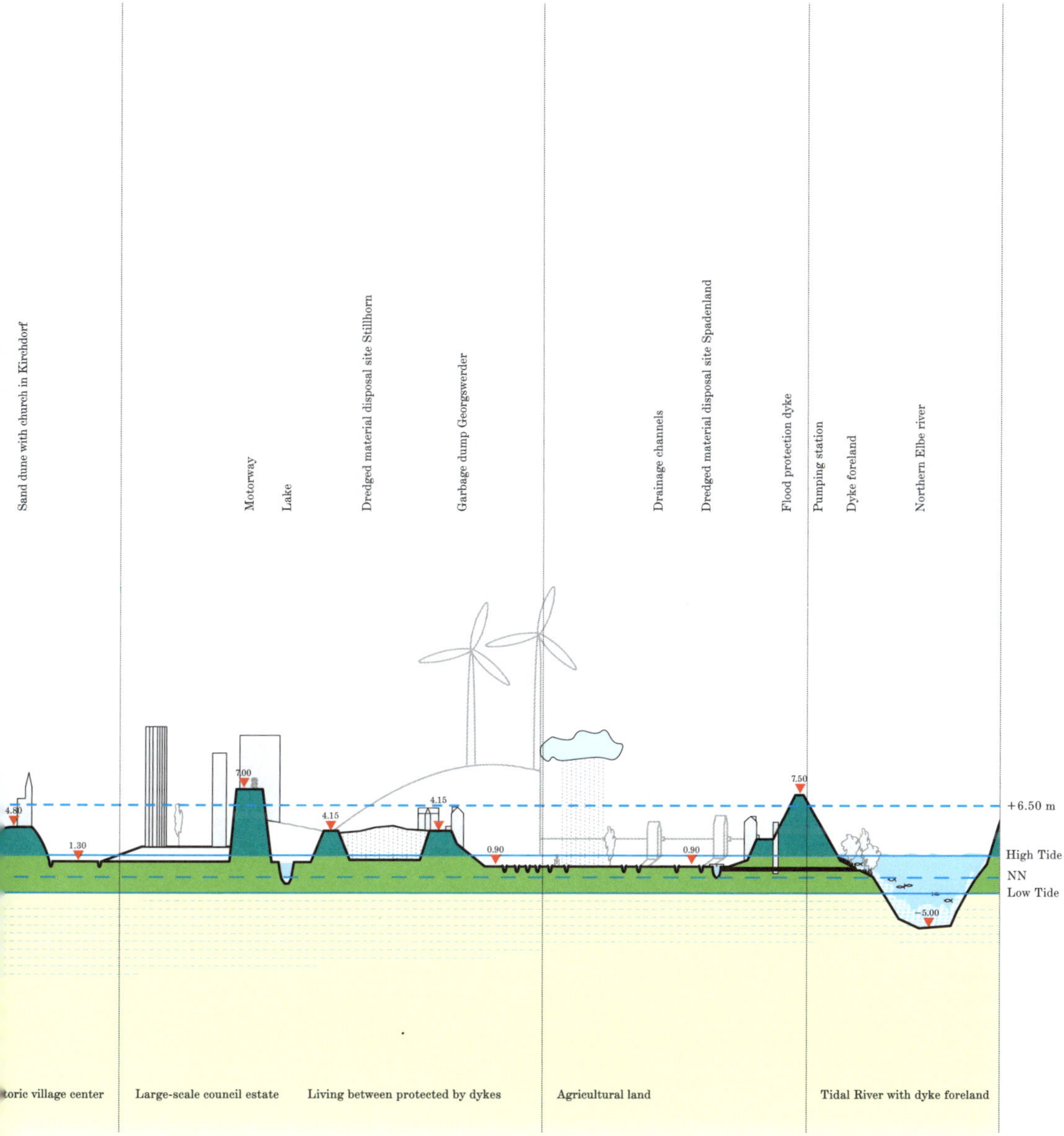

Sand dune with church in Kirchdorf
Motorway
Lake
Dredged material disposal site Stillhorn
Garbage dump Georgswerder
Drainage channels
Dredged material disposal site Spadenland
Flood protection dyke
Pumping station
Dyke foreland
Northern Elbe river
4.80
1.30
7.00
4.15
4.15
0.90
0.90
7.50
−5.00
+6.50 m
High Tide
NN
Low Tide
toric village center
Large-scale council estate
Living between protected by dykes
Agricultural land
Tidal River with dyke foreland

relationship between topography, water fluctuations and landscape structure, using three characteristic spatial layers: the water level below medium-low tide, (<-1.53 m), the water-land-layer between medium-low tide and high tide (-1.53 m to $+2.09$ m), and the land layer above the daily flood line ($>+2.09$ m). These spatial layers change form constantly in terms of their position, expansiveness, and height—but the inner logic of their topological spatial landscape structure remains constant despite the change in form. The first part of Water Atlas describes the characteristic landscape experience of the above-mentioned, three spatial layers. Photos, maps, diagrams, and texts illustrate the interplay of human influence, topography, and water dynamics, which, in relation to the respective layers, can form the basis of core questions and possible approaches for the future development of the Elbe Islands.

By looking at the Elbe Island as a topological space for opportunity, the existing structures are represented as a pictorial, topological interpretation of a changeable network, and not purely as the given spatial-physical characteristics in the form of aerial views, city maps, or master plans. A topological perspective reveals the structures of and the relationships between water, land, infrastructure, and buildings. This interpretation portrays the islands as a space for opportunity, which is defined and transformed by water and land dynamics. It also reveals design possibilities that can be indicated using design scenarios based on different approaches to managing these dynamics.

Designing various possible developments requires an understanding and a conscious, solution-oriented treatment and design of the dynamics that underlie the visual appearance of the Elbe Island's different landscape elements—because a design approach that ignores these dynamics and focuses purely on the appearance of the landscape will not develop long-term qualities. Representing these relationships based on their underlying dynamics and addressing existing structures based on their origins is a prerequisite for describing them in a new way, developing them further, and designing with them. In this respect, the Water Atlas serves as a water-conceived, spatial, and dynamic planning tool of the Elbe island.

In the context of the IBA laboratories, several design workshops were organized, which built on the perspectives and design methodology developed in Water Atlas, involving different professional disciplines as well as the public. They resulted in further projects for infrastructural spaces, such as a development strategy for the tidal city of Hamburg, based on the Hamburg Port Authority's Tidal Elbe Concept, or the Deichpark concept, in cooperation with the Landesbetrieb Straßen, Brücken und Gewässer (Hamburg Office for Roads, Bridges and Open Waters), which is responsible for building dikes (von Seggern 2012, Stokman 2013).

River. Space. Design.—Planning Strategies, Methods and Projects for Urban Streams

Many communities in Germany and in Europe are facing the challenge resulting from the current EU-Water Framework Directive and the EU-Floods Directive to develop their flowing waters to be more natural looking, and at the same time take account of increased flood protection requirements. These guidelines prioritize the aspects of water morphology and ecology. Yet these should not be examined in isolation because rivers and riverbanks are vital urban open spaces, which are important for the quality of life in increasingly urbanized societies. These extremely different demands often have to be reconciled in the smallest of spaces, which necessitates an integrative approach. Yet hydraulic engineering, nature conservation, landscape architecture, and urban planning do not often collaborate sufficiently to integrate the complex, dynamic water processes into the design of urban riverspaces.

This was the focus of "River. Space. Design."—a project sponsored by Deutsche Forschungsgemeinschaft (German

List of process spaces and design strategies

A Embankment Walls and Promenades

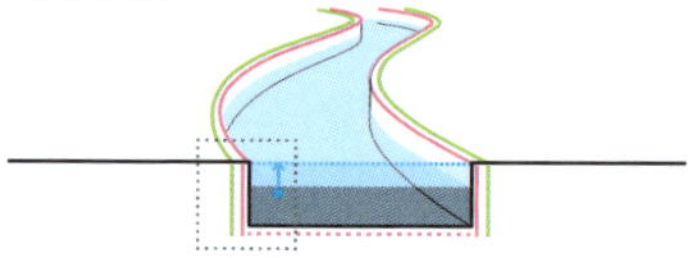

B Dikes and Flood Walls

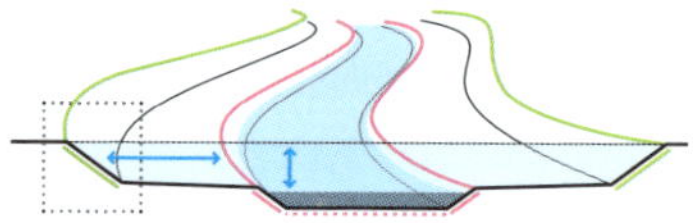

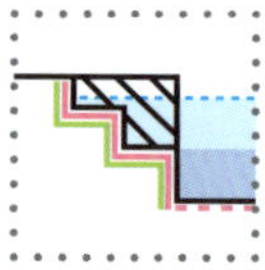

A1
Linear spatial expansion

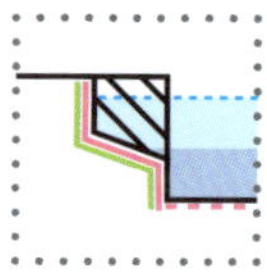

A2
Selective spatial expansion

A3
Temporary resistance

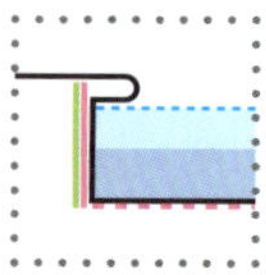

A4
Placing over the water

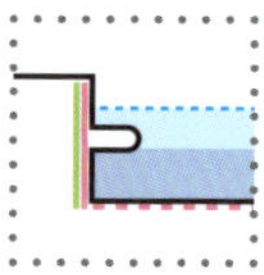

A5
Tolerating

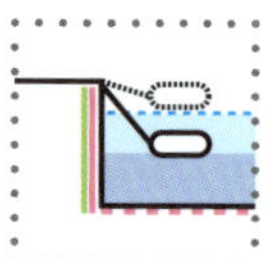

A6
Adapting

B1
Differentiating resistance

B2
Vertical resistance

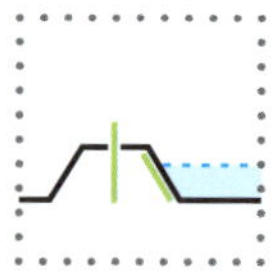

B3
Reinforcing resistance

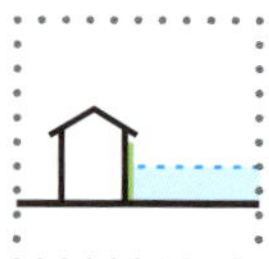

B4
Integrating resistance

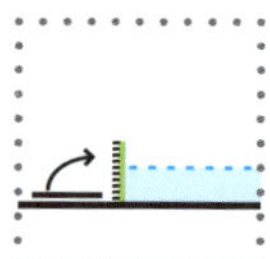

B5
Temporary resistance

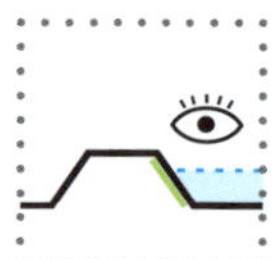

B6
Making river dynamics evident

C Flood Areas

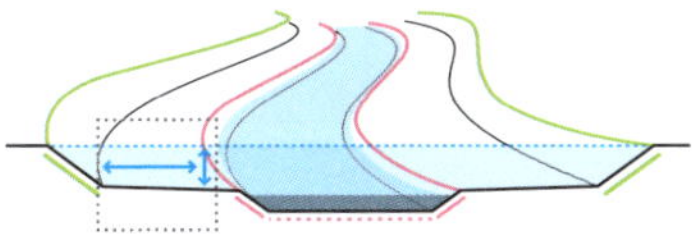

C1
Extending the space

C2
Placing over the water

C3
Tolerating

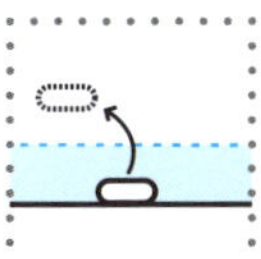

C4
Evading

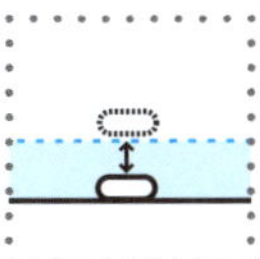

C5
Adapting

D Riverbeds and Currents

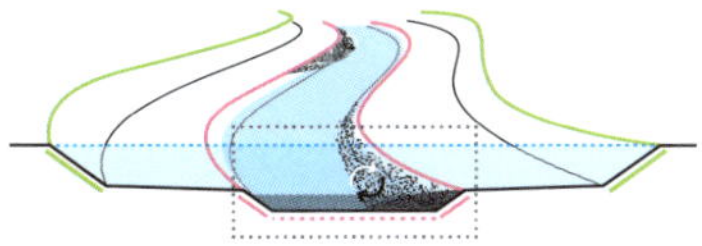

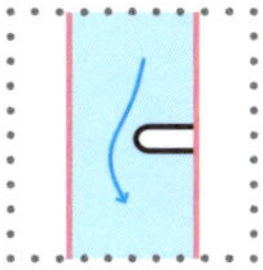

D1
Deflecting the current

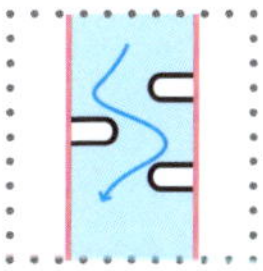

D2
Grading the channel

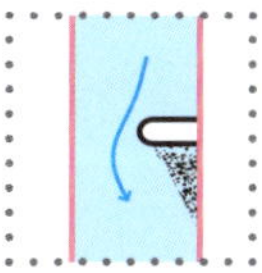

D3
Varying the riverbed

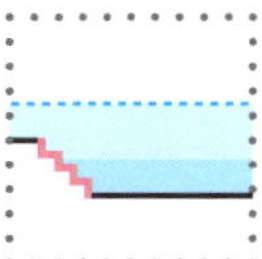

D4
Varying the bank reinforcement

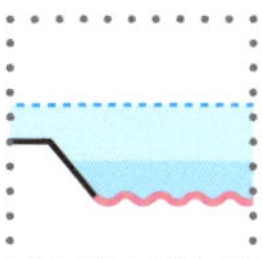

D5
Varying the riverbed reinforcement

E Dynamic River Landscapes

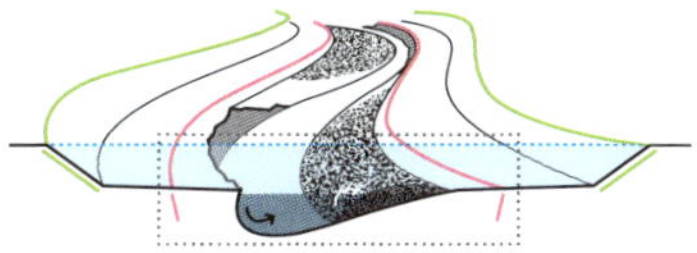

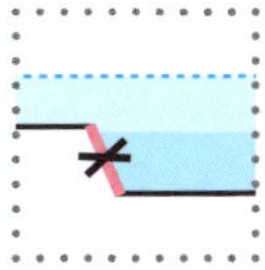

E1
Allowing channel migration

E2
Initiating channel dynamics

E3
Creating new channels

E4
Restricting channel dynamics

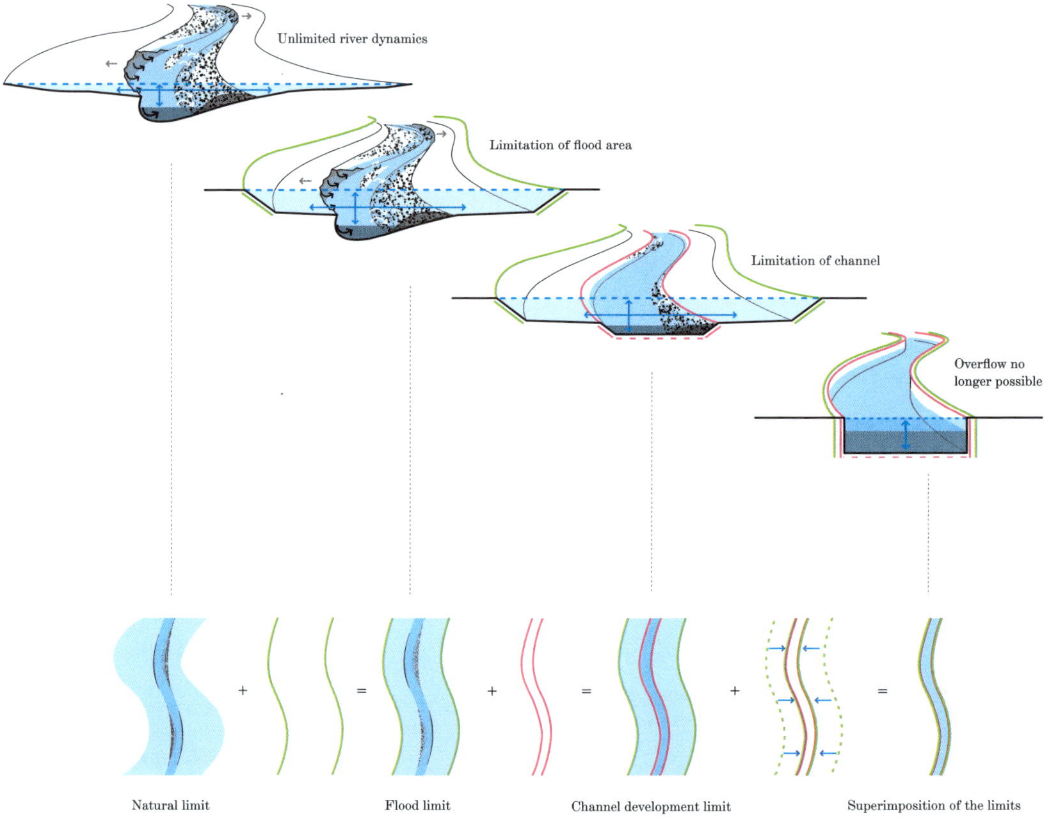

On most rivers natural processes have been either restricted or are completely controlled. The flood limits (green line), set for instance by a dike, delineate the flood area. The limitation of the self-dynamic river channel development (red line) through, for example, embankment walls or low weirs curtails any shifting of the channel.

Research Foundation)—which resulted in a book that serves as an important aid for designing urban streams. The project involved visiting approximately fifty built projects that all followed a process-oriented approach: their design incorporates the dynamic changes of water via water level fluctuation and morphodynamic erosion and sediment processes.

The selected projects were subjected to a comparative analysis in order to examine different design strategies and typological design methods in relation to their processual, reciprocal effects with water dynamics. These were systemized in a topological structure and presented in the form of a graphic network of logical if-then relationships, which could be combined flexibly for future design assignments. The different ways of dealing with process borders was identified as a key design parameter. These could be designed in various spatial interrelationships: lines, objects, or spaces—for instance in the form of bank reinforcements, dikes or floodplains—establish different borders for water processes, and thereby influence the processes of flooding, sedimentation, and erosion. Human-built borders and natural water processes relate differently to one another in the various projects. Case study findings isolated five types of process spaces that are characterized by how the positions of their varying borders relate to each other, and, subsequently, to assign different design strategies and design methods to each one. These demonstrate basic topological patterns and explain which design method should be applied to which situation and how these might be combined. Intelligent reconstruction, transformation, and expansion of process borders in the various process spaces generate a set of new dynamics that lead to a shift in the stream of flowing waters. Humans cannot completely control water processes, but they can influence them through understanding the process, and guide them along deliberately set borders.

The results were published in the form of a book which can be used as a Topological Atlas. The book consists of two interconnected sections that allow the reader to examine the systematic design catalog and project catalog simultaneously. The many illustrations, clear layout, and comprehensive glossary make it an easy-to-use, graphic reference book for the process-oriented design of urban streams. One important aim of the research was to develop new ways of publicizing and representing the results, because a linear sequence of texts and graphics—as is typical for standard books—would not have been able to conceptually represent the complex relationship between process spaces and design methods. Shifting the focus to the systematization of dynamic waters processes and their human-made borders led to the development of a design tool that aids in a fresh understanding and an innovative design of river spaces and their processes.

Prospects

Designing infrastructure systems as landscape is a practice of intertwining landscape with built infrastructure. Landscape takes on an infrastructure dimension and must be designed with this in mind. The lack of building culture, often criticized in the current debate concerning the relationship between infrastructure and landscape, cannot be blamed on the ignorance of engineers alone. Planning legislative procedures, technical necessities, and the political compulsion to act, all direct attention to the large-scale, strategic potential of qualified landscape development through infrastructure systems. The interdisciplinary and visionary levels this requires can and must be initiated by the spatial planning and designing disciplines. Urban planner Thomas Sieverts, in his speech on the occasion of the IBA prelude in Hamburg, emphasized the importance of "design and urban planning inclusion of large systems," because these "tend to be self-sufficient, almost autistic, self-referential and isolated." According to Sieverts, they are characterized by a "professional cronyism of experts and institutions that form a completely closed system that is almost impossible to penetrate by planning or civil society." And when asked which discipline is best suited to designing one of these urban landscapes that comprehensively and extensively integrate large systems, he replied, "There is a new discipline emerging in this field—Urban Landscape Architecture—and it is still open as to whether urban planners will play an important role or whether they will hand this over to the landscape architects" (2004).

Because landscape architects possess a comprehensive, synthetic understanding of design and landscape, they now have the opportunity to reposition themselves in the field and assume a leading role—in close cooperation with other disciplines. This necessitates developing new strategies in order to initiate the appropriate projects, in which landscape architects can take on the appropriate role. These strategies will be described below using the terms "Understanding," "Integrating," and "Influencing."

To recognize the design of landscape as infrastructure, or infrastructure in landscape, as an interesting future task for landscape architecture requires a great amount of "understanding" regarding the logics, specialist discourses, and conceptual approaches of different expert communities. Particularly important is awareness and knowledge about current challenges, changing paradigms, and new engineering technologies that are the essential starting points and drivers of change in infrastructure systems. Thus, for instance, new energy policies convey a move towards renewable, decentralized, more landscape-related forms of energy, as well as new routes and storage elements for the distribution and supply of energy. The EU-Water Framework Directive and the EU-Floods Directive demand an integrated view of water, city, and landscape, with the aim of establishing integrated management and flood control plans and determining the appropriate measures to achieve these goals. The level of knowledge of many landscape architects in relation to these current problems is often still too low to find specialist links and to participate on an equal footing by developing design solutions for these future tasks. An open and inquiring debate is essential to discovering the scope, potential, and possibilities for change within infrastructure issues, which seem to be purely determined by laws, regulations, and technical rules. For instance, does a dike have to be just a technical flood protection structure, or can it be designed as an attractive and multifunctional element of the city, of course under compliance with rules of technical security? Or, can dikes be constructed in a different process, with a different shape and height if floodwaters are given more space and the city is developed into a flood-adapted city?

The second strategy is that of "integrating." Based on understanding and new ideas for designing the variable network between landscape, infrastructure, and society, we need to actively integrate with the process of change and cooperate with the actors who greatly influence this change. We cannot wait until we are asked, nor can we expect to be asked. We have to devise strategies and actively approach the experts and institutions that do not open by themselves and traditionally form closed systems. To do this, we could attend interdisciplinary conferences and workshops, or events organized by other specialist disciplines, in order to familiarize ourselves with their conceptual approaches and projects and to talk with them. We need to find situations where landscape architects can make a decisive contribution, but have yet to be invited to do so; and identify connecting factors for new forms of collaboration with projects, institutions, or persons from other disciplines by connecting our proposals with their strategies. Therefore, we need to actively bring our ideas, about how we can contribute to the problem at hand and what the appropriate tasks might be, to potential clients and colleagues. It is essential here to emphasize the added value that such a collaboration would mean for all sides:

expressing appreciation, discussing on equal terms, and thinking in synergies. The objective is the collaboration and new alliances between very different actors in infrastructure and landscape development: agriculture and forestry, road and water engineers, industrial companies, environmentalists, residents, and municipalities—all contribute to shaping a common vision of landscape. Developing design approaches, images, and procedures for this is a very exciting task for landscape architects. One positive, prime example for such an approach is the collaborative projects between the Hamburg Port Authority and the IBA Hamburg. Their interdisciplinary project Kreetsand, a pilot project in the framework of the "Elbe Tidal Concept" of the Hamburg Port Authority (HPA), demonstrates how the once impenetrable and closed system of the Port Authority contributes significantly to the holistic development of connecting transition zones between land and water (Meine 2013).

The third strategy is "influencing" new task fields, procedures, laws, as well as initiating new projects. New ideas and approaches are met with considerable resistance by economic factors, as well as building and planning legislation. For all parties involved, collaborating on interdisciplinary projects is conceptually, procedurally, and legislatively new territory, and there are still countless questions regarding whether and how. Research is just beginning in many areas. Moreover, practice is often far removed from research and trapped in long-established routines. In order to reduce these obstacles in the long term, we need to develop new formats of cooperation and innovative pilot projects, working at the interface of research, practice, and education. Even on the level of education, it is important to promote action-oriented, transdisciplinary learning, and sensitize students in various courses of study for integrated approaches and tasks. Open-ended, experimental, and playful interdisciplinary knowledge production by students, whose minds are not yet constrained by the established practice, can contribute significantly. In order to promote a change towards interdisciplinary planning and design culture, research has to develop innovative forms of dialogue and cooperation between the previously separate spheres of different disciplines, which integrate these into the practice.

This requires a self-confident discipline of landscape architecture that is able to develop visions and implement them; that knows the procedures and rules and how to apply them—but also dares to break and re-invent them; that is able to cooperate and communicate; and, above all is passionate.

Blackbourn, D. (2006): *The Conquest of Nature. Water, Landscape and the Making of Modern Germany.* Jonathan Cape Press, London.
Dünne, J. (2009): "Geschichten im Raum und Raumgeschichte, Topologie und Topographie," in: Universität Potsdam (ed.): *Dynamisierte Räume. Zur Theorie der Bewegung in den romanischen Kulturen*, Potsdam.
Graham, S., Marvin, S. (2001): *Splintering Urbanism: Networked Infrastructures, Technological Mobilities and the Urban Condition.* Routledge, London/New York.
Günzel, S. (2007): "Raum—Topographie—Topologie." in: id.: Günzel, S. (ed.): *Topologie. Zur Raumbeschreibung in den Kultur- und Medienwissenschaften.* Transcript Verlag, Bielefeld, pp. 13–29.
Heidenreich, E. (2004): *Fließräume. Die Vernetzung von Natur, Raum und Gesellschaft seit dem 19. Jahrhundert.* Campus Verlag, Frankfurt.
IBA Hamburg / Studio Urbane Landschaften (eds.) (2008): *Wasseratlas. WasserLand-Topologien für die Hamburger Elbinsel.* jovis Verlag, Berlin.
Kaufmann, S., Blum, S. (2013): "Vulnerabilität und Resilienz," in: von Detten, R.; Faber, F.; Bemman, M. (eds.): *Unberechenbare Umwelt: Zum Umgang mit Unsicherheit und Nicht-Wissen.* Springer Fachmedien, Wiesbaden.
Loidl, H., Bernard, S. (2003): *Freiräume. Entwerfen als Landschaftsarchitektur.* Birkhäuser Verlag, Berlin.
Meine, M. (2013): *The Kreetsand project: a pilot for the "Tidal Elbe Concept" and integrated estuarine management in practice*, Hamburg.
Picon, A. (2005): "Constructing Landscape by Engineering Water," in: Institute for Landscape Architecture, ETH Zürich (ed.): *Landscape Architecture in Mutation.* Zurich, pp. 99–114.
Prominski, M., Stokman, A., Zeller, S., Stimberg, D., Voermanek, H. (2012): *River. Space. Design.* Birkhäuser Verlag, Berlin.
Schulz, H. (2004) "Stadt als Sukzessionsform. Wenn im Prozess des Schrumpfens Stadt zum Teil der Landschaft wird," in: *Planerin* 1/2004, pp. 58–60.
Von Seggern, H. (2012): "Towards Creative Knowledge," in: Dietrich, L., Hendriks, M., Kandjee, T., Moll, C. (eds.): *Touch. Landscape Architecture Europe.* Basel, Wageningen, pp. 194–200.
Von Seggern, H., Sieverts, T. (2006): "Gestaltung der Stadtregion als Landschaft," in: DGGL (ed.): *Regionale Gartenkultur. Über die Identität von Landschaften.* Callwey Verlag, Munich, pp. 14–19.
Von Seggern, H., Werner, J. (2008): "Designing as an Integrative Process of Creating Knowledge," in: Von Seggern, H., Werner, J., Grosse-Bächle, L. (eds.): *Creating Knowledge.* jovis Verlag, Berlin, pp. 35–66.
Sick, F. (2012). *Stadtraum, Stadtlandschaft, Karte.* Narr Verlag, Tübingen.
Sieverts, T. (2004): "Entwicklung der Metropolen im Zeitalter der Globalisierung im Focus von Siedlungsstruktur und Gesellschaftsentwicklung oder Unbestimmtheit im Städtebau unter den Bedingungen der dritten Moderne als kreativer Antrieb für eine Hamburger Bauausstellung".
Stokman, A. (2013): "Dike Park Elbe Island—Towards flood-adapted design strategies for Hamburg's urban coastline," in: ETH Zürich (ed.): *Rising Waters, Shifting Lands.* gta-publishers, Zurich, pp. 51–61.

Function, Fiction, Form, and Feeling On the "Aesthetic of Pleasantness"—[1] in Landscape Architecture

Wulf Tessin

1 See Wulf Tessin: *Ästhetik des Angenehmen—Städtische Freiräume zwischen professioneller Ästhetik und Laiengeschmack*, Wiesbaden 2008.

What role does beauty play for the user in relation to landscape and urban open spaces? How can one develop an aesthetic of landscape architecture from its use? Both of these questions will be addressed in the following essay, in which I would also like to somewhat vary and expand upon the well-known adage "form follows function"—first in relation to the meaning of the catchphrase "form follows fiction" within the context of postmodern architecture, and then regarding the theory that "form follows emotion" or "fun." This essay, in other words, focuses on the issues of function, fiction, form, and feeling.

1. Function: Pleasant Leisure Time Behavior

People obviously do a variety of things in landscape and in urban open spaces: they go for walks, hikes, they play, jog, lie in the sun, converse, celebrate, have picnics, read, take their dogs for walks, observe and enjoy nature, watch their children at play, look at clouds, and at everything creeping, crawling, and flowering. This list of outdoor leisure activities is obviously so long and heterogeneous that it is difficult to develop design ideas in direct relation to "form follows function," other than specific user programs and furnishing elements like pathways, benches, shelters, mini-golf courses, or nature trails.

Now, with the above in mind, if one generally questions the function of open spaces or landscape beyond specific outdoor activities, one arrives at paraphrases such as leisure, rest and relaxation, social reprieve, or what the Kaplans—[2] described as "psychological restoration." Their studies led them to the conclusion that people, when asked to describe places that make them feel particularly good, overwhelmingly preferred (apart from their "own homes") nature or landscapes or "green" areas as feel-good places. The subjects were then asked to describe in detail why such places made them feel so good. It was quickly established that these were places in which they sought and found various forms of "psychological restoration." Planted, green, outdoor areas serve as places of psychological restoration, as feel-good places within an urban environment that may be interesting, and might offer everything imaginable, but is often stressful and tiring. This is when the desire arises to retreat to "one's own four walls" or "hit the countryside" and get away from it all—where focused attention is not required, but at best casual, aimless attention, or even none at all, which, of course, leads to a great deal of psychological restoration. However, feel-good places such as these are still stimulating enough not to be boring, because if they were, the feel-good factor would soon be over. Hence, it only transpires if the space allows for and supports enough of the outdoor leisure activities that people enjoy, activities that possess strong somatic, physiological connotations such as fresh air to breathe, sunshine on the skin, physical exercise and relaxation.

2 Rachel Kaplan and Stephen Kaplan, *The Experience of Nature: A Psychological Perspective*, New York 1989.

The above description of the function of urban open spaces and recreational landscapes as feel-good places quickly leads to the ancient notion of *locus amoenus*, meaning a green and calm place in which one can relax and spend leisure time. Perhaps etymologically derived from *a-munus*, it also suggests that a *locus amoenus* includes the enjoyment of being freed from work and obligations. We would speak today of "suspensive behavior." In other words, our behavior is attuned to "leisure," to recreation. Even when hiking, jogging, or gardening, these activities are—different to our busy day-to-day experience—self-determined. We alone establish the degree of strenuousness, concentration, work demand, and how many various inconveniences we are willing to accept. This of course includes the freedom to decide ourselves where, when, and how long we spend time at a place. Interactions with other visitors, if there are any, remain superficial, friendly, uncommitted, and can be terminated at any time; in our conservations awkward subjects are avoided, but for the most part, we prefer to be alone, which is a great social respite. Therefore, people can have very allergic reactions to any deviating behavior such as noise, vandalism, and alcohol, which is seen as unpleasant, even disruptive.

Thus recreational landscapes and urban open spaces viewed from this behavior program perspective tend to be pleasant places: they provide the stage for pleasant leisure activities, rest, and relaxation. In this context, Werner Nohl once even spoke of the "eudemonia of a successful social practice" that "shines through"—[3]; and Martin Seel of the "good life" that we apparently anticipate in nature and landscape.—[4] This is clearly an overstatement, but it nevertheless identifies already the fictional aspect of landscape and urban open spaces and the related outdoor behavior, an aspect that needs to be given consideration next.

3 Werner Nohl: *Freiraumarchitektur und Emanzipation*, Frankfurt am Main/Bern/Cirencester 1980, p. 370.

4 Martin Seel: *Eine Ästhetik der Natur*, Frankfurt am Main 1996, p. 353ff.

2. Fiction: Nature as a Pleasant Setting

Landscape and urban outdoor spaces suggest ideologically not only eudemonia or a good life, a piece of freedom; they are usually more or less green, offer some aspect of nature, and thus decisively profit from the positive image of nature in relation to society. Although greenery/nature/vegetation has meanwhile been socially molded and appropriated in many ways, it essentially evades complete assimilation by society. Its simple, self-evident existence—which knows neither past nor future, neither guilt nor sin, neither joy nor suffering, and embodies neither ambitions, values, purposes, reasons, nor artistic endeavors—presents a fundamentally different form of existence to that of human-social reality; it is a type of counter-world, a dimension of the "Other." It thus becomes an object of human longing, a place to escape to: the "remaining rest of nature" in humans that wishes to evade total socialization finds its apparent parallel in the "remaining nature" in urban parks and gardens. It becomes a synonym for social respite and a metaphor for everything that wants to retreat from society and city. We love the fresh air of nature in contrast to air-conditioned offices or the urban stench; its stillness in contrast to the noise and rush of the city; the relative spaciousness of landscape and park in contrast to the tightness of the closed rooms in which we work and live; the life of and in nature in contrast to the dead materials of stone, concrete, metal, paper, and plastic that dominate the city; the diversity and change of seasons in contrast to the uniformity and monotony of the built environment. We long for the, so to say, indifference of and in nature, in contrast to the human system of values, ranking, and relevance that dominates our lives.

Thus, urban green and recreational landscapes symbolize something that urban day-to-day life has long extinguished: nature, or better yet, "pleasant nature," because this nice ideology of nature as contrast to society embraces the fact that we want the nature in recreational landscapes and urban open spaces to be pleasant. We usually prefer parks to urban barren lots, steer clear of them in cold weather, rain, storm, or darkness. Of course we like a cozy, nearby café. We avoid rough nature, preferring it to be green and colorful instead of bare and wilted; we would rather sit on a park bench than on a rock or a felled tree stump. We like deer, butterflies, and swans. But forget ticks. The dense forest was long feared as a *locus terribilis*, a sinister, shadowy, dangerous place; clearings, on the other hand, enjoy a rather high rating. Hence, we do not let the "love of nature" that we relish in landscape and urban open spaces get too "wild"; it is limited to its pleasant aspects, to a well-rationed, agreeable measure of "real nature," which of course includes the "right" weather: warmth, sun, blue skies, fresh air. Yes, precisely this pleasant, appropriate weather is so atmospherically important, that to feel good "outside," an amiable green setting of trees and other vegetation is even not always crucial. Often, the main thing is sunshine and a clear blue sky.

3. Form: The Pleasant Measure

Landscape and urban green areas are feel-good places because they provide the stage for pleasant leisure activities in amiable, Arcadian, and ideologically enhanced green environments. Therefore, the specific design of these open spaces is essential for this pleasant feeling. The pleasant side of nature has to be displayed, but this does not necessarily require a highly sophisticated garden design: one associates these open spaces more with "nature" than with "art," which is why a type of naturalness and a pleasant, agreeable open space design is particularly important in order to achieve a *locus amoenus* feeling. Good accessibility, good usability, a lot of green, quietude, good maintenance, a friendly peaceful atmosphere, and nice weather are all practically indispensable. If these are available, and if the design remains within the context of common taste, which includes planning nature as an amiable setting, then the visitor will experience his or her stay as pleasant.

But if the design is more than just pleasant, but beautiful (in the eyes of the visitors) people will feel more than just "good." They will feel even joy and delight demonstrating the relevance of beauty in open space design. Yet the design's significance can also be shown in the opposite case. People will even avoid an open space such as a barren lot if its design is "unappealing" or "not evident." Fortunately, however, most urban outdoor spaces are designed within the accepted corridor of conventional taste. They are more or less nice and green, and to achieve the feeling of pleasantness, this amiable, conventional open space design in general is adequate.

Yes, a pleasant place needs not always be a visually "beautiful" place. People rate places according to their level of "pleasantness" more than according to their level of "beauty." The general rule for open spaces is as follows: the greater the contemplative use, the more important the visual appearance or design; the greater the visitor's interests in physical exercise or social aspects, the less important the design. And, it follows that design is of different relevance for different social milieus. In general, women are more interested in the visual appearance of a park than are men, especially young men. For fringe groups, but also for young people in general (primarily male), who seem to feel comfortable even in "non-places," the "attractiveness" or the "good" state of maintenance of open spaces is of less significance. For them, the most pleasant aspect in this case is being together, undisturbed, and unburdened by swanky urban open spaces that conform to more "upright" behavior. This is why we find people in open spaces that no one would ever define as pleasantly designed, simply because the user here finds other aspects to be pleasant enough, such as location, accessibility, activities that can take place, or people you meet there. They are more interested in the social aspect, in all kinds of activities, and not in contemplation. They might even think that prettiness or good upkeep is too bourgeois and boring to be "cool." Thus, for example, the baroque garden design is certainly impressive for nearly all of us, but not everyone would call such a garden a pleasant place, because the leisure behavior is rather restricted to a pure visual experience. Some visitors may even feel small and somewhat controlled.

Therefore, pleasantness is a complex, mixed feeling, resulting from a situation-specific, precise amount of prettiness, maintenance, infrastructure, activities, people, nature, social control, etc. "Too much" or "too little" of everything can be counterproductive to achieving pleasantness.

Regarding the importance of design, one needs to understand that in an open space, which is not merely visited once but more or less day-to-day, the interest for the design of the park slowly decreases, and other less satisfied needs become more relevant to behavior. After a while, the beauty of the park becomes self-evident, freeing us to concentrate on other aspects, such as what is happening around us. We look at a cloud, a bird, a person walking through the park, a leaf floating in the wind, or we concentrate on what we are doing (e.g., playing football or reading a newspaper). This is how we avoid becoming aesthetically bored in outdoor open spaces, the design of which—now seen perhaps umpteen times and hence less visually stimulating—gives us less and less aesthetic variety. We enjoy the "all-inclusive leisure deal," which includes fresh air, nice weather, social respite, and our own activities, in an appealing environment and pleasant nature.

Pleasantness aims at mental relief or, at best, stimulation, but not at mental effort. Familiar attractiveness is pleasant, new things or new designs challenge us. They often seem like an annoyance or even a mental necessitation. For example: the proven, familiar design of landscape gardens, by which "form, function, fiction, and feeling" developed over two or three centuries into a cultural ideal, is still pleasing—but the new or the modern landscape design, if it deviates too far from this aesthetic convention, is more irritating than pleasing. But modern landscape architecture very often deliberately rejects these clichéd notions and their associated "Arcadian fictions" and "pleasant feelings"; it even aims to break them, deface them, and disclose them as ideological, outmoded, or even non-urban.

So it has become popular in modern landscape architecture to stage breaks and edges, never allude to anything "natural." Trees are planted in grids, their tops pruned into box-likes shapes, concrete is used, inclined planes cut into the terrain—do not dare create any natural-looking hills, plan them instead as cones, waves, or pyramids; have water always flowing in form through troughs, channels, or basins to avoid any danger of "wrong" idyllic associations with streams or ponds. Or by contrast, stage a "wilderness," and waive the idea of designing nature as something pleasant. Instead, opt to offer a quasi-"real nature experience."

Of course this kind of design is "new," even "interesting" and one can easily understand the need of landscape architects to be "innovative," but people, with their traditional, Arcadian-structured affinities in relation to urban green areas and landscape, certainly prefer the familiar and the pleasant side of nature, and will accept only moderate deviations in design, and only if the general impression is that of "pleasant." Some facets of modern landscape architecture are definitely not pleasant enough.

4. Feeling: Landscape Architecture in the Context of Pleasantness

The concept of pleasantness is often frowned upon in aesthetic discourses, especially when ambitious "artistic" landscape architects are involved. They are definitely not fans of feel-good architecture; they even see it as a curse word. The feeling of pleasantness is thereby, and quite rightly so, accused of being flat and shallow. It requires no inner concentration, does not presuppose thinking skills, knowledge, artistic taste, awareness of quality. It is considered straightforward enjoyment and therefore does not shock or delight, does not inspire awe. Pleasantness, in other words, is simple, unadulterated well-being, and hence has no sustainable consequence, no "depth."

In addition, pleasantness in this context is often suspected of harboring an overly snug relationship with the useful and everyday. The feeling of pleasure is not discredited alone because various simple or "merely useful" objects trigger pleasant feelings, but also because there is a specific cost-benefit calculation involved: pleasantness is often too easily achieved. It just happens, without any highbrow effort. Moreover, the feeling of pleasure is too often associated with the so-called lower physiological needs, such as sunshine, cool breezes, a cozy chair, and not with "higher" intellectual or even spiritual needs. Pleasantness is quietude, ease, relaxation—it's comfortable. Pleasant and simple, pleasant and comfortable are acknowledged synonyms.

Even if, from an artistic and aesthetic perspective, the feeling of pleasantness is not very much esteemed and seen as intellectually undemanding, of less artistic value and is often associated with shallowness, banality, usefulness, familiarity, and lower psychological needs, these are precisely the essential aspects of pleasantness and why this term so excellently qualifies as a description of the function of open spaces. Urban open spaces, particularly when they are used every day, satisfy people's wish to spend some time in outdoor places where they feel good. They are not visiting a museum or an art gallery and not looking for intellectual or artistic challenges. So the concept of pleasantness has a more complex scope than that of beauty or form. Pleasantness does not result alone from a "beautiful" designed open space: it always develops from the functions, fictions, and feelings with which the form of the place is associated; it is, so to say, an all-inclusive feeling. Even a not very pretty, but familiar place can be pleasant, just as a beautiful open place may not always be pleasant enough to spend much time there, if it does not allow for certain activities or an affective appropriation.

People of course would like to feel good everywhere (even in places where they are busy), but in relation to open spaces and landscapes as places of leisure, and rest and relaxation, they definitely expect—despite some resignation even there—that their stay will be a pleasant one or they abstain from going there. As we all know: people cherish and expect more pleasantness from landscapes they visit on a day trip or vacation than they do from the landscape in which they live and work. And, for instance, they expect more pleasantness from parks and gardens than from streets, playgrounds or sport fields, which are not so much associated with "psychological restoration" or even "Arcadia."

By the way: no one should be fooled. The "aesthetic of pleasantness" may seem like an undemanding design, which is why the concept is often rejected by "ambitious" landscape architects. But in fact, the exact opposite is true: designing an innovative and artistically interesting place, an ecologically valuable or a highly attractive space for all kinds of activities, should in fact be less challenging than designing one that is "merely" pleasant. Furthermore, it should be even more difficult to successfully design an open space that is sophisticated in terms of an artistic, ecological, and/or use perspective, but remains within the realm of pleasantness. Yet, is this not precisely the balancing act and challenge that landscape architects should face?

The "Aesthetic of Pleasantness" is more a design attitude than a design style, and has little to do with ecological naturalism, a trivial behaviorist functionalism, or an aesthetic formalism. Hence, it would be a valuable challenge to one's professional routine or level of professional innovation. Even if it were clear from the onset that "design" would never be more than a necessary, but not yet sufficient, contribution to a pleasant outdoor space. As shown above, pleasantness needs more than just good architecture and it sometimes occurs even without good design. Being open to pleasantness in a design process would mean putting the professional perspective and ones' own architectural ambitions into perspective. It would mean being open for a kind of "layman's aesthetic" and for people's wish to feel good in a pleasant outdoor surrounding. That means finding new professional, even ambitious standards and solutions without leaving the corridor of pleasantness and common taste, and without risking wide-ranging approval. It is all about finding the right, pleasant measure in everything and avoiding any exaggerations or imbalances. Unfortunately, many landscape architects consider themselves artists or ecologists, garden historians or planting experts, or even social workers. Yet it is just this "division of labor" or specialization within modern landscape architecture that tends to lead to those exaggerations and imbalances in design, which are often, so to say, one-sided. People like it more "all inclusive."

CHRISTOPHE GIROT is Professor and Chair of Landscape Architecture at the Architecture Department of the ETH in Zürich. He received a dual Masters in Architecture and Landscape Architecture from UC Berkeley, and was Chair of Design at the Versailles School of Landscape Architecture. His teaching and research interests span new topological methods in landscape design, landscape perception and analysis through new media, and contemporary theory and history of landscape architecture. At the ETH he co-founded the Landscape Visualization and Modeling Laboratory (LVML) with Professor Adrienne Gret-Regamey in 2010. His professional practice focuses on large-scale landscape projects, using advanced 3D GIS techniques that contribute to the design of more sustainable landscape environments such as the Alptransit Deposit in Sigirino and the Third Rhône River Correction in the Canton of Valais. He currently directs an advanced design research project on the Ciliwung River in Jakarta for the ETH Future Cities Laboratory in Singapore.

ANETTE FREYTAG is Senior Lecturer and Head of Research at the Chair of Landscape Architecture of Professor Girot at the ETH Zürich with whom she is working since 2005. Her dissertation on Swiss Landscape architect Dieter Kienast (1945–1998) has been awarded several prizes. The book will be published by gta/Zürich and Architectura&Natura/Amsterdam. Since 1997 she has been publishing many articles on contemporary landscape architecture as well as on historical gardens and sites. Her recent research interests are centered on the intersection of art, landscape architecture, and architecture between the 1970s and 1990s.

ALBERT KIRCHENGAST is an architectural theoretician who collaborated with Ullrich Schwarz at Graz University of Technology and Ákos Moravánszky at the Institute gta at the ETH Zürich. Since 2010, he works in the TheoryLab of Christophe Girot. He is a member of the Österreichische Baukulturstiftung, author of the book *Weiterbauen*, co-author of *Topologie/Topology*, and co-editor of *Experiments–Architecture between Sciences and the Arts*, as well as *Mies als Gärtner*. At present his research interest focuses on the role of landscape in the architecture of Mies van der Rohe.

DUNJA RICHTER worked for the Department of Historical Garden Preservation, Staatliche Schlösser und Gärten Hessen from 2005 until 2008 and issued expert reports on the preservation and development of historical gardens and landscapes. Since 2009, she has worked as an academic assistant at the professorship of Christophe Girot at the ETH Zürich. Her dissertation focuses on the history of garden design and landscape architecture in nineteenth century Switzerland, with a concentration on the trade and use of plants. She is co-author of *Topologie/Topology*.

ANNEMARIE BUCHER studied art history, ethnology, and philosophy at Zurich University and Landscape Architecture at the ETH Zürich. She has also been a research fellow at Harvard University. She is currently working as a reader in art theory and cultural theory at Zurich University of the Arts and as a freelance researcher and curator. She is the author of several books and articles on art, cultural theory, landscape, and theory. She has curated several exhibitions, such as "Why make Prints?" and "G59, the First National Garden Exhibition in Switzerland." Her recent activities apart from teaching include a transdisciplinary research project on the functions of art in a global context (together with Dominique Lämmli). Other current work features an exhibition project on the banana as a transdisciplinary and transcultural phenomenon and on landscape as process. She lives and works in Zurich.

GION A. CAMINADA was born in 1957 in Vrin, Graubünden. After completing an apprenticeship as carpenter and joiner, he attended the School of Applied Arts, then post-graduate studies in architecture at the ETH Zürich. Since 1988, he has worked at his architecture office in Vrin, since 1998 as assistant professor, and since 2008 as Professor of Architecture and Design at the ETH Zürich. He has received numerous prizes and awards including the International Architecture Prize for New Construction in the Alps, the Architecture Award for Sustainable Construction, the German Critics Prize, the Meret Oppenheim Prize, and the Culture Award of the Canton Graubünden.

STEFAN KÖRNER after studying horticulture, he studied landscape planning at the Technical University Berlin. He then worked as a landscape architect in Berlin. From 1994 to 2001, he served as research assistant at the Institute of Landscape Ecology of the Technical University Munich, while studying for his Ph.D. at the Technical University Berlin. From 2001 to 2005, he worked as a researcher at the Institute for Urban Ecology of the Technical University Berlin on several externally funded projects, while writing his habilitation thesis on the rehabilitation of landscape design as a cultural task. He also worked as an associate lecturer for the Department of the Cultural History of Nature in the Landscape Planning Program. Since October 2005, he has served as Professor of Landscaping/Vegetation Engineering (landscaping, landscape management, and vegetation development) at the University of Kassel (Endowed Professorship of the Federation of Gardens, Landscapes, and Sports Fields). Since 2010, he has served as Dean of the Faculty of Architecture, Urban, and Landscape Planning at the University of Kassel. Research interests include theory of landscape, planning theory, nature conservation and monument preservation, nature conservation theory, and urban use of plants.

WILHELM KRULL, Ph.D., is Secretary General of the Volkswagen Foundation. Previously, he worked as a DAAD lecturer at Oxford University and held a senior position at the Science Council and at the Max Planck Society. Since the late nineteen-eighties, he has been a member of numerous supervisory and advisory boards, including the OECD, the EU, the BMBF, the Max Planck Society, and the Science Council. From 2006 to 2008, he was also Chairman of the European Foundation Association (EFC) and since 2008 Chairman of the Board of the Association of German Foundations. He studied German literature, philosophy, educational science, and political science in Bremen and Marburg.

NORBERT KÜHN, Prof. Ph.D., was born in 1964. He first studied Landscape Management at the Technical University of Munich-Weihenstephan, then doctorate studies at the Department of Vegetation Ecology. From 1998, he worked as a senior engineer for the Department of Field Botany and Plant Use at the Technical University of Berlin, and since 2003 Head of the Department of Vegetation Technology and Plant Use. His main research interests are theory in the use of plants, extensive perennials use, spontaneous vegetation, green space management, and historical use of plants. Since 2006, he has served as Dean of the Landscape Planning module. He is a member of international committees and advisory boards, and since 2006 has served as Chairman of the Karl Foerster Foundation.

HANSJÖRG KÜSTER was born in 1956 in Frankfurt am Main. He studied biology at Stuttgart-Hohenheim University, from which he earned a doctorate degree as a Dr. rer. nat. (1985). From 1981 to 1998, he worked at the Institute for Pre- and Protohistory at Munich University. Since 1998, he has served as Professor for Plant Ecology at the Institute for Geobotany at Leibniz University Hanover. His main interests are ecology and landscape. He has published several books including *Die Geschichte der Landschaft* (Munich 2013); *Die Entdeckung der Landschaft. Einführung in eine neue Wissenschaft* (Munich 2012). His books have also been translated to Italian and French.

VITTORIO MAGNAGO LAMPUGNANI studied architecture at the Universities of Rome and Stuttgart and received his doctorate from both universities. From 1974 to 1980, he was a research assistant in Stuttgart, and from 1980 to 1984 adviser to the International Building Exhibition (IBA) in Berlin. From 1984 to 1985, he taught at the Graduate School of Design at Harvard University. From 1985 to 1986, he was a fellow at the Institute for Advanced Studies Berlin, and from 1990 to 1995, Director of the German Architecture Museum and a Professor at the Städel School in Frankfurt. From 1986 to 1990 he was also Assistant Editor of *Domus* magazine, and from 1990 to 1995 its Editor in Chief. Since 1994, he has held a full professorship in the History of Urban Design at the ETH Zürich, where he served as Dean of the Department of Architecture from 1998 to 2001, and since 2010, at the Institute for the History and Theory of Architecture (gta). He runs his own architecture firm in Milan (Studio di Architettura) and another in Zurich (Baukontor Architects with Mark Amman and Jens Christian Bohm). His most important projects include the housing group in Maria Lankowitz near Graz (1995–1999) with Marlene Dorrie and Michael Regner, the Audi Forum in Ingolstadt (1999–2000) with Wolfgang Weinzierl, the Novartis Campus St. Johann, Basel (2001 ff.), the underground train station in Mergellina, Naples (2004–2010), and the Richti Quarter in Wallisellen.

LOTHAR SCHÄFER, Prof. emer. at the University of Hamburg, was born in 1934. He studied mathematics, physics, and philosophy in Frankfurt, Freiburg, and Tübingen. In 1962, he earned his Ph.D. (*Kants Metaphysik der Natur*, Berlin 1966), and in 1971 received his habilitation in philosophy at the University of Tübingen (*Erfahrung und Konvention*, Stuttgart 1974). In 1976, he was appointed Professor with Chair of Philosophy at the University of Hamburg representing the fields of epistemology, philosophy of science, and natural philosophy. Since 1983, historical and systematic studies on the subject of Nature, Technology, and Responsibility. Cooperation with the DLR Stuttgart. See also: *Das Bacon-Projekt: Von der Erkenntnis, Nutzung und Schonung der Natur* (Frankfurt am Main. 1993).

JOSEPH SCHWARTZ has been Chair of Structural Design at the Faculty of Architecture of the ETH Zürich since February 2008. He studied at the Faculty of Civil Engineering of ETH Zürich. After receiving his diploma in 1981, he led experiments on the rotation capacity of masonry as a research assistant of Prof. Bruno Thürlimann, and graduated in 1989 with a thesis on the *Bemessung von Mauerwerkswänden und Stahlbetonstützen unter Normalkraft* (design of masonry walls and reinforced concrete columns under normal force), which was awarded the Silver Medal of ETH. He then studied stress fields for the design of reinforced concrete structures. In 1990, he worked as a senior assistant with Prof. Dr. P. Marti, and in the years 1989–1999 held several teaching positions at ETH Zürich and other Swiss technical universities. From 2001 to 2008, he was a lecturer at the University of Applied Sciences of Central Switzerland. He is co-author of Design of Concrete Structures *With Stress Fields* (1996), *Mauerwerk* (1998), and *Before Steel* (2010). From 1991 to 2001, he was associate partner of an engineering firm in Zug, Switzerland, responsible for the planning and design of several bridge and building construction projects. Since 2002, he has headed his own engineering firm with its headquarters in Zug, and works closely with several leading Swiss architects. He is a board member of the Section for Bridge and Structural Engineering and the commission of SIA 266 Masonry.

MARTIN SEEL is Professor of Philosophy at Johann Wolfgang Goethe-University, Frankfurt am Main. His main fields of research are epistemology, philosophy of mind and language, virtue ethics, art theory, and aesthetics in general. His publications include: *Eine Ästhetik der Natur*, Frankfurt am Main. 1991; *Versuch über die Form des Glücks*, Frankfurt am Main. 1995; *Ästhetik des Erscheinens*, Munich 2000 (*Aesthetics of Appearing, Stanford* UP 2004); *Sich bestimmen lassen. Studien zur theoretischen und praktischen Philosophie*, Frankfurt am Main. 2002; *Paradoxien der Erfüllung. Philosophische Essays*, Frankfurt am Main. 2006; *Die Macht des Erscheinens. Texte zur Ästhetik*, Frankfurt am Main. 2007; *Theorien*, Frankfurt am Main. 2009; *111 Tugenden, 111 Laster. Eine philosophische Revue*, Frankfurt am Main. 2011; *Die Künste des Kinos*, Frankfurt am Main. 2013 (forthcoming in September).

MICHAEL SEILER, Prof., Ph.D., was born in 1939. He studied geodesy at the TFH Berlin, horticulture and landscape design at the Technical University of Berlin. Since 1979, he has served as Director and then Head Curator of Peacock Island. In 1987, he earned his Ph.D. on the history of the landscape garden at Klein-Glienicke. Since 1989, he has been Honorary Professor at the Free University of Berlin, from 1993 to 2004 Garden Director of the Foundation for Prussian Palaces and Gardens Foundation Berlin-Brandenburg, and was awarded the Friedrich Ludwig von Sckell Ring of Honor in 2000 by the Bavarian Academy of Fine Arts. Since 2004, he has served as Chairman of the company Pueckler Berlin. He has written numerous publications on garden history and historic gardens.

ANTJE STOKMAN is a landscape architect, Professor of landscape planning and ecology at Stuttgart University, and member of the *Studio Urbane Landschaften*, an interdisciplinary research and teaching platform on the topic of urban landscapes. She studied landscape architecture at Leibniz University Hanover and Edinburgh College of Art, and was involved in teaching and research at Hanover University, Technical University Hamburg Harburg, Peking University, and Tongji University Shanghai, China. As a practicing landscape architect she worked in many national and international projects. Her recent work focuses on strategies to develop hydrologic systems as a basis for sustainable urban form and design of urban landscapes. She was awarded the Topos Landscape Award in 2011, the Lower Saxony Science Prize in 2009, and nominated as a member of the German National Advisory Council on Spatial Planning in 2010.

WULF TESSIN, Ph.D., was born in 1945. He studied sociology and urban studies in Munich and Dar-es-Salaam, Tanzania. He earned his Ph.D. in 1975, and his habilitation in 1985. He first worked as a research assistant at the University of Gottingen and the RWTH Aachen, and until 2010, was Professor of Sociology in Planning at the Institute for Open Space at the Faculty of Architecture and Landscape of Leibniz University Hanover. His area of research and practical work includes urban development, urban open-space planning, open-space cultural management, and aesthetics of reception. Major publications include *Der Traum vom Garten—ein planerischer Alptraum?* (1994), *Freiraum und Verhalten* (2004, 2nd edition 2011), and *Die Ästhetik des Angenehmen* (2008).

PICTURE CREDITS

page 34: René Magritte, La condition humaine (The Human Condition), 1933, oil on Canvas, 100cm × 81cm, National Gallery of Art, Washington DC
papes 54/55, 59–62, 65, 67, 69, 71, 73: Lucia Degonda
pages 64, 75: Gion A. Caminada
pages 83, 84/85: Pascal Werner, LVML, Chair of Landscape Architecture Professor Christophe Girot, ETH Zürich
pages 86/87, 88, 96/97, 98/99: Ilmar Hurkxkens, Atelier Girot
pages 100/101: Magda Osinska, Atelier Girot
pages 106/107: Matthias Knuser, Lukas Murer, Alain Weber, Design Studio Dordrecht, Chair of Landscape Architecture Professor Christophe Girot, ETH Zürich
pages 108/109, 110/111: Kristina Eickmeier, Annina Peterer, Design Studio Dordrecht, Chair of Landscape Architecture Professor Christophe Girot, ETH Zürich
pages 117, 126, 133, 134: Stefan Körner
page 120: Caspar David Friedrich, Landschaft mit Regenbogen (Landscape with Rainbow), c. 1810, oil on canvas, 59cm × 84.5cm (missing since 1945)
pages 123 top, 125: From: Lindner, Werner: Bauten der Technik. Ihre Form und Wirkung, Werkanlagen, Berlin 1927, p. 219, p. 188
page 123 bottom: From: Schultze-Naumburg, Paul: Die Gestaltung der Landschaft durch den Menschen, Munich 1992, p. 339
page 142: From: Echtermeyer, Theodor (ed.): Die Königliche Gärtnerlehranstalt Dahlem, Berlin 1913, p. 174
pages 150, 151: Norbert Kühn
pages 164, 166, 168, 170, 172, 174, 178: Hansjörg Küster
pages 190/191: From: Alphand, Jean-Charles Adolphe: Les Promenades de Paris, Paris 2002, Reprint, no page
pages 194/195: From: Belting, Hans, Blume, Dieter (eds.): Malerei und Stadtkultur in der Dantezeit, Die Argumentation der Bilder, Munich 1989, table III und IV
page 213: Toni Kotnik
pages 215, 222 top, 223 bottom: Joseph Schwartz
page: 216: From: Schweizerische Bauzeitung, 17 (11), 1891, pp. 66–67
page 217: Christian A. Natiez
pages 218, 224 top: Christian Menn
page 219: From: El croquis 124, Eduardo Souto de Moura, 2005, pp. 160–187
page 220: Chair of Structural Design Professor Joseph Schwartz, ETH Zürich
page 221: Éditions LAPIE St Maur
page 222 bottom: Claude Paulet
page 223 top: From: Brown, D.: Bridges, London 1996, p. 107
page 224 bottom: Christian Kerez
page 233: From: Gagosian Gallery (ed.): Andreas Gursky, New York 2010, p. 25
page 239: From: Engler, Martin (ed.): Malereien in Fotografie, Strategien der Aneignung, Berlin 2012, p. 65
page 245: Gerhard Richter: Abstraktes Bild (Abstract Painting), 1992, Sprengel Museum, Hanover
page 251: Stiftung Preußische Schlösser und Gärten Berlin-Brandenburg, SPSG, (Prussian Castles and Gardens Foundation in Berlin-Brandenburg), GK I 30330
page 254: Detail of the lithographed plan from 1862
pages 258/259: SPSG, collection of plans, no. 3674
page 262: From: Verhandlungen des Vereins zur Beförderung des Gartenbaues in den Königlich Preußischen Staaten, vol. 2., Berlin 1826, table IX and X
page 264: From: Verhandlungen des Vereins zur Beförderung des Gartenbaues in den Königlich Preußischen Staaten, vol. 2., Berlin 1826, table XIV
page 268: SPSG, collection of plans, no. 3705
pages 271, 277, 282: Michael Seiler (April 2009, May 2004, no date)
page 272: SPSG, collection of plans, no. 3639
page 274: SPSG, collection of plans, no. 14504
page 278 top: SPSG, plan missing (photography)
page 278 bottom: SPSG, collection of plans, no. 3725
pages 287, 292: Antje Stokman
pages 294 top, 294/295, 298/299: From: IBA Hamburg, Studio Urbane Landschaften (eds.): Wasseratlas, WasserLand-Topologien für die Hamburger Elbinsel, Berlin 2008, pp. 18, 29, 44/45
pages 302/303, 304: From: Prominski, Martin, Stokman, Antje, Zeller, Susanne, Stimberg, Daniel, Voermanek, Hinnerk: Fluss. Räume. Entwerfen, Planungsstrategien für urbane Fliessgewässer, Berlin 2012, pp. 41/42, 31

---

pages 29–32, 183–186, 323–326: Topology Symposium, Semper Aula, ETH Zürich, 11–13 October 2012, photographs: Klemen Breitfuss, Alexandre Kapellos

IMPRINT

Editing: Albert Kirchengast
Translation: Laura Bruce
Proofreading: Inez Templeton, Lynne Kolar-Thompson
Graphic design: Willi Schmid & Radim Peško
Typefaces: Landscript Condensed (radimpesko.com), DeVinne
Paper: Constellation Snow Vicenca, 350g (cover) and Planoart 115g
Printing and binding: Gugler GmbH

Bibliographic information published by the Deutsche Nationalbibliothek
The Deutsche Nationalbibliothek lists this publication in the Deutsche Nationalbibliografie; detailed bibliographic data are available on the Internet at http://dnb.d-nb.de

jovis Verlag GmbH
Kurfürstenstraße 15/16
10785 Berlin

www.jovis.de

ISBN 978-3-86859-212-2

This publication was supported by the Volkswagen Foundation, Hanover, Germany.